P9-APT-602

# A New History
## of
## Educational Philosophy

# A New History
# of
# Educational Philosophy

## JAMES S. KAMINSKY

Contributions to the Study of Education, Number 58

**GREENWOOD PRESS**
Westport, Connecticut • London

**Library of Congress Cataloging-in-Publication Data**

Kaminsky, James S.
  A new history of educational philosophy / James S. Kaminsky.
    p.  cm.—(Contributions to the study of education, ISSN
0196-707X ; no. 58)
  Includes bibliographical references (p. ) and index.
  ISBN 0-313-28430-X (alk. paper)
  1. Education—United States—Philosophy—History.  2. Education—
Great Britain—Philosophy—History.  3. Education—Australia—
Philosophy—History.  I. Title.  II. Series.
LB14.7.K36  1993
370′.1—dc20     92-25742

370
KAM

British Library Cataloguing in Publication Data is available.

Copyright © 1993 by James S. Kaminsky

Library of Congress Catalog Card Number: 92-25742
ISBN: 0-313-28430-X
ISSN: 0196-707X

First published in 1993

Greenwood Press, 88 Post Road West, Westport, CT 06881
An imprint of Greenwood Publishing Group, Inc.

Printed in the United States of America

The paper used in this book complies with the
Permanent Paper Standard issued by the National
Information Standards Organization (Z39.48-1984).

10 9 8 7 6 5 4 3 2 1

# Contents

# Preface

The first preface for this book was written some ten years ago while I was at the University of Hawaii on sabbatical leave. After my work in Hawaii it was impossible for me to believe that educational philosophy was connected to philosophy through some simple line of intellectual descent—the way the story is usually recounted. Between 1983 and 1986 I spent my time trying to disassemble my understandings about the origins of philosophy of education acquired in graduate school and trying to formulate a more useful and interesting construct with which to replace them. I found it a great deal easier to lose my faith than to find something to replace it with.

The impulse to write a different and new history of educational philosophy came from Stephen Toulmin's *Human understanding* (1972) and Harold Silver's *Education as history* (1983). Toulmin's idea of intellectual professions and their embodiment in various organizations—"The Professional Embodiment of Science"—was immediately suggestive. I began to investigate the possibility that the origins of educational philosophy were better attached to the organizations of its embodiment than to their annotated bibliographies. Further, Silver's work called my attention to the connection between the 1890s social reform movement, social science, and education—and therein educational philosophy. It was apparent that the origins of educational philosophy were tied not only to the professional organization of its embodiment but also to the social reform movement and social science as well. The work of Toulmin and Silver convinced me that educational philosophy had a much broader intellectual parentage than was commonly acknowledged. What followed from those two insights is this book, which is an intellectual history of the type Richard Rorty claims as his own. He writes, "In my sense intellectual history consists of descriptions of what the intellectuals were up to at a given time, and their interaction with the rest of society—descriptions which, for the most part, bracket the questions of what activities which intellectuals were conducting" (1984, 68). It is also a history of educational philosophy. It is doxography, an attempt to settle the question of who is a philosopher of education, what works deserve the honorific title of educational philosophy, and so on. In this version of the discipline the central issues are these: What intellectual activities have educational philosophers concerned themselves with? What strands of common interest unite the discipline? Is such and such stance correct? All of these concerns are central to this book.

This book is also an anthropology of the discipline. In this sense,

What we want to be told is whether that tribe has anything interesting to tell us— interesting by *our* lights, answering to *our* concerns, informative about what *we* know to exist. Any anthropologist who rejected this assignment on the grounds that filtering and paraphrase would distort and betray the integrity of the tribe's culture would no longer be an anthropologist, but a sort of cultist. He is, after all, working for *us*, not for *them*. (Rorty, Schneewind, and Skinner, 1984, 6-7)

As both anthropologist and cultist in one guise I hope no more than for the book to be "interesting by *our* lights, answering to *our* concerns, informative about what *we* know to exist" (Rorty, Schneewind, and Skinner, 1984, 6-7). In the guise of a cultist I hope it can suggest a version of educational philosophy that is less self-referential and less constrained by its history and its intellectual present. In this genre the book is more educational philosophy than educational history.

Several people have helped both directly and indirectly in the writing of this book and I would like to acknowledge their assistance. First and foremost I would like to acknowledge the technical assistance of Bonnie Ann Rasmussen who edited draft after draft of this manuscript—over the entire ten years of its writing. The other large debt that I must acknowledge is to Professor Alan Cumming an eminent department chair who supported this work during its early years when the project was very new and very fragile. I should also thank Tony Welch and other colleagues at the Department of Social and Cultural Studies in Education, University of New England in Australia, who provided intellectual support during those early days, and thank my colleagues in the Philosophy of Education Society of Australasia who thoughtfully discussed and offered constructive criticisms of several papers that foreshadowed various sections of this book.

In Britain I would like to thank Professor Paul Hirst, who granted me a sabbatical place at the University of Cambridge, Department of Education, where I concluded researching various aspects of philosophy of education in Britain. T. H. McLaughlin offered his personable assistance while I was at Cambridge and provided me with an opportunity to test my ideas at a meeting of the Cambridge Branch of the Philosophy of Education Society of Great Britain. After I returned to the United States, McLaughlin, acting as secretary of the British society, provided important archival records, for which I am very grateful. I would also like to note the assistance of John and Pat White at the Institute of Education, University of London. Pat was particularly instrumental in assisting me to gain access to an unpublished autobiography of L. A. Reid. I would also like to thank Nicholas Reid and Dr. F. M. Reid, Professor Reid's widow, for providing access to the autobiography.

In the United States I would like to acknowledge the support of my colleagues in the Southeast Philosophy of Education Society. The support of Robert Sherman at the University of Florida, C. J. B. (Jim) Macmillan at Florida State University, and Joe L. Green, at Louisiana State University in Shreveport was both timely and effective. They all offered professional and intellectual support in the last days of the project—at a time when it was sorely needed.

At this point it is also important to note the support of my colleagues in the Philosophy of Education Society in the United States. Denis Phillips at Stanford University assisted me in obtaining a sabbatical place at Stanford where I concluded research on the United States section of this book. Denis was as always the generous scholar and gentleman; I remember his assistance well. I would also like to thank Gerald Reagan and Richard Pratte at Ohio State University, who offered their general comments and support for this project over the years. I would also like to note the important counterpoint Harvey Siegel at the University of Miami provided for my work. My inability to convince Harvey of the central thesis of this work and his continued cheerful willingness to listen to my argument as the project evolved was a constructive element in this intellectual endeavor.

I would like to thank Edward Beauchamp at the University of Hawaii who suggested a publisher for this book. Finally I need to acknowledge my colleagues at Auburn University whose generous support and encouragement allowed me to concentrate on this work.

At this point I must also acknowledge my indebtedness to the editors of *Educational Philosophy and Theory, Educational Studies, Harvard Educational Review,* and the *Journal of Education* for allowing me to republish materials from those journals. The articles were these: James S. Kaminsky. 1986. "The first 600 months of philosophy of education—1935–1985: A deconstructionist account." *Educational Philosophy and Theory* (18) 2; 1988. "The first 600 months . . . revisited: A response to

Harris." *Educational Philosophy and Theory* (20) 1; 1988. "Philosophy of education in Australasia: A definition and a history." *Educational Philosophy and Theory* (21) 1; 1991. "Some antecedents of educational philosophy in Britain with particular reference to social science." *Educational Studies* (17) 3; 1992. "A pre-history of educational philosophy in the United States: 1861 to 1914." *Harvard Educational Review.* (62) 2; and 1992. (*in press*) "A new history of philosophy of education in the United States: A prologue." *Journal of Education.*

# Introduction

What is offered here is a new history of philosophy of education.[1] It is a history from the bottom up (see Stearns, 1988, 3-6). It is an international history.[2] While this is not a people's history of educational philosophy, it is at least a social history. Philosophy of education did not reach its mature form and standing in the premier research universities of America upon the shoulders of any one individual. This new international history maintains that the dialogues of educational philosophy can be best understood by reference to the broader intellectual, social, and political movements that were related to the practice of the discipline and to the individuals who were a part of or contributed to those movements than by reference to the arguments of its extended bibliographies alone. This study calls attention to the importance of the profession's "external" structures while remembering the significance of its "internal" logics. It acknowledges the profession's "inner circle," but it is also interested in the actors who were not part of the inner circle and in the relevant literature that did not flow from the inner circle. In an even more heretical tone, it claims a centrality for a literature that can only tacitly be called philosophical.

What is intellectually deceptive in contemporary and influential accounts of the discipline's prologue is the intimation that its antecedents are to be found in the internal logic of philosophy (e.g. Price, 1967, 230-243). While it must be conceded that certain comments on education share a certain literary style (turgid, prolix, and self-referential), intellectual genealogies (Greek and Roman), and doxologies (metaphysical and epistemological), upon close inspection it must also be granted that the concerns and reservoir of questions that constitute the discipline's first forms are as closely tied to the idea and possibility of social reform (the elimination of poverty, hunger, disease, drunkenness, ignorance, crime, and corruption) and the invention of social science (amelioration versus theory production) as they are to the intellectual history of philosophy.

The present rehearsal of educational philosophy's genesis is concerned with the manner in which social, cultural, and historical pressures affected and, in some sense, created the educational discipline that we know as philosophy of education, more than it is with the internal logic of its natural history and annotated bibliographies (cf. Passmore, 1967b). Educational philosophy is a complex discipline that has many points of contact with the intellectual and social movements of its period of genesis. There are several elements in its prologue: (1) the intellectual work of Herbert Spencer; (2) Victorianism; (3) the social reform movement of the 1890s; (4) social science; (5) the new class; (6) philosophy; and perhaps most important, (7) the institutions (professional societies) of its establishment.

## NONTRADITIONAL PERSPECTIVE

There are real advantages in thinking about philosophy of education from a nontraditional perspective. First (at the risk of belaboring the point), this approach separates the history of philosophy of education from the history of philosophy and calls attention to why it is useful to distinguish between the work of the two. Second, by focusing upon mechanism (the societies that are constitutive of educational philosophy's invisible college), the discipline's history can be extracted from its schizophrenic relationship with philosophy while still retaining a constructive link with philosophy, social science, and the schools. Third, this approach argues for reshaping the reservoir of questions that is constitutive of educational philosophy's program of research and, in most instances, for allotting the questions of philosophy to departments of philosophy. It also calls attention to a natural audience—professional educators. Last, it points the way toward a more productive relationship with the schools and professional educators.

A history of educational philosophy cannot be told without reference to philosophy, but more important, it cannot be retold without reference to its own history, the history of social science, and the intellectual matrix in which that history occurred. The natural history of philosophy of education does not exhibit a seamless link with philosophy. Various philosophical tracts partially pertaining to matters of education can be traced at least back to Plato in the Western intellectual tradition (see Ulich, [1947] 1982) but its intellectual pedigree cannot be traced with reference only to philosophy.

## PROTO-PHILOSOPHY

It is best to consider timeworn philosophical tracts concerned with education as a proto-philosophy of education. They share a certain literary style and language with educational philosophy, but they do not share the industrial context or the concern with social and political reform of industrial capitalism. In other words, philosophy is part of a different pool of questions that only overlaps the questions of educational philosophy. For some purposes it makes perfect sense to attribute educational philosophy to philosophy in general, if not to academic philosophy, given their common literary and linguistic styles. But this narrow view only can be maintained, however, by neglecting educational philosophy's important connections with social science, social reform, and political action. The social reform movement of the 1890s and social science provided a focused intellectual arena for the moral, social, and philosophical issues of schooling.

The questions raised in classical literature of philosophy were about a different set of questions and answers. For example, Plato's *Republic* and Aristotle's *Politics* essentially addressed education in aristocratic, agricultural, city–states. Although these texts had a certain metaphorical or analogical usefulness for Victorian social and educational concerns, they did not fit the reservoir of questions produced by industrial society: the questions of political economy generated by the acute poverty of its slums or the questions of social organization generated by urbanization.

## UNITED STATES

The economic and demographic origins of American educational philosophy are found in the period following the Civil War. The industrial revolution, urbanization, and the concentration of wealth that followed the Civil War dissolved the agricultural society that had been at the core of America's social order.

The intellectual origins of modern educational philosophy can be traced first to Herbert Spencer and collaterally to Charles Darwin and Alfred Russell Wallace, cofounder with Darwin of evolutionary theory. They fundamentally changed traditional concepts of the world.

Spencer wrote compelling descriptions of the Victorian social order and its educational system and legitimized them with the technical power of Darwin's and Wallace's work. Spencer fundamentally affirmed evolutionary explanations of the social order and challenged classical concepts of an education. At the turn of the century America's middle class discovered Herbert Spencer's evolutionary theory. Just as the universe was moved by evolution—a process containing so many variables as to be unpredictable—so was human destiny. Moreover, just as the ultimate end of the universe was unknowable, so was the ultimate end of humanity. To Spencer's mind intervening in the evolutionary processes was either futile or mischievous. Social intervention merely interfered with the general process of evolution. Intervention in society created social turbulence just as intervention in the physical world created unforeseeable and in many instances harmful side effects; that is, intervention created costs (problems) without the possibility of anything more than the most transient benefit. Thus, the good intentions of social reforms and those dedicated to humanitarian reform were, despite their surface appearance, socially and morally pointless, if not harmful to the social order. In Spencer's fundamental scheme of things order was placed prior to welfare.

The fatalism of Spencer's work, its indifference to the situation of many Americans who found themselves the objects if not the victims of the nation's social and economic reorganization, as well as his vastly appealing (anticlassical) educational thought were the intellectual predicates of educational philosophy in America. Spencer made education a philosophical issue in the United States. Insofar as educational philosophy and pragmatism had a consistent and focused intellectual predicate, its predicate was mortgaged to the thought of Spencer, whose writings, particularly *Social statics* ([1851] 1969), *Education* ([1861] 1897), and *Principles of sociology* (1876–1896) were the wellspring of educational philosophy.

Educational philosophy's political economy—the manner in which formal, cultural, and social politics and economics interact so as to affect ideology or social orientation—reflected a social reform politics. Its political economy was the social democratic politics of Populism and Progressivism, just as it was a reaction against Spencer's social Darwinism. Thus, a certain solidarity was established between educational philosophy and those who did not possess social and economic privilege. The discipline's political economy was a justification for a rational educational solvent of the social and economic differences that existed between America's "haves" and "have-nots." It was a stance that was warranted by "the conviction [of

Populists and Progressives] that they were thus assuring social unity and progress" (Glenn, [1987] 1988, 9). The political economy of American educational philosophy can be traced to the complex interaction of industrialism and urbanization. Wrenching social and technological dislocations followed the Civil War and brought about unprecedented material distinctions that threatened to create a permanent under-class and a class of permanent advantage—a new aristocracy of wealth. At the same time in the United States, social dislocations generated a new intellectual class with its own technical and intellectual agendas.

America's new intellectual class was also part of the history of educational philosophy. The new class allied their interests with those of the common people and consolidated, among other things, a program for universal education, that is, the common school movement (see Glenn, [1987] 1988, 9). In part, educational philosophy became the intellectual and politically articulate voice of the movement during the period between the turn of the century and 1940. Educational philosophers hoped to secure social progress and order without the kind of apocalyptic confrontations that they had witnessed during the American Civil War. Educational philosophy became the voice of rational social reform and social construction within the university and the institution of schooling.

Industrialism and urbanization brought an inordinate educational commitment to the nineteenth century; what it lacked was an educational system to match the commitment evident in the rhetoric of the period. The idea of the common school can be traced at least back to the seminal work of Horace Mann (Glenn, [1987] 1988). But it was the Progressives who would bring the common school to life in modern form. Mann was committed to the establishment of a common school that would foster American patriotism outside of the divisive sentiments of the church and the social distinctions of European society. The Progressives were committed to taming industrial modernism and the social injustices that threatened the peace of the social fabric. The Progressives' version of the common school was committed to the creation of a just and fair democratic society. It would provide a place where individuals could find their place in the world on the basis of merit, not station. *Education became their general theory of action* (cf. Mills, 1964, 331, 391-423, 447).[3] Philosophy of education began in the belief that there should be public schools for everyone.

In the period before the Civil War American philosophy of education explicitly referred to Enlightenment contract theorists such as John Locke, Jeremy Bentham, and James and John Stuart Mill, just as it had reference to great republican revolutionaries such as Thomas Jefferson, Benjamin Franklin, James Madison (Karier, [1967] 1986, 21-

42), and a group of less well-known American churchmen (Chambliss, 1968). Between the Civil War and World War I it referred to Herbert Spencer. After World War I—in its professionalized form—educational philosophy referred, normally, to the pragmatists: Charles Sanders Peirce, William James, and John Dewey.

Outside of academic circles influential educators such as William Torrey Harris—organizer of the St. Louis Philosophical Society and the *Journal of Speculative Philosophy*, superintendent of the St. Louis Schools, and most important, United States Commissioner of Education to Presidents Cleveland, McKinley, and Roosevelt—had reference to Hegel and explored his thought in his own journal and the *Journal of Social Science*. But in a very important sense Harris's Hegelianism was merely something to be transcended.

Progressives heard the call to arms in the work of "muckraking" novelists like Sinclair Lewis, Upton Sinclair, and Theodore Dreiser, the philosophy of the socialist Left. Muckraking novelists like Sinclair Lewis, Upton Sinclair, and Theodore Dreiser are all part of the discipline's early history. Thorstein Veblen's trenchant critique of business domination of the universities, *The higher learning in America* (1918), and Upton Sinclair's two polemics, *The goose-step* (1922) and *The goslings* (1924), are all part of a matrix that generated philosophy of education. They made fundamental education questions a public issue.

Philosophy also made its contribution to the discipline. American philosophy in general, and Peirce, James, and Dewey in particular, became increasingly disappointed with classicism and Hegelian idealism. By the same token they were increasingly at odds with Herbert Spencer's evolutionary metaphysics. Although they were initially fascinated by its materialism and naturalism and its unified theory of science, its implicit social fatalism and seeming indifference to the human condition alienated them from Spencer's work. Spencer marginalized mind, discounting it to the naturalistic functions of evolutionary forces. The pragmatists could not accept a philosophy that had no place for a vigorous voluntarism and abandoned the human condition to the "ghost in the machine."

At the turn of the century, both Charles Sanders Peirce and William James struggled to construct a more active and independent version of mind, and John Dewey integrated a radical (at least in comparison to existing academic conventions) democratic politics and a social conscience into the constitutive elements of pragmatism. Dewey argued for the school as a device for social reform, a device of social action. In the same manner as the radical utilitarians, Peirce, James, and Dewey all believed in the power of rationality and philosophy. But Dewey's faith seemed particularly strong ([1920] 1950). He instrumentalized that faith in his investigations of education (e.g. Dewey, [1899] 1959; 1902b; [1916] 1966; 1938). His stance was consistent with the best socialist, utilitarian, Fabian, and utopian tracts. The work of Peirce, James, and Dewey was a new beginning—or at least a strong set of new brackets—that abandoned Spencer's conservative social perspective just as it abandoned Hegelian idealism.

The twentieth century in America witnessed the fruition of the common school movement. It also marked the emergence of the belief that education could be investigated as a "laboratory science" as well as a new awareness that schooling was intimately involved in the nation's social order. These events as a part and function of the social reform movement of the 1890s "brought the talents of John Dewey and a group of less publicly known scholars and teachers that formed the backbone of the progressive movement in education" (Eaton, 1975, 73) into the public arena.

In the hands of Dewey and his colleagues at Chicago and Columbia, educational philosophy became the device for the realization of the fact and promise of the common school. As Glenn ([1987] 1988, 4-5) reminds us, on one level the common school agenda was a matter of providing free, secular, and universal education—public schools for all the children of a community, not schools of churches, religious foundations, and private enterprise. On another level it had to do with producing the common attitudes, loyalties, and values necessary for forging a new nation. And on still another level it had to do with the establishment of the schools as a public institution for transcending the unprecedented material distinctions brought about by the generation and concentration of vast wealth during the Civil War, wealth that threatened to create a permanent underclass in American society and that appeared to threaten the egalitarian and democratic focus of America's social order. In a sense then, the history of educational philosophy is part of a reconstructionist politics of community and social and economic opportunity.

In the period between the turn of the century and World War II reference must be made to the Great Depression. It was the catalyst that drove the discipline in the 1930s and explains its tryst with social radicalism of all varieties, just its unsuccessful tryst points the way toward its obsession with metaphysics, epistemology and analysis.

Further, the discipline's modern development cannot be rehearsed without reference to the sixties and its counterculture, writers and musicians, civil rights activists, and antiwar protesters. Included in this group are Richard Nixon's "Silent Majority"; writers and poets such as Tom Wolfe and Bob Dylan; activists such as Martin Luther

King, Jr., Malcolm X, Todd Gitlin, Abbie Hoffman, Angela Davis, and Herbert Marcuse, who authored the popular American statement of the ideology of the academic American New Left; Arlo Guthrie's gentle cinematographic icon of the "folk years," *Alice's restaurant, M.A.S.H.* (the movie), the rockopera *Hair*, and its less profane counterpart *Jesus Christ superstar* consolidated the zeitgeist of the sixties. During the sixties both America and educational philosophy changed fundamentally.

## GREAT BRITAIN

Educational philosophy's evolution in Great Britain is not simple or straightforward. It does not boast a solitary intellectual accomplishment that foreshadowed the discipline's mature form. But it does have a discrete starting point: its professional organization in the mid-1960s. (cf. Larson, 1977, 208). Its antecedents can be traced back to the Enlightenment, but its modern configuration was largely an event of the social and intellectual politics of the period following World War II.

During the reign of Queen Victoria, toward the end of the nineteenth century, the schools and education were beginning to find their way into social and intellectual discourse. The topic was part of a general social concern about the apparently desperate and intractable social and economic conditions being generated by industrialism. It was part of a more general discussion of political economy and social reform. But for the most part it was about finding tangible political solutions for the amelioration of the suffering and smoldering anger generated by the industrial world.

Educational philosophy's history in Britain has a complex and amorphous prologue. Social, cultural, intellectual, and historical pressures created a concern for social reform, and therein education. The conservative reaction to Victorian liberalism and radicalism, that is the Victorian response to the issues of social reform, established the reservoir of educational questions with which moral philosophy and political economy would contend during this period. The reaction also separated social science (and education) from philosophy. In other words, it created the possibility of education as a separate discipline just as it created the possibility of educational philosophy as an academic enterprise outside of moral philosophy and political economy. Conversely, questions of social, economic, and political reform provided whatever reference philosophy retained with education.

The study of social science (in the singular) and therein the study of education found collective public representation in the National Association for the Promotion of Social Science, an umbrella organization dedicated to social welfare founded in 1856. Its membership list extended to peers, MPs, fellows of the Royal Society, various baronets, knights, ministers of the Church of England, statisticians, administrators, reformers, politicians, and moral philosophers.[4] It was the association that was responsible for initiating a systematic study of society and its institutions—education among them.[5] Education's central role in this organization quite probably helped delay its establishment within the university until well after World War II.

In the time between the close of the Victorian period and the end of World War II government and the university establishment were the only sources of patronage capable of sustaining the academic study of education or its collateral superstructure, social science. Neither was interested in supporting the systematic study of education. The poverty-stricken teachers colleges were barely capable of supporting themselves let alone sponsoring an intellectual and professional initiative such as educational philosophy (cf. McNair, 1944, 13; Stewart, 1989, 69). Since neither sinecure was available to educational philosophy, insofar as the discipline took shape at all, it did so around an endless list of government reports and royal commissions and did so through the lives of a handful of highly charismatic individuals: James and John Stuart Mill and elitist liberals such as Beatrice and Sidney Webb, John Ruskin, H. G. Wells, George Bernard Shaw, Bertrand Russell, and the great intellectual families of Britain.

Prior to the 1960s educational philosophy was a "discipline in waiting." It could not emerge while educational philosophy's tasks were dispersed among diverse elements of the social reform movement, Britain's intellectual elite, and the civil service establishment. World War II provided the predicate for a systematic reappraisal of education's fundamental assumptions in Britain; the war brought a social environment in which the easy Victorian answers to social problems were less compelling and also brought a lower class that was unwilling to return to a time "before the war." Politically enfranchised and active in a way that they had never been before, the lower classes found patent political responses less plausible than they had seemed previously. This matrix of events suggested a reorganization of British society just as it suggested an intellectual reorganization of the ancient universities and the system in which they were the keystone (Marwick, 1982, 94-155; Stewart, 1989). The ancient universities were compelled to find a place for social science and a collateral—if not internal—place for the study of education and the training of teachers.

The discipline's prologue is important because it explains how the condition of Britain's wider social and intellectual order conditioned the fund of questions that would define the educational philosophy that R. S. Peters and Paul Hirst wrote and the Philosophy of Education Society of Great Britain developed (cf. Toulmin, 1969, 26). Although the social reform movement of the 1890s and the National Association for the Promotion of Social Science generated the same fund of questions that helped inspire philosophy of education in the United States, this reservoir of questions and answers germane to social reform did not find a "susceptible" environment in Britain. Although the educational philosophy was "ripe," the absence of a university environment that was, for all intents and purposes, supportive of education delayed the university study of the discipline. In a sense the discipline's prologue is an account of opportunities that were not taken up and an account of a conservative response to a quantity of fundamental research questions appropriated by the social reform movement and therein social science. Essentially, the discipline's history is a display of establishment solidarity and resistance.

Educational philosophy's modern British form was foreshadowed by a complex interaction of biography, enduring intellectual acts, and social movements. As in the United States, it is a discipline of mixed parentage. But British philosophy of education evolved out of a stronger link with academic philosophy than did its American counterpart. Under the guidance of R. S. Peters it was methodologically radical and intellectually conservative. It was more at home with a classical version of education than it was with the social reform versions of education evolving out of Wilson's Labour politics. The discipline in the United States had strong and immediate links with the social reform movement and therein social science. The discipline in Britain did not adopt similar linkages but maintained a strong allegiance to philosophy. British educational philosophy was a reaction to the attempt of social science to appropriate the language and thereby the study of education to itself. Of course, the establishment of educational philosophy in Britain was at least partially an attempt to attach the status and academic standards of philosophy onto teacher education.

The evolution of the discipline was erratic. But it would be wrong to claim that this was an effect of inadequate intellectual resources. Individuals of great intellectual capacity and accomplishment were deeply concerned with problems of education and, collaterally, social problems at every level of generality.[6] The critical difficulty was structural, not intellectual. The discipline's development was a problem of institutionalization or, more accurately, lack of it.

## AUSTRALASIA

The conjunction of the area's colonial history, its geographical position on the Pacific rim, fashioned Australasia into a European cultural anomaly wedged between Oceania and Asia. "The cultural baggage brought by the colonists provided the foundations for local norms and values; this umbilical link was infused by economic and political forms of dependency—trade, investment, immigration, foreign policy, and so on—that survived the construction of the colonial confederation in 1901 and the early decades of the new Commonwealth" (Head, 1988, 9). It created an academic establishment that revered European and later North American culture and followed the intellectual leadership of the great universities of Europe and North America.

The intellectual dependency of Australasia on the Empire and English-speaking superpowers in the period following World War II is a central factor in the explanation of intellectual work in both Australia and New Zealand (Head, 1988, 9). It partially was a function of the small size of its academic establishment: small postgraduate numbers, modest research resources, small staffs, and large academic work loads. Academic work in Australia and New Zealand was dependent upon Europe and North America for professorial leadership and postgraduate training. The area's best graduate students pursued their intellectual training overseas—the probability of an appointment in an Australasian university was vastly increased by foreign postgraduate training. Similarly, given the modest nature of academic opportunity in Australasia, many of the best academics left the area to pursue their careers in Europe or America (Bourke, 1988, 60).

But by the early sixties the entire system of Australian education was entering upon a period of qualitative transformation parallel to that of Australian society as a whole. Postwar economic expansion, immigration, and the new relationship with North America forced a reassessment of many establishment values and reinforced the "new" pluralistic values of postwar immigrants and of a newly emerging white-collar class (Barcan, 1980). The old ties to Empire and Victorian culture were radically modified. Egalitarian attacks upon Australian society and elitist versions of schooling soon followed. The postwar baby boom, the rise of industrialism with its white-collar class, and the consequential expansion of primary, secondary, and tertiary education transformed the educational establishment. Government policy led to a massive expansion of teachers colleges. The university system followed suit but did not expand quite as rapidly. Following the qualitative transformation, the Australasian academic establishment moved to generate its own intellectual identity.

In the humanities and social sciences the investigation of the continuities and discontinuities of Australasian culture was undertaken with a certain urgency:

This has been true of entrepreneurs and economists debating the most efficient policies to stimulate industry, exploit natural resources, increase population, and raise living standards; explorers and engineers who in different ways have seen the outback as a challenge to be tamed; social and political reformers who have dreamed of building a better world; artists and writers who have tried imaginatively to reconstruct, and make familiar, the experiences of life in a new environment; leaders of ethnic minority groups who try to articulate the complex relations between their own residual cultures and the dominant Anglo-Australian culture. (Head, 1988, 11)

Conservatives on the other hand emphasized the social and political continuities of Australasia to its colonial heritage. The attempt to craft a uniquely Australasian identity has been marked by a pattern of dependency and dissent.

The establishment of educational philosophy followed a similar pattern of intellectual work. Its prehistory in Australasia is tied to the intellectual work of John Anderson and C. D. Hardie, two academic immigrants from Great Britain. John Anderson accepted the chair of philosophy at the University of Sydney in 1927 and inspired a domestic interest in the study of philosophy and education. In 1942 C. D. Hardie's *Truth and fallacy in educational theory* was published in Britain. After the publication of this important work, Hardie was given the chair of education at the University of Tasmania. Hardie's appointment pointed the way toward the establishment of educational philosophy as a discipline in Australasia's colleges and universities. And of course, both men were examples of Australasia's intellectual dependency; neither was a native Australasian.

By the late 1960s many Australasian academics were directing the literary and linguistic style of philosophy at the idea of education. The pattern of the discipline's establishment followed a meter similar to that of the English experience. Its initial "disciplined" form was inspired by R. S. Peters. Further, many of the senior members of the Philosophy of Education Society of Australasia, following the traditional pattern of overseas postgraduate training, evolved outside of their own ecology and in terms of a peculiarly distinctive English environment, that is, they traveled to England, trained at the London Institute, and defined themselves in terms of questions and answers that were more often than not constitutive of, and pertinent to, the English scene and Peters's version of the philosophy of education.

Many of the Society's newer and younger members, who had been trained in Australia and/or the United States, by the mid-1970s found the research agenda and methodology of the "London Line" problematic. They sought to generate their own intellectual identity. They attempted to define an Australasian version of their own craft by "analysing the distinctiveness of their society—its goals and values, social hierarchy, life-styles, ethnic composition, landscape, etc." (Head, 1988, 11). In the discourse and arguments generated by questions of cultural identity, the New Left, and the counterculture, educational philosophy was transformed. By the mid-1980s the discipline had freed itself from its subordinate intellectual dependency upon Empire and constructed its own qualitative transformation.

---

## NOTES

1. As Harris (1988) points out, this history has philosophical consequences. Bruce Raup (1966) noted that a study of the history of educational philosophy is part of the study of the discipline itself. Part of the purpose of this history is to construct the groundwork for a version of educational philosophy that is less self-referential and less constrained by what Richard Rorty calls "Philosophy." In this version of things history, literature, poetry, and all of the enterprises of language have an important place in the discipline. Philosophy, then, is: a search for conceptual alternatives that will provide order and power among puzzling data in a world that confounds our purposes and intentions (see Hanson, 1972; Rorty, 1989, 9).

2. In the post–World War II period major contributions to the "invisible college" of educational philosophy came from the United States of America, Britain, and Australasia. The Philosophy of Education Society of Great Britain was established in the closing days of 1964, and the Philosophy of Education Society of Australasia was established in 1970. These societies exchanged research results and became the significant reference points for the conduct of educational philosophy. In other words, while it is useful and informative to say that American philosophy of education began with the John Dewey Society, a complete account of contemporary Western educational philosophy's evolution is an account of at least three histories in common or on parallel paths.

3. For example, George Counts proposed a theory of social action that was, essentially, a matter of education in general and schooling in particular (see, Gutek, 1983, 108-162). Harold Rugg proposed a similar theory in *Culture and education* (1931). Dewey added his support for a general theory of action that revolved around education in two books: *The public and its problems* and *Reconstruction in philosophy*.

4. Abrams (1968, 45) reports that the National Association for the Promotion of Social Science was composed of over thirty-five organizations as well as chambers of commerce, cooperative societies, temperance organizations, and educational groups.

5. After the demise of the National Association for the Promotion of Social Science the study of education lacked a historical environment that would demand an academic (university) reappraisal of education's fundamental assumptions—a traditional predicate for philosophical investigations. The social, cultural, and historical conditions necessary for the consolidation of fundamental investigations of education, that is, educational philosophy would not appear for generations.

6. John Locke, Jeremy Bentham, James Mill, John Stuart Mill, Matthew Arnold, Sidney and Beatrice Webb, John Ruskin, and Bertrand Russell, to name only the patently obvious, directed their attention to education. The advent of the discipline certainly was not delayed for a lack of individuals with great intellectual ability devoted to its questions.

Part I

# Philosophy of Education
# in the United States

# The 1890s Social Reform Movement in the United States

If educational philosophy's intellectual predicate was anticipated in part by philosophy (see Chambliss, 1968), the empirical predicate for educational philosophy was found in the turn-of-the-century demand for social reform and the invention of social science (Furner, 1975, 286-288). What follows is an account of how social science and educational philosophy developed a common intellectual and academic alliance and goals as a means of addressing some of the most pressing questions of urbanization and industrialization.

## SOCIAL REFORM

In the United States, philosophy of education initially was set within the context of the attempt to make the practice of schooling responsive to the demands of the social conditions of nineteenth-and twentieth-century America. At the most critical moments of its inception the discipline was mortgaged to the social reform movement; that is, it was closely related to attempts of social reformers to dissolve the long-standing monopolies of learning, to dissolve the arrangements that "made" some individuals affluent and "made" others poor. Therein the idea of the discipline was tightly tied to the idea of the common school movement and the social concerns that were part of that movement (Glenn, [1987] 1988).

The intellectual task was to dissolve the individualism, the "voluntarist philosophies" that made the monopolies of learning not only plausible but also commendable—a voluntarism that made membership in America's underclass a function of drunkenness, prostitution, brutality, and ignorance—and to replace it with a new philosophy and system of explanation that paid attention to the effects of social structure (cf. Haskell, 1977, 240-256). The social reform program focused upon the redistribution of opportunity and the development of both social policies and educational institutions as ways to shield individuals from the worst hazards of unregulated industrial economics and as an efficient means of improving their social situation (Haskell, 1977, 255).

The demand for social reform and the attempt to exchange the squalid world that the excesses of immigration, urbanization, and industrialism had generated for something better through objective rational means—solving the world through the collection of data and changing the world through social policy—created social science, and thereby numerous assorted disciplines, education among them. The plan was simple. If industrialism and urbanization were the cause of America's desperate social conditions then social science would provide the diagnosis and education would provide the cure.

The social reform movement was part of a complex social interaction of farmers, laborers, settlement house notables, novelists, academics, and labor organizers. The movement was the part of a version of Progressivism that belonged to the "well off" and the well educated. It part of a much broader social reconstruction and intellectual critique of America. The critique took to task both the practices and the values of Victorian America. This critique was part of—for lack of a better name—modern times. It was the beginning of a new ethos that signaled a new world and the decline of the Victorian period. In Schlesinger's words:

The Progressive era was an unprecedented time of popular education. The muckrakers in press and magazines disclosed the techniques of political and business corruption. And political leaders sought to show how honesty and intelligence might provide the remedy. Thus there arose Robert M. La Follette of Wisconsin, Charles Evans Hughes of New York, Hiram Johnson of California, James M. Cox of Ohio—typical Progressive governors, some Republicans, some Democrats, but all standing for the enforcement of middle-class standards of civic decency against greedy wealth and crooked politics. The greatest of them all in his public impact was Theodore Roosevelt of New York. (Schlesinger, [1957] 1988, 18)

By the turn of the century urbanization, industrialism, and a Victorian worldview that rationalized privilege and offered moral absolution for avarice and greed had ringed America's major cities with ghettos of poverty and had driven the small farmers from their fields. Populism and Progressivism were the organized form of the people's resistance to their dispossession.

Middle-class Victorians believed in the power of ideas (Mills, 1964, 331). They also believed like most Victorians that the drunkenness, prostitution, degradation, poverty, and ignorance that was endemic in America's urban slums was a function of individual weakness or wickedness. But this was a time of relative affluence, and the situation of the lower classes inspired moral guilt, indignation, and a call for fair play, if not justice. The juxtaposition of unparalleled affluence with unparalleled poverty was offensive to the nation's middle class. They knew that something was not quite right.

The social reform movement's intellectual assault upon Victorianism was driven by the generation of middle class and "well-off" Americans that came of intellectual age between the turn of the century and after World War I—John Dewey among them. In one form or another elements of America's intellectual aristocracy were involved in calling attention to the base social conditions in which millions of Americans were living. If they agreed about nothing else, they did agree that the shocking poverty in the nation's urban slums and single family farms was wrong. If America was to survive industrialism they knew that the economic dissipation of the nation needed moderation, regulation, and some moral boundaries.

The reformers were out to prevent the construction of a permanent underclass and to disestablish vested privilege—political and economic—just as they were out to find a place for themselves closer to the throne, a place of more profound authority and political influence when the issues of the social order were being discussed. Having constructed a place of authority for social science at the turn of the century—even if that place was not as salubrious or as close to the seat of legislative power as the place of social science in Britain—they sought to translate that authority into power (Haskell, 1977, 98).

The people's resistance to Victorian versions of society and social order in the United States was as much a matter of direct action as intellectual critique. The nation's alarming economic intemperance generated the social reform movement. The social reform movement represented a disappointment with Victorianism. It was a response of the intellectual establishment to those farmers and urban workers who had had enough and were demanding more—a decent living in the land of plenty. That element of America's intellectual elite who perceived the role of social and moral philosophy as well as social science as tightly related to the agenda of social reform had more sympathy for Eugene Debs than they did for John D. Rockefeller and Andrew Carnegie.

The social reform movement was adopted by the popular press and by socially conscious elements of America's literary establishment. They were individuals of Christian conscience or utopian cum socialist leaning who were disappointed with turn-of-the-century America. If America was the land of plenty, it seemed to them that the plenty was not being shared around very well. Insofar as educational philosophy was one element of the social reform movement, it was part of the critique of American Victorianism and the society it generated.

## AMERICAN SOCIAL SCIENCE ASSOCIATION

The country's new intellectual middle class responded to the demand for social reform both by articulating the need for change and by proposing solutions. The American Social Science Association was established to do just that: propose solutions to the social problems generated by industrialization and urbanization. The association was founded in 1865 by the Massachusetts Board of State Charities (Silver, 1983, 102). Samuel Gridley Howe and Frank Sanborn were key figures in the establishment of the association, but in a real sense, as Haskell (1977) notes, the American Social Science Association was Sanborn's organization.

Sanborn was the fifth child of seven born into a Unitarian family of moderate means and some social distinction in Hampton Falls, New Hampshire (Haskell, 1977, 51). He was educated at Harvard, and there he became a friend of Theodore Parker and came to know Samuel Gridley Howe, Thomas Wentworth Higginson, John Greenleaf Whittier, and Ralph Waldo Emerson (Haskell, 1977, 53). It was this circle of acquaintances that led him first to the Massachusetts Board of State Charities and then to his work with the association. Between 1865 and his resignation in 1898 Sanborn led the institution and gave it its distinctive character. To Sanborn's mind social science was a kind of reform activity that was hardly distinguishable from the kind of thing that was drawn from the pen of numerous socially conscious novelists.

The formation of the American Social Science Association (1865), and therein the formalization of social science, was a function of the self-evident demand for the social reconstruction (reform) of the nation's urban centers (Silver, 1983, 134). It was an attempt to solve America's social problems through the power of ideas. At the time of its organization there were no professional social scientists in America or any other country for that matter (Haskell, 1977, 24; Furner, 1975, 10-11). "The modern disciplines of economics, history, sociology and political science are based upon disciplined communities of inquiry that were brought into existence by the mundane labors of men like Richard T. Ely, Herbert Baxter, Herbert Adams, John Franklin

Jameson, Edward A. Ross, Albion Small, and Jeremiah W. Jenks" and the American Social Science Association (Haskell, 1977, 25).

The American Social Science Association was of course connected to the idea of social science. But it was the English version of the idea of social science that Americans found most attractive. Frenchman Auguste Comte was the first to present the idea of social science in his *Positive philosophy* ([1830-1842] 1893). Comte's version of social science was by modern standards relatively undifferentiated. He conceived of it in the singular without the academic divisions that eventually would evolve out of his version of positive philosophy; that is, he conceived of social science as one academic undertaking without its modern division into sociology, political science, economics, psychology, and so forth. Furthermore, he saw social science as an intrusive device through which government would intervene in the social order. Although such an intrusive version of social science seemed quite acceptable to the French, it was most certainly unacceptable to the British and just as certainly unacceptable to the Americans.

John Stuart Mill brought social science from the European continent to Britain. He presented a version of social science that was dedicated to the discovery of the "facts" that could be, he argued, a social palliative in themselves without the intrusive, dangerous, and socially corrosive invasion of government into private affairs (see Mill, [1848] 1891; [1867] 1985; [1843] 1884). Britain's social reform movement found Mill's version of social science compatible with their faith in ideas and laissez faire government. Once presented with Comte's ideas in acceptable philosophical garb, Britain's middle class immediately institutionalized the new approach to social reform through the establishment of the National Association for the Promotion of Social Science. Established in 1857, the British association was the institutional and intellectual model for the American Social Science Association, which would be founded in 1865.

The American Social Science Association claimed license to John Stuart Mill's adaptation of social science (Burns, 1959; Senn, 1958). The combined sense of the reality of social laws, the accessibility of social data, and the regularity of social behavior implied the possibility of successful intervention in human affairs and the amelioration of social distress (Silver, 1983, 104). Social institutions became legitimate objects of academic inquiry. This ethos identified education as a central instrument of social reform and as worthy of investigation in its own right (Silver, 1983, 136).

Social science and philosophy at the turn of the century retained a close relationship. Nothing demonstrates this better than the reverent and respectful eulogy for John Stuart Mill that was published in volume 5 of the *Journal of Social Science* (1873). The eulogy is instructive. It portrays the intimate relationship of philosophy and social science:

John Stuart Mill. By the death of this eminent man, which took place at Avignon, on the 8th of May last, this Association has met a great loss. In 1865, he was elected a corresponding member, and he accepted the office, by a cordial letter dated March 5, 1866. Everything in this country interested him, for he saw that the great moral and political truths, to the investigation of which he had devoted himself, were here to be subjected to the freest experiment. He congratulated us upon the attempt to form an association for the more careful consideration of these truths, and he offered to assist us in any way in his power. Such an opportunity was not to be lost and he was freely consulted. (American Social Science Association, 1873, 136)

The honest sense of concern and loss expressed by the American Social Science Association upon the death of John Stuart Mill indicated the close social, professional, and intellectual commerce that still existed between philosophy and social science.

"Social science" and "education" were related concepts in mid-nineteenth century Europe and America. They had a common ancestry in social and moral philosophy (cf. Bryson, 1932a, 19-27; 1932b, 304-323; 1932c, 26-36). Social science emerged from philosophy as a familiar and accessible concept and an organized discipline in the second half of the nineteenth century. This is a crucial factor in understanding the establishment of the systematic study of education on the one hand and philosophy of education on the other—first in the social reform movement and then in the United States' universities.

From 1865 to 1885 the American Social Science Association represented the multifarious interests of those dedicated to the study of society. By the 1880s various elements among the association attempted to establish a common curriculum for social science, but members' varied purposes and diverse perceptions of themselves and their mission defeated the project (Furner, 1975, 10-12). In addition the association was unable to compete with its various specialized elements that were rapidly professionalizing.

The American Social Science Association articulated the questions of moral philosophy to social reform, social practices, and institutions of everyday life (Furner, 1975; Haskell, 1977). The association's original goal, the generation of social facts, represented a not inconsiderable faith in the power of ideas. This naive faith in ideas was a conceit of influential members of America's middle class that led to the belief that information would somehow conjure away poverty and its ancillary evils, or failing that, legislate them away (Furner, 1975; Haskell, 1977; cf. Silver, 1983, 100-131).

The response of the association's members was "motivated by a complex mixture of decency, guilt, and fear" (Furner, 1975, 23) and most assumed that the disadvantaged deserved the assistance of those with excess means. When it became apparent that charity was not equal to the task of remediating the ills of industrial society they directed the association 's investigations toward the uses of *formal education* as a means for the development of a patriotic, moral, and self-sufficient citizenry (Furner, 1975, 22). The banishment of ignorance from urban and industrial society through education seemed an elegant and economical solution to problematic social conditions.

The American Social Science Association was divided into four departments: education, public health, social economy, and jurisprudence. The literature of the association published in the *Journal of Social Science* was replete with examples of the moral critique of nineteenth-century America's social and institutional realities. The investigations with which the Department of Education were charged were these:

1. Under the Department of Education will come everything relating to the interests of Public Schools, Universities, and Colleges; to Reformatory, Adult, and Evening Schools; to instruction in the useful Arts; to Systems of Apprenticeship, to Lyceums, Pulpits, and the formation of Societies for the purpose of Public instruction. In this department will be debated also all questions relating to Classical, Linguistic, and Scientific Studies, in their proportion to what is called an English Education; and the bearing of National and Patriotic Memorials upon Popular culture. (ASSA, 1866, 15)

Economics, political science, sociology, social welfare, public administration, and education among others evolved out of the association's divisions. During its most productive years the *Journal* devoted roughly 10 percent of its articles to education.

It was a profoundly conservative organization, evident in an "Introductory note" in the *Journal of Social Science* that read:

Social Science, or the Science of Society, treats of man as a social being. It fulfils its functions just as other sciences fulfil theirs, by collecting facts, applying principles, and reaching the general laws which govern the social relations . . . [But] social science is not Socialism. The latter deals with Society destructively pulling down rather than building up, and reducing the higher grade to the lower, instead of raising the lower to the higher. The former, by a reverse process, seeks to uplift whatever is low, and indeed whatever is already high, by placing both on a firmer foundation, and rearing them in larger and loftier proportions. It is essentially constructive, and aims at strengthening, rather than undermining, the constitution of society. (ASSA, 1869, 1-2)

The political sentiment of these articles was largely conservative and elitist. Of course, the authors were, in most instances, members of the middle class demanding change on behalf of the less socially fortunate. But between 1850 and the turn of the century the journal consistently addressed the role of the school in society and the school in social reform. William Torrey Harris addressed philosophical and educational issues in the association's journal. Harris, among others (see *Journal of Social Science*), saved a place for philosophy in one of social science's dominant departments—education. Numerous articles in the *Journal* addressed topics that foreshadowed a reservoir of questions and answers like those addressed by Dewey's "The school and society" ([1899] 1959) and echoed the moral tone of "My pedagogic creed" ([1897] 1959).[1] The journal's concern for social reform and the instrumental role of education is identical to the tone of the work of utilitarianism's radical philosophers: Jeremy Bentham, James Mill, and John Stuart Mill. Motivated by a Christian sense of moral concern, but untrammeled by the religious and economic dogma of privilege; empirical, material, and teleological in their philosophy—both the radical utilitarians and those who were members of the American Social Science Association were concerned with freeing the underclass from ignorance, poverty, and moral depravity in all its forms.

The demand for social reconstruction and social reform in Victorian America opened the niche for social science in American higher education. Although the initial effort to inveigle Johns Hopkins University to give a home to social science—in the singular—failed, a suitable niche was constructed by dismantling social and moral philosophy into the various social sciences and then establishing them one by one in various American universities (Bryson, 1932a, 19-27; 1932b, 304-323; 1932c, 26-36; Furner, 1975; Silver, 1983, 120).

The American Social Science Association separated social science from moral philosophy by the traditional means of intellectual specialization. The areas of specialization that the association would sponsor would eventually professionalize, focused upon the production of theory and knowledge rather than social reform or moral philosophy (cf. Furner, 1975, 278-324). The professionalized version of social science that the association sponsored, with its ethos of empirical research and theory construction, firmly detached moral philosophy from social science.

The social and intellectual forces in which the American Social Science Association was embedded virtually ensured its initial success just as surely as they ensured its eventual dismantling. It was a transitional organization that acted as a clearinghouse, defined issues, focused inquires, intensified the issues of social reform, and sponsored more specialized academic societies. It was a clearinghouse for independent research, and as such it was unable to generate highly disciplined and focused research. In the end it was unable to recognize the functional forms of explanation that were beginning to dominate social science (Haskell, 1977, 234-35). It was an organization for amateurs in a world that had turned professional. In the 1880s every aspect of the association advocated systematic study, and those more interested in humanitarian purposes shifted their energies to single-purpose reform societies.

Industrialism, urbanization, and the rise of professionalism sponsored the dissection of the American Social Science Association into the various social sciences (Haskell, 1977, 27). The association met for the last time in 1909. Finally, it was necessary to beg space on the program from one of its descendants, the American Sociological Association, to announce its passing. The various new social sciences were still committed to social reform, but since they had been willingly co-opted into the university, reformist zeal was tempered by the conservative realities of membership in academic institutions that were dominated by the economic giants of the period. Nevertheless, the various specialty areas were still committed to socially useful knowledge as long as it was not critical of social elites or the institutions they owned and operated.

## PHILOSOPHY OF EDUCATION AND SOCIAL SCIENCE

Social and moral philosophy in American universities continued to apply to the work of scholars laboring in the classical tradition, usually in departments of academic philosophy. Nevertheless, "moral philosophy became an important source for the origin and development of what later developed as political science, economics, philosophical ethics, psychology, anthropology, and sociology" (Sloan, 1980, 6). These subspecialties of moral and social philosophy eventually established themselves as independent departments in their own right, largely in the period between 1890 and 1940.

Initially the construction of social science out of philosophy in the United States was attempted for the purposes of addressing the empirical issues of social reform and avoiding the seemingly endless entanglements of metaphysics. By the turn of the century the social sciences had abandoned or were abandoning contentious social and moral questions in the name of methodological purity, the collection of data, and the construction of theory (Furner, 1975, 286-288). But the separation of the various disciplines was not easy. Sociology, economics, and political science labored for a generation or more to escape the constraints of moral philosophy and to distinguish themselves from each other (Furner, 1975, 278-312). The unwillingness, at least initially, of the social sciences to take up the moral questions of social reform was one element of their appropriation of a professional identity distanced from philosophy.

Although social science in America and Great Britain found its initial point of establishment in the social reform movement, the social sciences found a home in the American university establishment. They crafted a place for themselves on the basis of the success of their investigations of American society. Later, American pragmatism provided it with a fundamental rationale. The intellectual legitimation and general description of social science was based upon the salient work of John Dewey. He was social science's preeminent philosophical spokesperson (Haskell, 1977, 252-253). Dewey joined social science and social reform to inquiry (see Dewey, [1927] 1954; 1935; 1939) and defined its logic (see Dewey, [1938] 1982).

Dewey's powerful and "socially acceptable" philosophy gave social science a common mission and explained and justified a common *scientific* method at a time when many of those devoted to social science could not agree on a common method or mission (cf. Furner, 1975, 10-34). What was novel in Dewey's thought was not merely methodological; what was really novel was the manner in which he tied the logic of social science to political ethics and social reform (Feuer, 1959, 545-546). Dewey's emphasis upon scientific thought—at a time when the distinction between systematic study and experimental method was only starting to emerge—tied an ethics of social responsibility and egalitarianism to the conceptual primitives of science. Dewey's ideas were the "raw stuff" to which the "legal realism" of Oliver Wendell Holmes, Jr., the political economy of Thorstein Veblen, and the social democratic economic history of Charles Beard gave common allegiance. It gave intellectual support to their work as something more than interesting literature and justified its opposition to the powerful special interests of industrial capital in society and the schools. He justified the place of social science in the university.

The belief that the evils of industrialism were beyond social control created conditions that propelled social science onto the campuses of American universities. These changes only waited for individuals whose work bridged the gap between a moral critique and a factual description of the appalling social conditions that industrialism and urbanization had generated. Postsecondary training institutions had to become specialized research-oriented organizations providing professionals to give expert social advice. Social science also awaited a community that would recognize and give its assent to that advice. The several disciplines of its modern form—economics, history, sociology, and political science—transformed the shape of the country's campuses and the intellectual disciplines that were constitutive of those campuses.

Political Science would find a niche in the rise of public administration as an area of the civil service and industry in the 1890s (Furner, 1975, 278). The study of government, a major part of moral philosophy in the mid-1800s, evolved into political science under the pressures of nationalism in the post–Civil War period and the demands of an expanding government establishment. Francis Lieber helped establish political science at Columbia University mid-century (Furner, 1975, 279). Andrew Dickson White established a department of "History, Political and Social Science" at Cornell in 1868 (Furner, 1975, 230). Charles Kendall Adams founded a department of political science at the University of Michigan in 1881 (Furner, 1975, 280).

In 1892 Albion Small was appointed to head the first sociology department at the University of Chicago. A couple of years later Frank Giddings opened a department of sociology at Columbia. With the publication of Small's *American Journal of Sociology* and books such as Lester Ward's *Pure sociology* (1903), the discipline was firmly launched in America. The American Sociological Association was formed in 1905. It was Small who exchanged seminal ideas on education with John Dewey (see Small, 1897). And the influence, of course, was reciprocal.

Albion Small, a colleague at the University of Chicago, shared Dewey's concern for the social role of schooling. Small, who was professor of sociology, wrote "Some demands of sociology upon pedagogy" (1897). In it he delineated a view of pedagogy remarkably like Dewey's:

Sociology, like charity, ought to begin at home, but, like charity, it ought not to stay at home. The rational method of observation, recognizing the real concentration of life around each member of society, explores the concentric circles of social activity from the actual standpoint of the observer. The child should begin to study economics,—literally, the law of the household,—he should learn the civics and ethics and history of the household, in the practice of normal household relations. The economy and politics and ethics and history of the school, and then of the parent's shop, and then of the neighboring factory, and later of the whole town, are the best educational material that the sociologist can recommend. In other words, the social desideratum is that the developing member of society shall become analytically and synthetically intelligent about the society to which he belongs. (Small, 1897, 848)

The parallel with Dewey's work is haunting. Without prior warning one might presume that the former quotation was lifted from the first section of Dewey's "The school and society" ([1899] 1959). It would not be unreasonable to conclude that the inspiration for the first sections of

"The school and society" flowed directly from Dewey's childhood experience of school (Jane Dewey, 1939) and was influenced by Small's comments on pedagogy. For that matter what later appears in Dewey's *Democracy and education* (1916) seems to shadow some of Small's remarks about economics, history, and geography.

Social science was an important influence upon the inventory of research questions and answers that educational philosophy would call its own. American and English investigations of industrialism and urbanization usually had reference to education as a device for the amelioration of social conditions and reconstruction of industrial society. Thorstein Veblen in economics; Albion Small, Lester F. Ward, Edward A. Ross, and Charles H. Cooley in sociology; and Charles A. Beard and J. Allen Smith in history and political science made claims to the study of education. John Dewey was heavily influenced by economists such as Veblen, historians such as Beard, and sociologists such as Small. Social scientists like George Counts and Harold Rugg were influential members of the John Dewey Society and important influences on the investigations of the Society.

Social science, education, and therein educational philosophy were understood by this group of Progressive intellectuals to be instrumental elements of social reform. Their connection to social reform in America opened the niche for educational philosophy on American campuses. Educational philosophy was a foundational element of schools of education. The Universities of Iowa, Michigan, Minnesota, Chicago, Ohio State, Harvard, Illinois, Berkeley, Yale, and Columbia Teachers College all boasted an early concern for educational philosophy. It was a concern that separated colleges of education from the high schools and normal schools. In the new schools of education, philosophy of education was part of both the demand for social reform and the intellectual critique of inequity, poverty, and deprivation of nineteenth century industrial society.

But the familiarity of social scientists with the undergraduate lecture promoted the mischievous idea that primary and secondary teaching was a self-evident activity. It also encouraged the university community to reach the further conclusion that there was nothing to know about education. Any skills necessary for effective teaching were seen as the kind of things that any intelligent man or woman could work out for him or herself. The inability of the social sciences to take the investigation of teaching seriously left the systematic study of teaching to faculties of education. Thus the social sciences abandoned the study of education as they focused upon the demands of the experimental treatment of social data to consolidate the establishment of their place in the university.

The consolidation of an empirical and statistical profile forced the social sciences to abandon the moral questions of education as well. The last decision left a vacant niche for educational philosophy. When economics, sociology, and political science failed to make successful claims to the study of education (cf. Furner, 1975; Haskell, 1977) and education continued the presence it had established in its own name within the American university, moral and social questions of philosophy at least insofar as they pertained to education remained within its domain. But unlike the other social sciences, education did not shed its connection with social and moral philosophy. The traditional place of social and moral philosophy within education was left relatively intact, and the study of education remained within departments of education.

Social science anticipated a radical educational philosophy that academics like George Counts, who grew up on a Kansas farm, and Harold Rugg, a scholar who traced his roots to New England, would support. Both men had been influenced by the social and economic critiques of Beard and Veblen (Bowers, 1969a, 85). Both Counts and Rugg, among other educators and social scientists, wrote searching commentaries about the educational reproduction of social inequalities.

The work of George Counts is the classic example of similar studies conducted by American educators. Counts was directly inspired by the work of Charles Beard, who was a close friend (Dennis, 1989). Beard had written an iconoclastic study of the American constitution, interpreting its articles and sections in terms of how they secured the economic and social advantage of America's founding fathers. Counts did the same thing for the American school. In *The selective character of American secondary education* (1922), *The social compositions of boards of education* (1927), *Secondary education and industrialism* (1929), and *The American road to culture* (1930), Counts demonstrated the relationship of the control and structure of the common school to the social and economic advantage of America's privileged elite. Similarly, from the perspective of social science—tempered by the bohemianism of Greenwich Village—Harold Rugg published with Ann Shumaker *The child-centered school* (1928). This work railed against the commercialism of America's schools. Their work was an important and original empirical extension of the theses of Veblen and Beard.

George Counts (a social scientist by trade) was the editor of *The Social Frontier*, educational philosophy's radical early voice. Harold Rugg, a sociologist cum educator, was in his own way as influential as Counts. The meld of philosophers and social scientists was not accidental. It was a function of their common ancestry in moral and social philosophy and the research questions in which they shared a common interest. It was also a function of the fact that the discipline's establishment was taking place at a time when the boundaries of philosophy and social science and the various social sciences themselves were not as rigid as they were to become in their modern form.

All that remained was for someone to demonstrate that education was a domain in which real and fundamental social (philosophical) questions were worthy of intellectual investigation and to claim those questions for education and therein educational philosophy. John Dewey, of course, did just that. In doing so, he provided the intellectual means to establish educational philosophy in its own right just as he allied the discipline's reservoir of research questions to those of social science as well as to those of philosophy. Dewey's "My pedagogic creed" ([1897] 1959) and "The school and society" ([1899] 1959) foreshadowed a new academic discipline.

## NOTE

1. William Torrey Harris, U.S. commissioner of Education, Daniel Coit Gilman, president of Johns Hopkins University, and other important educators were associated with the ASSA. It seems quite unlikely in such a state of affairs that Dewey was unaware of the *Journal of Social Science* or its social reform stance.

# 2

# Intellectual Antecedents

In one sense Populism and Progressivism were critiques of America's version of Victorianism. They were a "people's" critique. They may have been a "class" movement as well, but their intellectual heroes were domestic and their ideologies were "homegrown." Even if, like their European counterpart, they were driven by one element of socialist ideology or another, they rejected or at least held in abeyance revolutionary solutions.

The common point of reference in the social reform movement of the 1890s was Edward Bellamy's socialist utopia *Looking backward* ([1887] 1926). Bellamy's prose was crisp and powerful. Describing the world he saw, he wrote:

I cannot do better than to compare society as it then was to a prodigious coach which the masses of humanity were harnessed to and dragged toilsomely along a very hilly and sandy road. The driver was hunger, and permitted no lagging, though the pace was necessarily very slow. Despite the difficulty of drawing the coach at all along so hard a road, the top was covered with passengers who never got down, even at the steepest ascents. These seats on top were very breezy and comfortable. Well up out of the dust, their occupants could enjoy the scenery at their leisure, or critically discuss the merits of the straining team. Naturally such places were in great demand the competition for them was keen, every one seeking as the first end in life to secure a seat on the coach for himself and to leave it to his child after him. (O)n the other hand there were many accidents by which it might at any time be wholly lost . . .

Commiseration was frequently expressed by those who rode for those who had to pull the coach, especially when the vehicle came to a bad place in the road . . . At such time the passengers would call down encouragingly to the toilers of the rope, exhorting them to patience, and holding out hopes of possible compensation in another world for the hardness of their lot. (Bellamy, [1887] 1926, 10-11)

*Looking backward*'s ideology was as utopian and arcadian as it was socialist.

Edward Bellamy was powerfully influenced by the Fourierist craze that swept America in the late 1800s. When Bellamy joined the staff of New York's *Evening Post* in 1871, he more likely than not met the Fourierist, Parke Godwin, still on the paper's editorial staff (Guarneri, 1991, 401). Guarneri reports that "It *is* known that Bellamy was introduced by his brother Frederick to Albert Brisbane, whose theories, according to Frederick, 'interested him deeply.' Brisbane's son reported that the aging Fourierist 'closeted himself for long sessions' with the budding socialist" (1991, 401). Bellamy's *Looking backward* ([1887] 1926) was deeply influenced by Fourierism. The assemblage of industrial armies, the emphasis upon voluntary and peaceful social reconstruction, and the practical economies of blending private and communitarian living styles that are prominently featured in *Looking backward* trace their intellectual heritage to François Marie Charles Fourier (Guarneri, 1991, 404).

In an attempt to make his version of socialism popular Bellamy separated his work from the cultural radicalism, subversive (French) cultural text, and sexual novelties that were essential characteristics of Fourierism (Guarneri, 1991, 404; cf. Klier). Nevertheless, it was Bellamy's call for action on a national scale and the pioneering Fourierist communities of Texas that bound his version of utopian socialism to the Farmers Alliance. It was obvious to the nation's small farmers just as it was obvious to Edward Bellamy that only governmental action on a national scale could protect them from national industrial and financial organizations that had been generated by the Civil War.

Populism and Progressivism had similar utopian cum socialist ideologies, even if their emphasis upon collective action and legislative programs was the antithesis of Fourierism's decentralized communitarianism. The movements were as suspicious of the unions as they were of big business. Both were suspicious of the city and industry. Populists and Progressives were representatives of the "little guy," the small capitalist on the farm and the industrial laborer in the city (Mills, 1964, 328). They were the same people Thorstein Veblen remembered in *The theory of the leisure class* ([1899] 1922). Direct action for them resulted in the McKinley, La Follette, Roosevelt, and Wilson elections (Mills, 1964, 328). The movements were concerned with domestic philosophy and domestic politics. Their task, as Populists and Progressives saw it, was a matter of extending the American creed to all parts of society while keeping a weather eye on the social politics of greed and avarice.

It is significant . . . that the most successful socialist or semi-socialist parties in the United States—the Socialist Party of Oklahoma, the Non-Partisan League, the Farmer-Labor Party of Minnesota—based their attack on capitalist economic structure, not in terms of a Marxian doctrine of class struggle, but as a continuation of the traditional struggle of farmers and workers, the common people, against "the vested interests" of eastern bankers and Wall Street, the symbol of concentrated wealth. North Americans have shown their willingness to organize against capitalist power in order to protect their opportunities to have a good job or to run their own farm or small business; but propaganda designed to appeal to a permanently exploited proletariat of workers and landless or mortgaged farmers has made little impression. (Lipset, [1950] 1968, 190)

Populism and Progressivism began a movements for the popular extension of the franchise and the political base of American democracy. Under President Taft a graduated income tax and the direct election of Senators would be made possible by the Sixteenth and Seventeenth Amendments to the Constitution. As part of the extension of democracy intrinsic to Progressivism, John Dewey would explore the educational requirements of democracy (Cremin, [1961] 1964, 120). One aspect of his exploration resulted in his classical statement of Progressive education: *Democracy and education* ([1916] 1966). This period presented the American archetype of direct political action by the working class, the strike. By the 1920s the precedent for direct political action was established in American politics just as it established the trade union movement's interest in electoral politics.

In the late 1890s the Chicago Teachers Federation (in 1916 it became part of the American Federation of Teachers) had sued the city of Chicago to enforce the collection of tax directed toward the financing of the city's educational system. Several public utilities and the Pullman Palace Car Company had evaded paying municipal taxes for years. Acting for the Chicago Teachers Federation, Margaret Haley and Catherine Goggin brought the city of Chicago again and again to court to secure the collection of tax. And finally in 1898-1899 they obtained a judgment ensuring the payment of tax (see Murphy, 1981). The Chicago Teachers Federation and later the American Federation of Teachers supported a vast array of progressive issues including items as diverse as public support of education, women's suffrage, trade unionism, and equal treatment for blacks and black teachers (Murphy 1990). It should be remembered that the American Federation of Teachers was a willing vehicle for the implementation of John Dewey's thought.

Populism and Progressivism foreshadowed a different America, an urban industrialized nation. The Farmers Alliance,[1] the Grange,[2] the Knights of Labor,[3] and other less stable events expressed the people's criticism of the Victorian world and its industrial and urban improvidence. It was an expression of the stupendous confrontation between capital and labor that marked the politics of America in the 1890s. Its expression was to be found in those historical forces that were flirting with insurrection—the 1892 Homestead Strike,[4] Coxey's army of 1894,[5] the 1894 Pullman Strike,[6] and so forth.

Insofar as elements of the social reform movement were Populist, they were advocates of agrarian socialism (Hofstadter, 1963, 7; Mills, 1964, 328-329). Agrarian socialism in North America (located primarily in the wheat belt in the United States and primarily in Saskatchewan and the western provinces in Canada) sought to shelter farm ownership and income from a prejudicial system of free trade that left farmers to compete without government assistance in world markets, while paying heavy prices for high tariff goods and high interest to banks for the capital to pay for those goods (Lipset, [1950] 1968). Agrarian socialism was a fight for economic independence in which socialism meant one dollar for a bushel of wheat and liberalism meant seventy cents for that same bushel (Lipset, [1950] 1968).

## POPULISM

Populism began in a Texas depression. In 1877, impoverished and disconsolate white Texas farmers formed the "Farmers Alliance." The cooperative cum socialist/utopian ideology of the alliance was brought to Texas by Etienne Cabet, a disciple of Robert Owen and Victor Considerant who brought a fusion of the dreams of the English utopian Robert Owen and the French cooperative socialist François Marie Charles Fourier to Texas in the 1850s (Klier; Guarneri, 1991, 399-404). The resulting ideology denied fatalism, focused upon the genuine possibilities of the American frontier, and accepted both the freedom to and the responsibility for building a better world. Members of the alliance, like the Fourierists, sought to avoid both plutocracy and anarchy through voluntary and peaceful social reconstruction (Guarneri, 1991, 399-404). But this cooperative cum socialist/utopian ideology was tempered by the rabid individualism of the American transcendentalists. The predicate of the alliance was socialist, utopian, and transcendental.

The alliance system was to become the beginning of America's rural political radicalism—Populism (Zinn, 1980, 279). By 1887 resistance to the brutal crop-lien system, the company store, and the smothering interest rates of the banks generated a membership of 200,000; the alliance's educational lecture series reached two million farm families (Zinn, 1980, 280). Committed to direct action, the Farmers Alliance was a radical organization. Its more conservative counterpart was the Grange.

American Populism as evident in the Farmers Alliance and the Grange found support in Canadian Agrarian Socialism. The ideology of both movements combined and spread across the Plains tempered by French socialism, English utopianism and American transcendentalism. It generated a low-key resistance that captured state governments if not the political machines of those states across the nation's agricultural belt. It helped organize the People's party. As a political force it organized those who worked and created a demand for governmental protection from the economic exploitation of the monied classes. It was a powerful movement that by 1896 enticed William Jennings Bryan to run against McKinley for president of the United States (Zinn, 1980, 289). It was a movement convinced of the benefits of collective action and collective resistance to domination by the big money interests of the East.

As much as the Farmers Alliance and the Grange were divided over the issues of tactics, they were united in their concern for education and their demands for social reform. Both were concerned with the application of science to agriculture (Cremin, 1988, 471). But, perhaps even more important, the lectures organized by the Grange and the alliance informed farmers' perceptions of themselves and fundamentally altered their political relationship to government (Cremin, 1988, 472). The educational activities of both groups were consistent with the educational emphasis of Populism. Although the educational opportunities offered by these organizations were only utilized by a minority, the emphasis on education as a device of social and economic reform could not be missed. It foreshadowed a radical educational politics that men like George Counts would espouse and that John Dewey, would justify philosophically.


## PROGRESSIVISM

Progressivism was the urban counterpart of Populism. It found its base in the city in the same manner that Populism found its base in the "heartland." Populism shared its utopian and socialist genius with it. Populism and Progressivism never questioned the goodness of American society although they were more than willing to castigate some of its principal institutions. They questioned the necessity of the vast social inequities in America's rural and urban landscape (see Morrison, 1895; Riis, [1903] 1970). Arthur Schlesinger, Jr. noted that Progressives could be divided into at least two groups—politicians and ideologues ([1958]

1988, 130-131). Among the politicians, Robert La Follette, George Norris, and Al Smith dominated the politics of liberalism. They were the loyal opposition to the Republican presidency. Among the ultraliberal ideologues, John Dewey, Herbert Croly, Thorstein Veblen, and Charles A. Beard dominated Progressivism's intellectual structure. The ideologues questioned the morals of the "leisure class" (see Veblen, [1899] 1922), its laissez-faire economics (Beard, 1913), and its politics of privilege and advantage, and Croly popularized Progressivism and appealed to the conscience of the middle class. His tool was the *New Republic*, which he edited. In the end, the movement convinced most of the middle class and those in Washington that big business was in need of federal regulation.

However reluctantly embarked upon, the Progressive Era was a period of reform directed toward the control of America's economic buccaneers (Zinn, 1980, 341-346). The Hepburn Act was passed to regulate railroads and pipelines, the Pure Food and Drug Act to control the adulteration of urban America's food. The Mann-Elkins Act regulated and consolidated the nation's telephone and telegraph industry. Wilson's administration created the Federal Trade Commission and the Federal Reserve to curb some of the excesses of the banking system. This period also marked the extension of the federal government's interest in education. The federal government acted to extend education to those who were not proceeding on to college. The Smith-Hughes Act (1917) established vocational education. As part of the general extension of educational opportunity during the Populist and Progressive period, modest and humble land grant colleges established for the sons and daughters of farmers and mechanics in Minnesota, Michigan, Wisconsin, Iowa (in the midst of the Populist redoubt), and other places developed into institutions that significantly challenged the prestige of elite private colleges—e.g., Harvard University, Stanford University, Johns Hopkins University, and so forth.

It was a period of affluence and social confrontation. There was little sympathy for the bitter strikes of the 1890s. The Pullman strike (1894), the Homestead strike (1892), the Haymarket bombing (1886) in conjunction with the eight-hour-day movement, and Coxey's Army (1894) frightened America's intellectuals. What the brutal confrontation between labor and capital did not accomplish, World War I did. The easy ideology that promised social peace and industrial order that flowed from the social reform movement was shattered in the closing years of the nineteenth century and the early years of the twentieth. The disillusionment that began in the vicious strikes of the 1890s, and the equally vicious response of the Pinkertons, state militias, and local police was consolidated by the war and the Russian Revolution. There was little sympathy to be found for socialists, feminists, pacifists, or trade unionists in the confines of America's universities.

On the other hand, America's universities were not monolithic. They did have a number of intellectuals who spoke for and professed a solidarity with America's ordinary people. Academics like Charles Beard, Richard T. Ely, and John Dewey sympathized with the plight of the common people and supported—as a matter of Christian conscience and social democratic principle—the politics of their discontent. The Progressives systematically opposed petitions for "the special management of democracy on the grounds of mass biological incompetence" by the eugenicists and social Darwinists in the name of liberty, equality, and fraternity. The simple humanism of both Populism and Progressivism made the work of eugenicists unthinkable and the work of Spencer impossible to support. Evolutionary social science's reactionary support for privilege and its indifference to the fate of the working class made its antieducational stance abhorrent and its implicit political economy detestable. The work of Beard, Ely, Dewey, and sociologists such as Albion Small and Frank Lester Ward was the intellectual counterpoint to the social Darwinism of Herbert Spencer and William Graham Sumner. Lester Ward's *Dynamic sociology* (1883) made a case for education as the "panacea" for social ills and provided a counterpoint to the evolutionary fatalism of the social Darwinists.

The importance of Populism and Progressivism for educational philosophy was that it forced the pool of questions that had constituted social and philosophical comments upon education into a political economy and ethics that the radical utilitarianism had been unable to transcend and the conservatives had adopted as their own.[7] The first tentative phrasing of that domain would be found in Dewey's "My pedagogic creed" ([1897] 1959) and "The school and society" ([1899] 1959). But others inside and outside of what could be called the inner circle would suggest questions and answers.[8] Some would be adopted, others would not.[9] The original research domain would be partisan, socialist, utopian, transcendental, and material—based in experience.

Populism and Progressivism made education a political issue. Educational philosophy's prehistory was immersed in the politics of social reform. It was a role educational philosophy clung to until the patriotic fervor of World War II created the social and historical conditions that caused the discipline's partisan social democratic politics to implode.

## MUCKRAKERS, ACADEMICS, AND INTELLECTUALS

The Populism and Progressivism of American's Victorian period was launched by the nation's workers, but the middle class became their orators, publicists, educators, and politicians. The muckrakers were their publicists. Muckrakers were disappointed with turn of the century America. If America was the land of plenty it seemed to them that the plenty was not being shared around very well. New Americans of the period had left the European underclass with the hope of better things in a new land. They were not willing to be the "raw material" of a new American underclass.

The popular yellow press gave a partisan education to the masses. Unlike the genteel magazines of the time, the popular press replaced Victorian escapism with a genre of realist literature that featured America's less perfect aspects: dirty schoolrooms, fly-specked kitchens, and broken men in down-and-out flop-houses. They were for the "people." Reading, previously a luxury reserved by the cost of hard cover books and expensive magazines for the well off was extended to all by prices that were within the reach of even a meager pocket.

Muckraking was sensationalized in the yellow press and legitimized in literary magazines. E. W. Scripps, Joseph Pulitzer, and William Randolph Hearst made careers out of playing up scandals and advising the poor of the realities of their situation. *McClure's, Cosmopolitan,* and *Munsey's Magazine* ran feature after feature exposing the social, political, and economic misbehavior of the trusts. Ida Tarbell, Lincoln Steffens, and Ray Stannard Baker became journalists of great standing by muckraking America's corporations. Muckraking was an activity in which the sons and daughters of immigrants of the working class played a significant role. For example, Theodore Dreiser was born in an immigrant and working-class environment, S. S. McClure was an immigrant from Ireland, and Jacob Riis was an immigrant from Denmark (Elliot, 1988).

Jacob Riis's *How the other half lives* ([1903] 1970) galvanized the interest of the intellectual establishment to the plight of those condemned to exist in America's industrial urban slums. Robert Hunter's *Poverty* ([1904] 1965) delivered a detailed study of life among the less than well-to-do in America. Riis's and Hunters's graphic exposure of poverty drew national attention.

Some of the nation's best creative writers took the issue up and would not let it rest (Filler, [1968] 1976). This theme was explored graphically in Stephen Crane's *Maggie* ([1893] 1896), Frank Norris's *Octopus* (1901) and *The pit* (1903 [1956]), Upton Sinclair's *The jungle* (1906), and Theodore Dreiser's books *The financier* (1912) and *The titan*

(1914). What America's realistic writers were doing to expose the plight of America's dispossessed and disenfranchised began with Crane's *Maggie* and ended with Steinbeck's *Grapes of wrath* (1939). This "realistic" fiction was paralleled by the "yellow" manuscripts appearing in the popular press. Lincoln Steffens, and Ray Stannard Baker directed an extended investigation into the malignant relations that existed between business, politics, and the unions. Ida Tarbell presented a ruthlessly honest portrait of the corrupt and malignant oil industry entitled: "History of the Standard Oil Company" in *McClure's* (1902, 1903, 1904). Thomas Nast went after Tammany Hall, just as Hamlin Garland's *Spoil of office* (1892) explored state corruption (Filler, [1968] 1976). Henry Demarest Lloyd's *Wealth against commonwealth* ([1894] 1936) was a brilliant piece of muckraking. It carefully described the attempt of business to suborn federal, state, and local government. America and its people discovered scandal, corruption, and poverty in the yellow press.

Jack London's work was an intellectual halfway house for the middle class and the "people" (see Foner, 1947). He brought a graphic picture of poverty and oppression to the middle classes and a socialist text to the working class. London's work bridged the gap between those who read the yellow press and the middle classes who read the *New Republic* and the *New York Times*. It brought the meaning of Marxism to an American context for both "ordinary Americans" and the middle classes. But it was a version of Marxism that never questioned America. Patriotic and competitive to the core, London only asked the chance to beat the bosses at their own game (Foner, 1947). His experience of poverty and deprivation, the killing work of unskilled labor, and the brutality of the police was autobiographical: experiences, catalogued in his novels *Martin Eden* ([1908] 1957) and *The iron heel* ([1934] 1948), were an enduring intellectual force in the Progressive period.

London's literary style displayed his partisan and socialist stance. First in books like *The people of the abyss* (1903), a profile of life in London's East End, and later in short works like "Apostate" appearing in the *Woman's Home Companion* in September 1906; or "The dream of Debs" in the *International Socialist Review* (1909), London painted a picture of endemic ignorance, child labor, and dark places where the light of education did not enter. Short essays brought his work to the attention of America's intellectual establishment and alluded to the reasons why the destitute and disenfranchised were choosing against a life of what was called "honest labor." [10]

Nor were the schools ignored. Joseph Mayer Rice's *The public-school system of the United States* (1893) documented the details of an administratively incompetent and intellectually bankrupt system. Rice was one of the first to connect educational misconduct with the social reform movement as both national in scope and related to the broader questions of urbanization, industrialism, poverty, and deprivation (Cremin, 1988, 227-228). *The public-school system of the United States* was classic rhetoric. It was partisan, factual, portrayed a vivid picture of urban public schools, and relied upon firsthand data for its credibility.

Rice was not alone. Robert Hunter's *Poverty* ([1904] 1965) is particularly noteworthy for its discussion of the lives of poor children and, among other things, their education.[11] The book presented a chilling picture:

It will be recalled that in those streets and courts and alleys in which the inebriated, the blind, the crippled, the consumptive, and the aged—the ragged ends of life—live, there also live the half-starved, underclad beginnings in life. The poverty which kills, which makes terrible the end of life, is not so terrible as the poverty which blackens and stifles childhood and casts a shadow over all the after life ...
The half-starved, beaten, and neglected child of the inebriate, the physically weak child of the consumptive, these are most to be pitied ... Guidance and supervision of the parents are impossible because they must work; the nurture is insufficient because there are too many mouths to feed; learning is difficult because hungry stomachs and languid bodies and thin blood are not able to feed the brain . .. There must be thousands—very likely sixty or seventy thousand children—in New York City alone who often arrive at school hungry and unfitted to do well the work required. (Hunter, [1904] 1965, 190, 216)

In true muckraking fashion, the hand of business in corrupt school administration was reported by Upton Sinclair. Sinclair's exposés of criminal corruption in the management of education followed the tone of what the muckrakers were doing in the press. In *The goose-step* (1922) and *The goslings* ([1924] 1970) Sinclair critiqued America's universities and its school systems. The intellectual adulteration of higher education in the name of the business interests of the Stanfords, Rockefellers, and Carnegies, to cite only the most important, was chronicled in Thorstein Veblen's *The higher learning in America* (1918). While Sinclair was concerned with corruption and cronyism, Veblen was concerned with the undue influence of the American "leisure class." These writers would not let educational misconduct pass without public comment.

Veblen delivered the most academic and extended critique of the American university. In *The higher learning in America* (1918) Veblen detailed the specter of business in the affairs of practically every aspect of the university. Business was eroding both classicism and the classical independence of the university. According to Veblen an alien presence haunted the university and was suborning it (Veysey, 1965, 346-347). Financial support was constantly sought and often won on the promise that the academic departments and laboratories that were set up would be of direct benefit to business (Veysey, 1965, 348-349). Philanthropists like Leland and Jane Stanford who erected an entire university to the memory of their son not only directly hired and fired members of the professoriat but also made sure they followed the party line in what they said and thought.[12] For the Stanfords the party line was prorailroad and proprivilege. The party line was a matter of personal economic privilege. It was only secondarily concerned with free markets, that is, it was only secondarily procapitalism. For that matter, the economic party line on both the East Coast and the West Coast was similar. For example, Alfred D. Chandler, Jr. (1977) has demonstrated that when J. P. Morgan organized the railroads through the manipulations of his bank he was more concerned with regularizing his position of economic privilege and monopoly than he was with ensuring the free play of capital markets. As a matter of fact Morgan's primary concern was to make sure that markets were not free, and competition was carefully controlled and monopolized. Free competition, like socialism, as Morgan knew only too well, was the enemy of economic privilege, monopoly, and, most importantly, profit (see Chandler, 1977). As far as they were concerned the business of the universities was business. A sober John Dewey noted that something important was being lost when the intellectual independence of the university was surrendered to business (1902a).

It was the yellow press that indelibly marked the social and moral issues of education in the public mind and America's academic establishment. It brought the ghastly conditions of those who toiled to the attention of America's academics and thereby to America's educational philosophers.[13] It was the muckrakers who made Progressivism, and therein progressive education, a public issue. The public advertisement of the socially corrosive effects of ignorance, poverty, drunkenness, prostitution, corrupt industrial practice, and the appalling conditions of America's industrial cities encouraged the development of a professional intellectual class that was expected to solve the problems of industrialism and urbanization that were so obviously out of control. The muckrakers identified education as part of the problem and part of the solution to the situation that industrialism and urbanization had created in the United States.


## HULL HOUSE AND EDUCATIONAL PHILOSOPHY

The social reform movement of the 1890s was the intellectual and middle-class counterpart of Populism and Progressivism. The movement was part of a complex interaction of settlement house notables, novelists, and academics, all responding to the political, economic, and social misconduct of great wealth. In a more academic voice it was a response to the monopoly consolidation of the enormous wealth and industrial development that had flowed from the Civil War (Hofstadter, 1963, 7-9). That element of America's intellectual elite who perceived the role of social and moral philosophy as tightly related to the agenda of social reform had radically different social and political goals than those who served privilege. Hull House was a critical gathering point for those who felt that special sympathy for the American underclass.

The Settlement House Movement was begun by Samuel Augustus Barnett, vicar in London's St. Jude's parish. Barnett and his wife "settled" in a destitute area of London for the charitable purpose of "elevating the poor." They established Toynbee Hall, the first settlement house. They counseled the destitute, made home visits, formed clubs, and taught classes on various subjects. After visiting Toynbee Hall, Jane Addams and her traveling companion Ellen Gates Starr decided to establish a settlement house in Chicago. Upon returning to the United States they acquired a house built by Charles Hull in 1856 and finally moved in in 1889. Over the years the social reform role of Hull House expanded, and Addams worked for the regulation of juvenile labor, shorter working hours for women, and social justice for immigrants and blacks. She researched the causes of poverty and crime. For her work she was cowinner of the Nobel Peace Prize in 1931.

Along the way Hull House became more than a settlement house. Under the dynamic leadership of Addams the mission and educational program of the house attracted all manner of academics and intellectuals from around the world. As a result Hull House became a venue for social debate and the contest of ideas as well as a settlement house. It came to serve as an important gathering point for Chicago's liberal intellectual elite and radical intellectuals from around the world.

The Hull House circle was the American analogue of the Fabian salon (Feuer, 1959, 557).[14] Dewey was a trustee of Hull House (Wise, 1935, 169-170). It was there he met the people, alluded to in his autobiographical essay, who influenced him more than books while he was a young professor (see Dewey, [1930] 1962, 22). At Hull House the intellectual salon—not the settlement house—Jane Addams would confirm what Dewey already suspected about America's "leisure class." The collection of yellow journalists, muckrakers, liberals, unionists, anarchists, socialists, and communists that made Hull House a common point of meeting for intellectual encounters was critical for the tone of Dewey's social and educational philosophy. Their thought was a key challenge to the intellectual assumptions of the then young professor (Addams, [1935] 1974, 50).

Dewey soon came to terms with foreign radicals, the revolutionary proletariat, as well as the not quite respectable institution of the socialist Left, the trade union movement. Jane Addams played a critical role in tempering his social conscience. If Hull House was his tutor, Addams was his guide. "John Dewey was a regular visitor as was Henry Demarest Lloyd" (Levine, 1971, 55). At Hull House Henry Demarest Lloyd presented his exposé on Standard Oil, and Henry George and members of the Chicago Single Tax Club exchanged views and debated all comers.[15] John P. Altgeld, the new governor of Illinois, who demonstrated incredible political courage by pardoning the condemned Haymarket martyrs, often came to dinner, as sometimes did Clarence Darrow (Levine, 1971, 55). In 1901 Prince Kropotkin presented his anarchist views and charmed the settlement and all who visited it (Levine, 1971, 55). Richard Ely, the Wisconsin professor who was bringing a social concern to economics, sketched pictures of national economics with a social conscience (Levine, 1971, 55-56). And Jane Addams presented the pure and good spirit of the destitute and disenfranchised—a powerful antitoxin to the Victorian explanations of poverty, destitution, drunkenness, and prostitution that assumed individual wickedness as a primary cause (Levine, 1971, 126-143; Wise, 1935).[16]

When Dewey left Chicago for New York and Columbia University, his contact with social radicals continued at Henry Street, a New York settlement house run by Lillian D. Wald. "Tagore; Madame Naidu, an associate of Gandhi; Madame Suradji; Prince Kropotkin; and Ramsay McDonald all came to Henry House" (Dykhuizen, 1973, 146).[17, 18] Many came to meet Dewey, but they also came to contest the smug social conceits of American industrialism and present their own causes.

Dewey was sure that education was the key element to transcending the poverty, ignorance, and hopelessness of life on "mean street." Dewey's stance in those early days was an amalgam of socialistic ideals and Calvinist individualism (see Dykhuizen, 1973, 1-116). His educational philosophy was launched in "My pedagogic creed" ([1897] 1959). In the conclusion of that little tract he wrote:

I believe, finally, that the teacher is engaged, not simply in the training of individuals, but in the formation of the proper social life.

I believe that every teacher should realize the dignity of his calling; that he is a social servant set apart from the maintenance of proper social order and the securing of the right social growth.

I believe that in this way the teacher always is the prophet of the true God and the usherer in of the true kingdom of God. (Dewey, [1897] 1959, 32)

The Calvinist ethic of his childhood was never more obvious.

Originally Dewey's educational thought was driven by his Calvinist ethics, the social reform movement in general, and the people of the settlement houses. But by the time he left the University of Chicago his work was driven by a combination of socialist and utopian politics. Going to Columbia in 1905 he emerged as the spokesperson of the democratic left-wing of American education (Feuer, 1959, 561). His politics and his educational philosophy moved decidedly to the left and moved even further during and after his tenure at Columbia (Dykhuizen, 1973; Hook, 1987).

## HERBERT SPENCER

The reciprocal influence of Britain and the United States upon the practice of education and social reform is well known (see Armytage, 1967). In Britain philosophers of education looked to the intellectual traditions of the continent: Rousseau, Pestalozzi, Froebel, Kant, Fichte, Herbart, as well as homegrown intellectuals like John Locke, Jeremy Bentham, James and John Stuart Mill, John Ruskin, Matthew Arnold, and others. All the former and especially the Mills were central among the social and intellectual antecedents of educational philosophy; but it is Herbert Spencer who is the linchpin in the story of educational philosophy in the United States.

The intellectual fascination with Spencer's philosophical work marked, in a sense, the American intellectual establishment's break with speculative philosophy. Slightly more technically speaking, the acceptance of Spencer's metaphysics marked the passing of the intellectual dominance of American transcendentalism and the parallel rejection of the newer philosophical idealism inspired by Hegel and championed in the United States by William Torrey Harris among others. Spencer was one of the first thinkers to offer a modern and general (material, empirical, nonteleological, and without reference to final causes) theory of science and therein, of course, a modern and general theory of social science. He also presented the case that the task of science and social science was the production of general and systematic theory, not facts.[19] Spencer argued that evolution was the general description of the organization and vector of change evident in all empirical and material events.[20] According to him, physics, biology, psychology, and sociology were all amenable to description and, eventually, explanation within a theory of evolution.

In Spencer's world education did not, as many classicists insisted, exist for anything metaphysical; it existed for the purposes of survival (Low-Beer, 1969, 17). In a general sense "an education" was a historical description of one apparent means of human survival. Thus the justification of any person's education or system of education was in terms of its instrumental function in the maintenance of human life. Education was related to self-preservation and its collateral demands (Spencer, [1861] 1897).

At the turn of the century in the United States it was impossible to avoid reference to the work of Herbert Spencer in any serious study of philosophy, science, social science, or education (Cremin, 1988, 387). Spencer was the most influential writer of the time on man's place in nature (Kennedy, 1978, 25). Spencer's work had a serious influence upon the country's entire intellectual and academic community. The influence of Spencer's thought was partially due to the compelling strength of his prose and the manner in which it articulated the Victorian worldview. But its enormous influence was also the result of the manner in which Darwin's *Origin of species* ([1859] 1860) offered massive support for the general theory Spencer had held and written about for decades prior to the publication of Darwin's work. Darwin provided Spencer's theory of evolution with the one thing it lacked—a mechanism to explain organic evolution, that is, natural selection (Carneiro, 1967, xix). Spencer returned the compliment by providing Darwin with the term evolution, which did not appear in the first edition of *Origin of species* ([1859] 1860). He also extended the application of Darwin's mechanism to the social order. Articulated to the social order, Spencer's thought was the intellectual fetish of the period. Evolution was not something to think about, it was the manner in which science addressed the world. It was not just a matter of influence, it was a matter of intellectual orientation.

Herbert Spencer, an English polymath, wrote exhaustively upon diverse topics. His books, on everything from evolution to education, were well known on both sides of the Atlantic. He was an individual of enormous intellect and an important member of the English intellectual establishment. Although Spencer never became a member of the Royal Society of London, upon Thomas Huxley's invitation Spencer became a member of the X Club.[21] Membership in the X Club brought Herbert Spencer onto a familiar footing with most of Britain's eminent scientists and philosophers. At club dinners he conversed with Huxley, Tyndall,

Hooker, and Lubbock just as he did with casual visitors like Charles Darwin and Wilhelm Helmholtz.

In the United States Edward L. Youmans, an ardent supporter, founded *The Popular Science Monthly* at least partially as a device to publish Spencer's work (Kennedy, 1978, 25). He also enlisted D. Appleton and Company as Spencer's sympathetic publisher (Hofstadter, [1944] 1945, 14). One of the most influential publishers of intellectual material in America, Appleton secured Spencer's prestige in the United States. In America's great colleges the work of Herbert Spencer, John Stuart Mill, Thomas Huxley, Charles Darwin, and John Tyndall usurped the place once held by members of the Victorian literary guild, Tennyson, Browning, Arnold, and Dickens (Hofstadter, [1944] 1945, 21). Spencer's *Education* ([1861] 1897) accelerated utilitarian tendencies in American education and influenced the efforts of  Charles Eliot the president of Harvard, on behalf of the "new education" in secondary schools (Cremin, 1988, 390).

Herbert Spencer's American popularity and public fame probably peaked in 1882 during his triumphant tour of the country (Hofstadter, [1944] 1945, 48). The thunderous and appreciative public reception of Spencer's social philosophy cannot be uncoupled from its impact upon America's intellectual elite as well as the moral absolution it offered to America's capitalists (Hofstadter, [1944] 1945, 46). In *A people's history of the United States* (1980), Howard Zinn points out that the Victorian establishment was under siege from a sea of Grangers, Greenbackers, Single Taxers, Knights of Labor, Populists, Progressives, and socialists who were determined to restructure privilege and redistribute the country's wealth. But in Spencer's sociology the middle classes and their economic betters were delighted to discover that they did not owe the underclasses anything. And for the well off and the well-to-do it was even better to discover that meddling in the affairs of those who inhabited America's industrial slums and farm shanties was quite likely to cause more harm than good. In words appended in the postscript to the text of *The study of sociology,* Spencer wrote:

Fostering the good-for-nothing at the expense of the good is an extreme cruelty. It is a deliberate stirring-up of miseries for future generations. There is no greater curse to posterity than that of bequeathing them an increasing population of imbeciles and idlers and criminals. To aid the bad in multiplying, is, in effect, the same as maliciously providing for our descendants a multitude of enemies. It may be doubted whether the maudlin philanthropy which, looking only at direct mitigations, persistently ignores indirect mischiefs, does not inflict a greater total of misery than the extremist selfishness inflicts. ([1873] 1904, 314)

In the scheme of things that Spencer constructed, all things—social and political—would work out for the best, in the long run, if government did not interfere (Spencer, [1873] 1904; [1892] 1940). Spencer's work was a wonderful rationale of existing social distinctions and a justification for their maintenance (Hofstadter, [1944] 1945, 31-66; Noble, 1958, 16). His social fatalism was vastly appealing. In this light, it is no surprise to discover that it was Andrew Carnegie, in the company of Spencer's American acolyte Edward Livingston Youmans who saw Spencer off at the pier upon the conclusion of his American lecture tour.

The industrial freebooters and entrepreneurs that took president Grant as their hero took Spencer's philosophy as their own (Cremin, 1988, 389). The laissez-faire worldview implicit in Spencer's work and made explicit in William Graham Sumner's provided a solid rationale for educational monopolies and elitism of the nineteenth and twentieth centuries. Many agreed with Spencer in that they believed that the schools did not have a direct role in social reform. Social welfare, including education, generated so many unintended social consequences that it was uncontrollable and politically dangerous, or so it was argued (cf. Abrams, 1968, 74).

Spencer's *Education: Intellectual, moral, and physical* ([1861] 1897) was an extension of his general and systematic doctrine of evolution to education with some extensions that his reflections upon his father's life as a teacher provided (Royce, 1904, 127; Carneiro, 1967, introduction; Kennedy, 1978, 11-13). Victorian versions of schooling whose curriculum revolved around, to his mind, effete classicism contributed little to the struggle for existence (see Spencer, [1861] 1897; Kaminsky 1967, 527). Spencer's evolutionism, his emphasis upon the struggles of industrialized society, and his caustic criticism of classical education fitted nicely within the technological and utilitarian American ethos and endeared him to the age (Carneiro, 1967, introduction). But even more important than his attack on classics was the ceaseless war he waged against the state per se, against free libraries, free education, and the extension of public activity into the entire idea of social welfare (Spencer, [1892] 1940). While Spencer argued that elementary education for all was a necessary requirement for a pacific laboring class (a class in which people knew their place) and for responsible political activity within a democracy, the provision of further education extending into the esoteric air of secondary education or the provision of free libraries was unnecessary and perhaps dangerous, inasmuch as such provision would only fan the socialist ideas of the dangerous classes (Spencer, [1892] 1940, 39-40). This thinking provided a rough and ready manifesto for abandoning the dangerous classes to their own devices, educational and otherwise.

Herbert Spencer made education an intellectual and a philosophical issue.


## JOHN DEWEY

Before the twentieth century the work of European educators Pestalozzi, Herbart, and Froebel formed the basis of American educational thought and practice (Chambliss, 1968, 3). But the intellectual content of their pedagogical thought, for the most part, was irrelevant to the initial formulations of American educational philosophy. Pestalozzi's work was uncritically adopted in the realm of educational method. Herbartianism was accepted axiomatically by its most ardent advocates. The most serious philosophical work devoted to Herbartianism was largely critical (Chambliss, 1968, 3). And no sophisticated or systematic Froebelian philosophy of education was written by any American during this period (Chambliss, 1968, 3).

Educational philosophy as an element of pragmatism was part of the intellectual gambit that took social reform as its purpose and the self-evident abuses of industrialism as its predicate. It was a gambit it shared with turn of the century social science. Pragmatism's interest in education was part of its theory of action (cf. Schlesinger, [1957] 1988, 131). Pragmatists believed in ideas and the power of ideas (Mills, 1964, 331). Education delivered ideas. The problem to be addressed was twofold: first, the schools had to be reformed such that educational practices relied upon theory that was educationally potent (Dewey, 1902b; [1916] 1966); and second, the schools could not be allowed to remain socially unconscious and indifferent to the fate of their public clientele (see Dewey, [1899] 1959). What followed from these concerns, once ordered, was a new academic discipline—philosophy of education. Its initial serious and systematic development can be traced to the work of John Dewey. Its form was distinctly American.

Dewey was profoundly influenced by the evolutionism of Herbert Spencer. In college Dewey read Spencer more often than any other author (Feuer, 1958, 557; 1959, 545). His undergraduate study was tempered by the evolutionary geology of James Dwight Dana, dean of American geologists (Hofstadter, [1944] 1945, 18; Jane Dewey, 1939, 10). After a long struggle Dana was convinced of the efficacy of evolutionary theory. His *Manual of geology* ([1894] 1896) played the same role in American thought as Charles Lyell's *Principles of geology* ([1830] 1889) played in Britain at an earlier point in time. Both books provided the intellectual leverage necessary to abandon biblical chronologies of creation and presupposed an extended chronology that could provide the expanses of time necessary for evolutionary processes. These convincing books provided evolutionary explanations with plausible domestic intellectual support. Dewey was also deeply influenced by John Tyndall and Thomas Henry Huxley, who presented the case for evolutionary theory in journals such as *Fortnightly, Contemporary Review, Nineteenth Century,* and the *Westminster Review.* Both Tyndall and Huxley shared their colleague Spencer's faith in the explanatory and descriptive power of evolutionary theory. Jane Dewey (1939, 39) wrote that her father was heavily influenced by John Tyndall and T. H. Huxley's thoughts, which he encountered in those popular English journals. She argued that those encounters were as important in shaping his thought as his college courses in philosophy (11). Dewey also studied Spencer with George Sylvester Morris (Dykhuizen, 1973, 321). Later, as a young professor, he reorganized the curriculum at the University of Michigan to pay closer attention to Spencer's work (Dykhuizen, 1973, 45). The influence of Spencer, Dana, Tyndall, and Huxley was evident in his early papers on ethical theory. In 1897 Dewey delivered two lectures on "Ethics and evolution" reported in the *Monist* (1898) and *Chicago Record* (1902) (Dykhuizen, 1973, 99-100) in which his evolutionary concerns were quite obvious.

Fascinated and outraged with Spencer's work, Dewey, like William James, spent years engaging him and disentangling evolutionary theory from Spencer's theory of mind and his social and economic politics. "Spencer became the foil against which James would fashion his philosophy of activism, empiricism, pluralism and free will" (Cremin, 1988, 401). James's ([1896] 1904) effort to come to terms with Spencer's philosophy of mind is found in his long essay "The will to believe." Dewey's effort to come to terms with Spencer would begin with "The reflex arc concept in psychology" (1896), receive elaboration in *Experience and nature* ([1925] 1958), and would not rest until he marked some concluding statements about the constitutive social elements of logic and thereupon mind in *Logic* ([1938] 1982).

Both William James and John Dewey constructed their investigations of mind as a response to Spencer's evolutionary social science. Both were repulsed by the short term social fatalism and the long-term indeterminacy of Spencer's version of evolutionary theory. If the universe was ultimately open as Spencer argued, the idea that it was immediately closed as he also argued seemed a rather crass rationale for privilege and a disingenuous apologetics for the indifference of wealth to the suffering only too evident in America's industrial slums. Dewey's contribution to the discourse of pragmatism was to develop the work of Peirce and James and infuse pragmatism with a radical social

politics. It was a matter of formulating a socially acceptable
alternative to Spencer's indifferent social Darwinism. Education, of
course, would be a central element in that socially conscionable
alternative.

Dewey argued—like Samuel Alexander (1920) in Britain and John
Anderson (see Baker, 1986) in Australia—for an empirical metaphysics
(Dewey, [1925] 1958) and an empirical ethics (Dewey, [1922] 1957).
Philosophy, as far as he was concerned, was about the problems of men.
In this line of argument moral philosophy was not a surrogate for
divine commands; Dewey saw ethics as an aid for people—unchurched
and unschooled since childhood—who found it difficult to know right
from wrong and refused the moral solace of taboos, folkways, and
circumstance. He also saw moral philosophy as a mode of inquiry that
was active in the world. For Dewey inquiry was a social activity that
was socially conditioned and had social consequences ([1938] 1982, 20).
It was a mode of human activity that might or might not facilitate
inquiry into existence and the conditions necessary for its reconstruction
([1938] 1982, 58). And in its academic form moral philosophy was a
mode of activity that might or might not allow for its own
reconstruction ([1938] 1982, 58). In other words, all too often moral
inquiry was subordinated to a scheme of uses and enjoyments of a social
elite, all too often it was a little more than moral absolution by
intellectual sleight of hand ([1938] 1982, 58). To Dewey's mind it was a
mode of academic conduct that was all too often—wittingly and
unwittingly—tied to the economic advantage of America's ruling class.
The core of his philosophy was its social democratic politics.

The idealism that Dewey imbibed as a student of the St. Louis school
of philosophy he rejected when faced with Hall's psychology and
Spencer's evolutionary biology. His sensitive perception of
industrialism's complex interdependencies, and the waning of the
world he had known as a child forced him to define a new and mature
stance that rejected the causal determinism of Spencer's evolutionary
thought and the "otherworldliness" of Hegelian idealism. Both of the
former had come to seem irrelevant in an increasingly scientific and
industrial world (Haskell, 1977, 10-16). Dewey's focus upon
interdependence of social effects provided a viable alternative to an
intellectual establishment that had previously relied upon theories of
autonomous individualism to explain and describe individual, class,
ethnic, and religious differences (Haskell, 1977, 15). His emphasis upon
interconnectedness called attention to social structures and economic
realities that marginalized action and compromised the integrity of
individuals. Dewey's historicism and cultural organicism linked
Oliver Wendell Holmes, Jr., Thorstein Veblen, James Harvey Robinson,

Charles Beard, and other Progressive scholars to a common intellectual stance. It also provided a logical thread that tied the work of these men and others into something called social science (cf. Safford, 1987, 175-196).

In 1894 John Dewey was appointed to lead the University of Chicago's Department of Philosophy, Psychology, and Pedagogy. His appointment allowed him to leave the comparative intellectual wilderness of Michigan for the highly charged intellectual life of Chicago (cf. McCaul, 1959). In Chicago social reformers were demanding universal suffrage and universal education. Dewey's appointment was at least partially a response to those demands. It allowed President William Rainey Harper to provide leadership for the Department of Philosophy and formally consolidated his commitment to the study of pedagogy within the university (McCaul, 1959). The establishment of education as a professionalized element of social science was a response to the pressure for professional social expertise. Urbanization, immigration, and industrialism had created a demand for social workers, journalists, city planners, lawyers, and teachers.

At Chicago, Dewey published "My pedagogic creed" ([1897] 1959) and "The school and society" ([1899] 1959). Later at Columbia he wrote *Democracy and education* ([1916] 1966), his most important and influential educational tract. It was Dewey's work in the schools and his unorthodox philosophical writings that would inspire American educators—arguably, into the 1990s.[22] John Dewey's contribution to the New Education movement, "The school and society" (1899) is representative of his *moral critique* of nineteenth-century American society and its institutions. But it is also a contribution to his *political critique* of nation and its institutions. His concern for progressive schools would be expanded in *Schools of to-morrow* (1915), which he wrote with his oldest daughter, Evelyn. His work established a close sympathy with Rousseau's *Emile* ([1762] 1907) and *Sophie*. While Rousseau's romantic work was part of Dewey's thought, it was the commitment to political philosophy much as one finds it in Rousseau's *Social contract* ([1762] 1987) or Hobbes's *Leviathan* (1651) that remained the enduring element in his educational thought. These abiding concerns reappeared in Dewey's *Public and its problems* ([1927] 1954), and *Liberalism and social action* (1935). In both of these works Dewey rehearses and stylizes the reciprocal relationship between social reform and education while developing his political philosophy. Although explicitly concerned with the schools, "My pedagogic creed" ([1897] 1959) and "The school and society" ([1899] 1959) were part of that more general educational literature that provided an intellectual impetus and organizational form to his philosophical thought.

The professionalization of educational philosophy that John Dewey's work foreshadowed had reference not only to the sociology of Herbert Spencer but also to the political economy of Jeremy Bentham and England's radical utilitarians. It moved away from metaphysical vagaries, argued specific cases, subordinated the law to humanity rather than vice versa, and promoted all issues of social reform. Dewey's opposition to the formalism of Jeremy Bentham and John Stuart Mill was largely ideological. It was Bentham and Mill to whom Dewey's *Liberalism and social action* (1935) addressed itself. He was concerned with the inability of the radical utilitarians to address democratic social reform. Their version of democracy was more at home in elitist and aristocratic Britain than in Dewey's United States.

It was John Stuart Mill who defined social science for the English-speaking world (cf., Senn, 1958; Burns, 1959) and inspired the idea of social science. But utilitarianism never was able to transcend the fixed and final supreme end—property (Dewey, [1920] 1950, 143). As Dewey wrote,

The reforming zeal (of utilitarianism) was shown in criticism of the evils inherited from the class system of feudalism, evils economic, legal and political. But the new economic order of capitalism that was superseding feudalism brought its own social evils with it, and some of these ills utilitarianism tended to cover up or defend...

Utilitarian ethics thus afford a remarkable example of the need of philosophic reconstruction... Up to a certain point, it reflected the meaning of modern thought and aspirations. But it was still tied down by fundamental ideas of that very order which it thought it had completely left behind...

If a few words are added upon the topic of education, it is only for the sake of suggesting that the educative process is all one with the moral process, since the latter is a continuous passage of experience from worse to better. ([1920] 1950, 144-145)

It was apparent to the pragmatists that if educational thought was to address the "problems of men" it would need a new tack. It was apparent that educational thought had to transcend its preoccupation with property and its suspicion of the dangerous classes.

## THE DEMOCRATIC LEFT-WING OF AMERICAN EDUCATION

Educational philosophy was tied to America's indigenous, and as yet still adolescent intellectual establishment. "The school and society" ([1899] 1959), one of Dewey's most influential early texts was part of the attack upon Victorian industrialism (cf. Cremin, 1988, 444). In "The school and society" Dewey wrote this:

How many of the employed are today mere appendages to the machines which they operate! . . . At present, the impulses which lie at the basis of the industrial system are either practically neglected or positively distorted during the school period. Until the instincts of construction and production are systematically laid hold of in the years of childhood and youth, until they are trained in social directions, enriched by historical interpretation, controlled and illuminated by scientific methods, we certainly are in no position even to locate the source of our economic evils, much less to deal with them effectively. ([1897] 1959, 46)

The conflict of class interest was practically self-evident to Dewey by the turn of the century. Dewey's concern for social reform and education revolved around the common concerns of social reform. Both were part of the intellectual disestablishment of Victorianism.

John and Alice Dewey established a Laboratory School in 1896. The Laboratory School merged with the practice school of the Chicago Institute after the death of Colonel Francis W. Parker in 1902. The merger created an imaginative humanist form of politically conscious progressive education. John Dewey contributed a social politics that called attention to the school's role in community reform. What was new at the Laboratory School under Dewey was its politics, not just its method (Feuer, 1959, 559); what was distinctive was its commitment to social democracy. Dewey's social reform politics would, of course, contribute to his undoing as head of the Department of Philosophy, Psychology, and Pedagogy at the University of Chicago as well as his tenure as head of the Laboratory School. When Dewey appointed Alice, his wife, to the position of principal of the Laboratory School the ensuing controversy finished his tenure at Chicago. The appointment of his wife showed bad judgment, probably inspired by the financial difficulties of the Dewey household (Dykhuizen, 1973); it smacked of nepotism. By the time the controversy had had time to boil, Dewey had resigned from the University of Chicago and taken a position at Columbia.

At Columbia, Dewey's department attracted many of the most able educators in the country and turned out many of the nation's top school administrators and philosophers (Potter, 1967, 428). Advanced educational training was in one way or another dominated by Dewey's colleagues or students. American philosophy and philosophy of education was dominated by Dewey's thought not merely because of its intellectual stature, but also because it was integrated into the teaching of Teachers College Columbia and Columbia University, arguably the most influential university in the United States.

The evolution of Pragmatic thought was also part of Dewey's self-effacing, modest New England character, a part of the compassion he felt for ordinary people and the Calvinist morality that was part of his home and his childhood. He grew up in a rural New England town, knowing individuals both from well established families and from homes of more humble means. He was moved by the plight of new, poor, and disenfranchised Americans and saw them as the victims of the nation's chaotic industrialism and urbanization. His thinking and its basic political and social intent was directed toward—to characterize it with C. Wright Mills' words—the "recommunalization" of American life, an aspect of living lost in the hurly-burly of turn-of-century industrial America (Mills, 1964, 279-280).

John Dewey was born in Burlington, a then small town in Vermont, to a farmer turned groceryman. Dewey's boyhood experience of a small town and the sense of community and caring it implied was a central feature of his life and intellectual thought (Dykhuizen, 1973, 1-10; Mills, 1964, 279). But unlike many of their compatriots of humble origin Dewey's family identified with the town's "cultivated" society. The books of Milton, Burns, Lamb, and Thackeray were no strangers to his home (Mills, 1964, 279). His family mixed easily with "old Americans," the community's elite, an elite that claimed a minimum of exclusiveness. His childhood left him with a broad social horizon and a gentle respect for people, rich and poor (Dykhuizen, 1973, 1-10). What John Dewey learned about poverty in Burlington was given final form by a trip with his mother to join his father in northern Virginia in the last year of the Civil War. The devastation and deprivation of northern Virginia made a lasting impression (Jane Dewey, 1939, 7).

By the same token, the social radicalism that informed his educational philosophy was also part of the anger he felt for a conservative elite who showed such small charity toward fellow Americans who, unlike themselves, had so little. The suspicion he felt toward the industrial establishment was begun in his youth. Dewey's attitude was not unique. It was part of an international phenomenon that Feuer (1959, 546) calls the back-to-the-people movement. Dewey's educational activism was part of a social concern for America. This concern certainly originated in his early years as a teacher in Oil City (see, Dykhuizen 1973, 19-20) and later as a new faculty member at the University of Michigan where, sent to inspect local secondary schools, the hard conditions of rural life confirmed what he had seen in Oil City (Dykhuizen, 1973, 19-51).

His wife Alice Dewey (née Chipman) possessed a deep sense of social justice. She was, perhaps, even more aware of the lurid realities of American life than was her husband. She had been raised by her grandparents Frederick and Evalin Riggs. The Riggses had a people's sense of the religion, politics, and social issues of the Midwest and beyond. They were familiar with the land that was the home of the Farmers Alliance and sided with native Americans in their attempts to achieve some semblance of social justice (Dykhuizen, 1973, 53). Raised in such an atmosphere, Alice Chipman could not ignore poverty in the slums of Chicago or suffragettes in the streets of New York (Dykhuizen, 1973, 149). She ran a house in which apathy and indifference were poorly suffered. In Alice's house an academic focus on "The pantheism of Spinoza"[23] was hard to sustain if it excluded the politics of social justice.

Dewey was challenged by the realities of Chicago's and New York's slums and the plight of those who dwelled in them. Like many Victorians Dewey was struggling with the idea of personal failure as a function of individual wickedness while trying to comprehend the same social facts as a function of urbanization, industrialism, and laissez-faire government that is, structure. Dewey's stance in those early days was a strange amalgam of utopian cum socialist ideals and Calvinist individualism (Dewey, [1897] 1959, 30-32).

For Dewey the school was the means of realizing a just social democracy. "All that society has accomplished for itself is put, through the agency of the school, at the disposal of its future members. All its better thoughts of itself it hopes to realize through the new possibilities thus opened to its future self. Here individualism and socialism are at one" (Dewey, [1897] 1959, 34). The common reference of Dewey's thought is to social science and social reform, as much as it is to the perennial intellectual classics of the West. If central questions of philosophy such as justice and fairness can be teased out of these questions, they largely were bracketed and presented in a new language of social justice, social responsibility, and social welfare far removed from their classical form. Educational philosophy found its authority and research agenda in social science and social reform in the same way that economics, sociology, and nonpatrician history found theirs.

Like social science, educational philosophy was a response to new times, new questions, and new social conditions. The old Victorian formulas that attributed the desperate conditions of the industrial underclass to individual wickedness were no longer compelling explanations. Ignorance could no longer be written off to natural differences of "wit," just as poverty could no longer be written off to some personal defect. It was obvious to the new Baconian social science that something more was at work—even if it defied description or explanation. Initially social science was an attempt to find some expedient to regain the arcadian simplicity of the preindustrial era.

Later it was an attempt to answer the social questions generated by industrialism. And still later, when social science had evolved into the social sciences, the new disciplines were still involved in the attempt to limit and control the excesses and civil transgressions of industry, even though the social sciences had found a new commitment to the construction of theory that made their commitment to social reform somewhat less compelling.

## NOTES

1. The Farmers Alliance was an agricultural cooperative that began in Texas in 1877 as a form of resistance to commercial credit arrangements that, for all intents and purposes, had indentured small farmers to the banks or wealthy members of the community. One of the direct antecedents to the Populist movement, its ideology contributed to the socialist tone of politics in the agricultural Midwest, and by 1887 its members and sympathizers numbered in the hundreds of thousands. It was one of the early forms of direct resistance to the social and economic exploitation. The alliance opposed bankruptcy sale of family farms and collateral chattels, boycotted merchants who failed to grant further credit, and occasionally burnt out stores with a particular mind to the merchant's credit records so as to escape a debt they believed to be created by exorbitant prices and usurious interest rates. It also participated in ordinary politics. For example, the success and support of the alliance encouraged Minnesota's Ignatius Donnelly to establish the Populist party in 1891.

2. The Grange was the oldest of all the agricultural organizations. Organized in 1867 by Oliver Hudson Kelley, it was at first conceived of as a social and educational organization. Its membership was originally concentrated in the Northeast, but at its peak it had over 800,000 members all across America. It sponsored lectures, supported the Progressive Education Movement, lobbied for legislation, and supported the Land Grant Colleges' agricultural mission. It was influential in the passage of the Interstate Commerce Act and the Sherman Anti-Trust Act.

3. The Knights of Labor was organized in 1869 by Philadelphia garment workers. Its membership grew slowly until the railroad strikes of 1877. Although the strikes were initially unsuccessful, they provided the impetus for the realization of the union. The Knights of Labor was one of the first large labor organizations. The union admitted all, irrespective of race, sex, nationality, or production skill. Membership peaked at about 700,000 in 1885 after strikes at the Gould railways. After the Haymarket Square Riot in which sixty-six police officers were wounded by a bomb, seven of whom later died, the Knights of Labor slowly lost membership and eventually dissolved.

4. The Homestead Strike of 1892: In a lengthy strike in 1892 the Amalgamated Association of Iron, Steel, and Tin Workers sought a new labor agreement with the Carnegie Steel Company, then managed by Henry Clay Frick. After the protracted negotiation failed, Frick laid off the entire work force, and the workers in response laid siege to the plant. Frick called in a small army of Pinkertons to retake the plant. On the night of 5 July, 1892 and the following day a battle ensued, and there were dead and wounded on both sides. The National Guard was called in in support of the Pinkertons, the siege was broken, and the strike soon failed. Over 150 of the strikers were tried, and the strike leaders were charged with murder, although all serious charges were dismissed by friendly courts. Unions were kept out of the Carnegie plants well into the 1930s.

5. Coxey's Army 1894: In response to widespread unemployment, Jacob Coxey, a wealthy Ohio quarry owner, proposed in 1894 that the federal government print $500 million to pay for a nationwide public works project. Coxey organized a march on Washington, D.C., in support of his plan. Support for a march spread around the country, and the army marched on the nation's capital. Arriving on 1 May 1894, supporters were beaten and disbanded and Coxey was arrested before he could read a paper in support of his plan.

6. Pullman Strike 1894: This nationwide railway strike began in 1894 in a company town at the Pullman Palace Car Company owned by George Pullman, just south of Chicago. The workers were protesting high rents and low wages. Frustrated in their demands, the Pullman workers struck. Eugene Debs and the American Railway Union initiated a boycott of all Pullman cars in support of the strike. The result was to halt all railway traffic out of Chicago. In response, on 30 June 1894 Attorney General of the United States Richard Olney agreed to send two thousand deputies to break the strike on the proviso that the General Managers Association, which represented the railways, would agree to pay the deputies. Later President Cleveland ordered federal troops to Chicago. On 6 July hundreds of railway cars were burned and trains were stopped by strikers in response to Cleveland's order. On the following day the state militia broke the strike. Debs was arrested for contempt, thirteen people were killed, and numerous individuals were wounded.

7. Later on in the post–World War II period educational philosophy would become ontological or metaphysical. But initially, it was largely sociological and political.

8. William Heard Kilpatrick, Harold Rugg, George S. Counts, John L. Childs, R. Bruce Raup, Goodwin Watson, Edmund deS. Brunner, Jesse Newlon, Harold F. Clark, and F. Ernest Johnson and John Dewey—the Kilpatrick Discussion Group—might reasonably be called members of the inner circle.

9. For example, Harold Rugg's (with Ann Shumaker) bohemian aesthetics published in *The child-centered school* (1928) would never become part of educational philosophy's central agenda. On the other hand, George Counts's address, pamphlet, and monograph, *Dare the school build a new social order?* (1932) would become quite central to educational philosophy's social democratic cum Marxist politics. And perhaps in the most contrary profile of all, William H. Kilpatrick's "Project method" (1918) would be both in and (at a later point in time) out of the central order of things.

10. London's influence was not confined to the turn of the century. As Sidney Hook, one of America's most celebrated philosophers, noted, it was in the novels of Jack London that he discovered socialism (1987, 30).

11. It is appalling to discover Samuel G. Freedman's *Small victories* (1990) describing contemporary social conditions in the Five Points area of New York not dissimilar to those described by Robert Hunter in 1904.

12. Jane Stanford's dismissal of E. A. Ross for his political opinions, which were not always compatible with the Stanfords' railroad interests, is the classic case in point (see Furner, 1975, 229-259).

13. It is interesting to see an allusion to *McClure's* in William James's seminal essay *The will to believe* ([1896] 1904, 5).

14. The Fabian Society was founded in 1883-1884 in London. It was dedicated to the establishment of a socialist and democratic state in Great Britain through education. Although its membership was always small it attracted some of the most important intellectuals of the period. They hoped to solve Great Britain's social difficulties through meetings, lectures, discussion groups, and conferences— that is, primarily through education—although they were not averse to generating and supporting strikes and other forms of direct resistance and social protest. And, of course, as an intellectual movement of the middle class, the Fabian Society frequently gathered in various cafés and private salons in the better parts of London to debate their ideas. Fabian salons became famous as hothouses of radical social thought.

15. Henry George (1839-1897), American journalist, economist, and social reformer, was best known for his advocacy of the "single tax." Following Ricardo's doctrine of rent he proposed that government abolish all economic rent (taxes) except for a "single tax" on the improvements on bare land. He argued that so much economic activity escaped all tax, that his "single tax" would provide a

simple means of generating more than enough money to pay not only for government but also for whatever social reform programs government should choose to establish. The Chicago single tax club was a vocal proponent of George's idea of the "single-tax" in the Midwest.

16. Dewey wrote *Liberalism and social action* (1935) and dedicated it to the memory of Jane Addams. The dedication was indicative of a close friendship, not a distant respect.

17. Rabindranath Tagore (1861-1941) won the Nobel Prize for literature in 1913. In 1901 he founded a school in Santiniketan near Bolpur where he sought to present the best of Indian and Western culture. And in 1921 he inaugurated Visva-Bharati University. In the last twenty-five years of his life he travel extensively and lectured in the Americas, China, Japan, Malaya, and Indonesia.

18. Ramsay MacDonald (1866-1937) was elected to the House of Commons in 1906. He was forced to resign his seat in 1914 for raising moral objections to Britain's declaration of war on Germany. Returning to politics in 1922 he became the first Labour prime minister of Great Britain. He was prime minister between the years of 1924 - 1929 - 1931 and 1931 and 1935.

19. The idea that social science was about the production of facts and social remediation was the stance of the National Association for the Promotion of Social Science and the American Social Science Association, not Herbert Spencer. Spencer belittled and despised both organizations.

20. Evolution is the progressive organization of events and dissipation of random motion moving from "incoherent homogeneity to a relatively definite, coherent heterogeneity" (Spencer, [1862] 1880 par. 144).

21. A dinner club of a few of the most prestigious members of the scientific community. The X Club provided Spencer with membership in the exalted group of scientists when he failed to gain membership in the Royal Society of London in 1856. He was a respected friend of Thomas Huxley and John Tyndall, just as Charles Darwin and Wilhelm Helmholtz knew Spencer as an admired associate. The X Club allowed Spencer to extend his reputation and contacts within the invisible college of Britain's intellectual elite despite the fact that he never became a member of the Royal Society himself.

22. Dewey not only provided the intellectual gambit for the rethinking of America's primary and secondary schools, but he also provided the rationale for restructuring social thought and collaterally America's colleges and universities (Rorty, 1982, 63).

23. "The pantheism of Spinoza" was John Dewey's second published article. It appeared in W. T. Harris's *Journal of Speculative Philosophy*.

# 3

# The Professional Embodiment of Education

Numerous agencies and associations were concerned with education and the politics that surrounded the institution of education during the period of American Victorianism. The most interesting, ones were the Western College of Professional Teachers founded in Cincinnati in 1830, the American Lyceum Association organized in New York in 1831, and the American Association for the Advancement of Education formed in Philadelphia in 1849 under the direction of Horace Mann (Wesley, 1957, 20). These agencies were followed by associations that had a more modern form: the National Education Association (NEA), and the Progressive Education Association. Nevertheless, these agencies had agendas that were only collaterally related to those of educational philosophy. They were never dedicated to the theoretical investigation of education and at best would only parallel the academic heading that the university and therein educational philosophy would define for itself.

The NEA, founded in 1857, reflected the politics of sectionalism, the patriotism of Civil War reconstructionism, and the furious individualism of the Populists (Wesley, 1957, 3). Inside this politics the NEA's Department of Superintendence, took a leading role in the discussions of social reconstruction and played an active role in the support of educational philosophy's utopian political projects. Nevertheless, the Department of Superintendence's major concern had to do with monopolizing the professional representation of educators. This task took precedence over issues of social or professional reform (Cremin, 1988, 238-239) and over the task of the theoretical explanation and description of education (cf. Haskell, 1977).

The NEA was largely indifferent to philosophy of education and to educational theory, it was concerned with educational practice. As educational philosophy slowly and gingerly initiated work in curriculum theory, the NEA slowly turned its attention to educational theory. The NEA's concern for curriculum theory began with the work of Dewey, Kilpatrick, and Rugg—who wrote some of curriculum's most interesting, systematic, and important early texts—but that interest ended with the social reform politics or political affiliations of those same men during the depression (Wesley, 1957, 51). During the depression political differences and different educational priorities completed the alienation of the National Education Association and its Department of Superintendence from the educational and intellectual stance of academics like John Dewey, George Counts, and Harold Rugg. Progressives were about the reconstruction of American society and its politics the NEA was about the day-to-day business of schooling.

In the depression the NEA's political concerns were comparatively modest but perhaps even more important than the agendas of the Progressives for the future of the common school in America. The NEA, particularly the Joint Commission on the Emergency in Education, was concerned with sustaining American schools by assisting teachers to protect themselves from the attempts of local governments to refinance their local debts by abandoning their commitment to the common school—marginalizing teachers' already meager salaries or dismissing them altogether, stripping the schools of assets or closing them if possible.

Nevertheless, the NEA's Department of Superintendence was the critical sponsor of the John Dewey Society. Without its patronage the Dewey society would not have been established. The backing of the department for the John Dewey Society and its social democratic politics during the rocky days of the depression was critical for the maintenance of the idea of educational philosophy and its public voice, *The Social Frontier*. Be that as it may, the NEA as a whole felt a positive antipathy for the social-democratic politics of the discipline's most prominent educational philosophers. The "socialist" comments of John Dewey, Harold Rugg, George Counts, and Charles Beard were unacceptable to them. Despite Kilpatrick's call for an end to radicalism in *The Social Frontier* in 1936, educational philosophy and the NEA fixed their eyes on different stars. The NEA's Department of Superintendence delivered three yearbooks in the period from 1932 to 1947 on the topic of social reconstruction, *Social change and education* (1935), *The improvement of education* (1937), and *Schools for a new world* (1947). These books favored social planning, but that was about as far as it went; they preferred moderation. The volumes were liberal in their content, privileging neither the Right nor the Left (Connell, 1980, 293). Although the radicalism of the Department of Superintendence would generate some support for educational philosophy's politics, the department was already listening intently to conservatives like I. C. Kandel and awaiting the conservative message that would be delivered from the University of Chicago's Robert Hutchins and other conservatives like Jacques Maritain, Arthur E. Bestor, and Mortimer Adler. Kandel's work in particular illustrated the conservative establishment's smoldering distaste for educational philosophy's politics.

As far as the NEA was concerned, educational philosophers were being diverted by "pie-in-the-sky" politics and metaphysical threats to democracy. In the years immediately following World War I the NEA was concerned with saving public education. It was concerned with preventing a ruinous reduction in school taxes. The NEA's Commission on the Emergency in Education appointed in 1918 and the Legislative Commission of 1920 did just that. The NEA dedicated itself to conservative or atheoretical politics, "playing it by ear," while educational philosophy dedicated itself to an intellectualized theoretical politics, "playing it by the book" (cf. Broudy, 1987). The NEA was out to save the schools from "real" threats; philosophers of education could, as far as they were concerned, save them only from metaphysical ones.


## PROGRESSIVE EDUCATION ASSOCIATION

The Progressive Education Association—the "other" organization in the helix that surrounded educational philosophy, the John Dewey Society, and *The Social Frontier*—was closely identified with John Dewey; yet it was really Stanwood Cobb's organization. The organization was more in tune with the work of Francis Parker than John Dewey. But like the Chicago Laboratory School, it became inextricably tied to the name of John Dewey.

The Progressive Education Association, organized in 1919, took early and liberal use of John Dewey's name and his theory of experience, which they innocently understood as the "child-centeredness" of his philosophy. Philosophy of education "stood away" from the Progressive Education Association (Beck, 1965). Reconceptualizing Dewey's theory of experience while turning a blind eye to early texts like "The school and society" ([1899] 1959) allowed the Progressive Education Association to incorporate Dewey's thought into the "child-centered" theories of education they had adopted from Europe and to remain innocent of the social and political intent of his educational thought (Graham, 1967, 60-79). The general stance of the Progressive Education Association was more directly related to the work of Stanwood Cobb or European educators such as Froebel, Pestalozzi, and Herbart (Graham, 1967, 79). The Association's great weakness as far as Dewey was concerned was directly related to the fact that it acknowledged no agenda of social or political reform (Graham, 1967, 65).

Professional associations like the PEA or the NEA were not significant referents for Dewey, although they were reasonably important for others such as Jessie Newlon and William Heard Kilpatrick, who had a close connection with the schools. Dewey never played an active role in the PEA although he was offered and reluctantly accepted the honorary presidency of the organization in 1927 after Eliot's death (Cremin, 1961, 246, 249). In his 1928 presidential address Dewey censured the PEA's socially unconscious educational agendas. Educational philosophy was not intellectually tied to either the PEA or the NEA, two of the very significant institutional elements in American's educational history. It was tied to the ideas and institutions of social science and social reform: Jane Addams and Hull House and the Chicago Laboratory School were the incubators of Dewey's social and political thought and thereby his educational philosophy.

The differences between the social reconstructionists and the child-centered members of the association remained a fundamental unresolved element in the dynamic of the Association. But toward the end of World War II when the PEA had changed its name to the American Education Fellowship the issues became explosive.[1] After the war teachers disclaimed the progressive politics of the social reconstructionists. Teachers and administrators were no longer willing to accept the social politics of the "Dewey faction." In addition, the child-centered members were outraged by B. O. Smith's editorship of *Progressive Education*. To their mind Smith had turned it into *The Social Frontier* of the late 1940s. In the end, the PEA disbanded itself over its internal ideological differences (Wesley, 1957, 203; cf. Benne, 1966; 1988).


## JOHN DEWEY SOCIETY

Prior to the Civil War philosophical comment on education was part of the contest between secular and sacred elements of the American community—American clerics and a few social reformers—over control of the nation's schools (see Chambliss, 1968; Ulich, [1947] 1982). After the seminal work of America's founding fathers, domestic philosophical comments about education in the United States existed as a group of rather discontinuous, unsystematic, and by and large intellectually unimportant adventures. The work was principally part of the church's attempt to retain its control over education. After the Civil War their work was mostly forgotten. Philosophically and educationally it was unimportant. In a sense the church is part of educational philosophy's pre-history, but mostly it is germane to an understanding of a battle between clerics and secular interests over the education of the public. Insofar as it is part of the history of educational philosophy it represents the conservative establishment's opposition and resistance to educational philosophy's socialist, utopian, and transcendental politics.

Following the Civil War, important philosophical comments on education were borrowed from the work of Herbert Spencer. And of course, partially responding to the evolutionary theory of Spencer, their own intellectual biography, and the questions and problems that American industrialism and urbanization had generated, Charles Sanders Peirce and William James articulated an American philosophical voice that John Dewey would press into the service of education. But apart from Dewey's seminal work there was little else. Education's place in the universities of America was almost nonexistent. Educational philosophy's presence was merely foreshadowed. Few if any academics were interested in education and philosophy, graduate students and research were almost completely absent, and universities sponsored no journals interested in education and philosophy. Resources for the university study of education were so small and inauspicious that scholars interested in education left the country to pursue their studies overseas.

Partially, educational philosophy originated through the efforts of faculties and schools of education in the nineteenth and twentieth centuries. It tended to be educational philosophers who initially brought respectability to the newly established schools and faculties of education. When they spoke, they spoke as philosophers. And it was philosophy that provided the most serious and systematic studies of human nature, social forces, progress, marriage and family relationships, economic process, maintenance of government, international relations, elementary jurisprudence, primitive customs, history of institutions, religion, ethics, aesthetics, and education (Bryson, 1932b, 304). Philosophy spoke to the educational questions of the nineteenth and twentieth centuries. To distinguish themselves from the educational faculties of normal schools, university faculties of education emphasized philosophical and theoretical aspects of education (Clifford and Guthrie, 1988, 64). Philosophy of education was that element of education that looked and sounded the most like what colleagues in the various faculties of arts and letters were accustomed to seeing and hearing in the academic confines of the university.

The John Dewey Society was the beginning of philosophy of education as we now know it—a bureaucratic organization, housed in various institutions of tertiary education, supported by salaried chairs and lectureships, discoursing through the books and journals of the academic press, meeting from time to time to discuss the intellectual issues of the moment. It was the society that would first gather together the pool of talent and shape the questions and answers that would constitute philosophy of education. Philosophy of education was established by the rationalization of philosophical discourse by a group of professional educators dedicated to the application of the genius and literary style of philosophy to the practice of educating and the specification and acceptance of a program of research and action consistent with those goals. That program was charged with breaking the class monopoly on secondary education and building a curriculum that would allow America's workers to identify and recognize the evils of urbanization and industrialization that systematically disadvantaged their lives; it would suggest means to deal with those social and cultural evils successfully.

Once established in a professional format, philosophy of education adopted a stance antithetical to Spencer's fatalistic social science. In its professional form it had direct reference to America's Populist and Progressive social reform movement, to the professionalization of social science and therein academic expertise as represented in the initiatives of the American Social Science Association, and to the indigenous metaphysics of Peirce, James, and Dewey. While educational philosophy adopted a version of science and social science that was closer to Spencer's than the version espoused by the American Social Science Association, it retained the association's concern for social reform. The version of educational philosophy that evolved out of all this was at home with Otto Neurath's *International Encyclopedia of Unified Science* just as it was at home with Upton Sinclair's politics. For Dewey education was anticlassical, a matter of public initiative, scientific, and a matter of social reconstruction.

Despite its complex genesis and an amorphous prologue, the discipline has a definite beginning. Philosophy of education began at the Hotel Traymore, Atlantic City, on Sunday, 24 February 1935. On that day a group of superintendents many of them without advanced academic qualifications, and academics, established the John Dewey Society (Harap, 1970; Johnson, 1977). The predicate of the society was a belief in the pending economic collapse of Western society. The individuals who gathered at the Hotel Traymore hoped to find within John Dewey's philosophy a powerful and positive role for the institution of schooling in the reconstruction of American society.[2]

Interestingly enough, the John Dewey Society, and therein philosophy of education, was a child of the education establishment, not the American Philosophical Association (Johnson, 1977, 74). The period from the turn of the century to the Great Depression was one of philosophical heroism, social prophecy, and moral pronouncement for the philosophical establishment. Philosophy was involved with cosmic matters. Addressing the questions of education was deemed to be banal. The important new philosophical journals of the period, *Philosophical Review, Journal of Philosophy and Psychology,* and *Scientific Methods,* failed to recognize and almost never published manuscripts concerned with educational matters (Chambliss, 1968, 4). Philosophy did not have much time for education (cf. Macmillan 1991, 191).

The group of men who founded the Dewey society were an assemblage of Populists and Progressives who used "pink" rhetoric in the name of agrarian and urban industrial democracy. They wanted a secure title to the family farm and a secure price for farm produce on the one hand, and a fair wage, benefits, and security of unionism and social welfare on the other. The men who founded the John Dewey Society were homespun nationalists. They were not interested in Marx in the way that their intensely intellectual European colleagues were (cf. Larson, 1977, 147). They were still inspired by a combination of French socialism, utopianism, transcendentalism, and fundamentalist Protestant humanitarianism. Although they were sympathetic to the more radical call to action of radical socialists like Upton Sinclair, they ignored the necessity of class conflict and clung to the Christian ideals of universal brotherhood and personal salvation (Larson, 1977, 147). Or, like George Counts—although labeled a Marxist by Elizabeth Dilling in *The red network* (1934)—they embraced a social democratic politics that had primary reference to American intellectuals critics such as Thorstein Veblen and Charles Beard, not Karl Marx (Dennis, 1989, 3).[3] Counts's socialism was primarily referenced to American intellectuals, and like many liberals he was only secondarily concerned with European intellectuals (Dennis, 1980).[4]

When the New York professors (the core of the Dewey society) met to discuss social questions that seemed to resist any resolution in classical Victorian terms, they made reference to the socialist Left and

America's nascent intellectual establishment, not to the intellectual heroes of the Progressive Education Movement, Froebel, Pestalozzi, and Herbart. The discussion group was an aspect of the New York intellectual establishment. The significant domestic intellectual contacts of this group were with

men like Charles A. Beard and J. Allen Smith in history and political science, Richard T. Ely, John R. Commons, Simon Patten, Guy Rexford Tugwell, and the acidulous Thorstein Veblen in economics; John Dewey in philosophy and education; Lester F. Ward, Albion Small, Edward A. Ross, and Charles H. Cooley in sociology; and the admirers of Oliver Wendell Holmes, Jr., in jurisprudence. (Hofstadter, 1963, 7)

These men were developing a social critique that opposed the deterministic and socially indifferent fatalism of Spencer's evolutionary sociology and the laissez-faire economics of industrial America. Ward, Ross, Cooley, and Small in sociology attacked the socially fatalistic assumptions of social Darwinism and natural-law laissez-faire individualism. Ely, Commons, Patten, Tugwell, and Veblen argued for the structural reform of American economics. Their work was conducted in the light of Veblen's insight that scarcity will always be the result of an economic system in which "industry" is sacrificed to the purposes of "business," that is, profit. John Dewey convinced them all that reason was the tool of the future. And Dewey, Small, and Ward argued for education as the panacea for most social ills.[5]

In 1929, the Great Depression began in America. By the mid-1930s even America's educators were thinking about taking direct action: They believed they were faced with the imminent collapse of the nation's socioeconomic system and the systematic disestablishment of the public school system, and they sought to take an active part in the reconstruction of what they saw as a basically good society that had somehow come undone. They could no longer believe that the troubles that bedeviled society and pilloried the schools were merely "technical" social and economic difficulties. They believed that the only manner in which society could be set to rights was through the political, social, economic, and moral reform of American society.

In the eyes of those who would found the John Dewey Society in 1935, the institution of schooling had failed. It was not just that the institution was somehow technically ineffectual but that it was somehow unequal to the "Enlightenment faith in reason." The institution was, in some sense, the American equivalent to the medieval church; that is, insofar as the church was the instantiation of the medieval faith in God, the common school in the early twentieth century was the American instantiation of the "Enlightenment's faith in reason." But if the institution of the school had failed, the schoolies' faith in the central credo of the Enlightenment had not. It was "reason" not "revolution" that would do the job. Thus, the task at hand was to solve the puzzling questions related to the school's role in the reconstruction of both reason and society.

Having defined their task, that concerned group of educators set about its realization. A preliminary meeting in Cleveland was called to plan the infrastructure of an organization to solve this question of the school's role in "reason" and the reconstruction of society. The meeting in Cleveland was suggested by Henry Harap of Western Reserve University and organized by Paul R. Hanna and Jesse H. Newlon at Teachers College, Columbia. In February 1934 the individuals contacted by Newlon met in connection with the meeting of the National Education Association's Department of Superintendence in Cleveland to determine whether or not there was enough support for an association of like-minded individuals (Harap, 1970, 137-140; Johnson, 1977, 65).

The meeting was exciting but accomplished less than Harap would have liked. Nonetheless, a proposal was passed to establish a society "to discharge our responsibility in the present era of social change" (as quoted by Harap, 1970, 160). In view of the motion, Newlon organized a follow–up meeting in April. This meeting was postponed and eventually held in the Hotel Pennsylvania in New York on 6 and 7 October, 1934. The group was attempting to determine the role they might play in the reconstruction of American society. Shortly thereafter, a letter signed by George S. Counts, Jesse H. Newlon, and Harold Rugg dated 6 February, 1935 gave notice to all of the participants of the Cleveland and New York conferences of a meeting at the Hotel Traymore, Atlantic City, on Sunday, February 24, 1935 (Harap, 1970, 160-161). At this meeting critical issues confronting education were to be considered and definite steps taken toward launching a strong national society for the scientific study of school and society (Harap, 1970, 161).

The ultraliberals who met in  Atlantic City had contacts with the Progressive Education Association, Kilpatrick's discussion group, and New York's intellectual and educational establishment through *The Social Frontier*. They also had a close association with the superintendents of America's most important school districts, who were in effect the school's establishment. At the February meeting in 1935 the John Dewey Society would be established.

Despite all the talk about "socialism" and "planned economies" that would mark their debates and fill the pages of their writings, they were at heart children of the Enlightenment who found it easier to listen to the voices of Thorstein Veblen and Charles A. Beard than to the strange voices of the European Left. The American Left was only tangentially related to Europe's intensely intellectual establishment. From a European perspective the American Left was a strange amalgam of socialist, utopian, and transcendental politics embedded in a very different social, cultural, and historical matrix. There was no escaping the impact of the European Left, but it was tempered by its American interpretation. Thoreau's essay "Civil disobedience" ([1849] 1866), with its overt political implications, "Walking" (1863), his adulation of rural life, and "Life without principle" ([1863] 1866), an expression of revolt against urban society, balanced the Populist and Progressive faith in planned economies with a simple utopian faith in the virtues of arcadian life. Just as Locke's political economy was designed to provide the intellectual solvent to dissolve feudalism, the European Left's tenets were designed to dissolve the vested economic industrial interests of aristocratic classes: Junkers, Magyars, as well as Czars and kings. But in America class was a more fluid phenomenon and the hard divisions of economic interests protected by private economic institutions and special legal privileges were still being perfected by J. P. Morgan and persons like him. The enmity between social divisions was not so profound nor were they tempered by time and history, the way they had been in Europe.

The connection between the Atlantic City group and its antecedents is usually drawn between the schools and the Progressive Education Association (Graham, 1967), but it also had strong connections to the American Social Science Association. The most obvious connection was between William Torrey Harris who was superintendent of schools in St. Louis, organizer of the St. Louis Philosophical Society, founder of the *Journal of Speculative Philosophy*, U.S. Commissioner of Education, member of the Committee of Ten along with Charles Eliot (president of Harvard, who was also active in and head of the American Social Science Association, Department of Education) (Furner, 1975, 24; Karier, [1967] 1986, 72; Cremin, 1988, 159).

The Atlantic City group, in the best sense, was aware of the plight of ordinary Americans and was torn by the grievous suffering of these people. But the group retained a fundamental faith in America, its democracy, and its people. They were latter-day Populists and academic Progressives of the day (Hofstadter, 1963, 7); that is, they traced their roots to the political economy of the American and Canadian frontier but found their voice in America's cities (Hofstadter, 1963, 7). Essayists, historians, political scientists, and philosophers of the country's nascent intellectual class spoke for the Progressives and that segment of the population who could not articulate their experience of the anguish generated by capitalism's new ways (Hofstadter, 1963, 7-9). Novelists such as Upton Sinclair and Jack London spoke for them and to them. Scholars such as Thorstein Veblen, Charles A. Beard, and John Dewey taught them and their children. And lawyers such as Louis Brandeis, Frank P. Walsh, and Samuel Untermyer attempted to wrest sovereignty and capitalism from the ruling class—the Goulds, Mellons, Rockefellers, Vanderbilts, and others.

When the John Dewey Society was established its agendas remained consistent with those that had launched social science. Its intellectual task was to be social reform, and specifically the social reconstruction of America's political economy. As Progressives, the Atlantic City group had different purposes. Just as Populists were concerned with a "new social order"—a new agrarian order—Progressives were concerned with a "new industrial order." As educators their goal was to redefine the social role of the school in a society that was increasingly being defined by the requirements of urbanization and industrialization. They accepted the new industrial order but were "politely bent upon" curbing the more outrageous excesses of the new industrial order.

The problem of Progressivism was that it was a divided movement. One half of the movement was dedicated to a benign "Toryism." The Tory half of the Progressive movement would have returned, in the best of all possible worlds, to a pre–Civil War agrarian society with all of its attendant civilities and "virtues," without giving up, of course, the new drama of life that had been generated by industrial society. The "progressive wing" of the Progressive movement, led by men such as William Jennings Bryan and Louis Brandeis, hated big industry and feared the tyranny of big government almost as much as that of big industry. Nevertheless, this second group of urban Progressives looked to government to establish a new relation between employer and employee, a "just relation, that would diminish social inequities" and thereby make aright an industrial world that was, to their mind, inevitable (Hofstadter, 1963, 2-3; Morison, 1965, 811–821).

The educational revolution that Progressivism was stirring up would not have found its way into the schools without the work of men such as Frank McMurray, William Heard Kilpatrick, Jessie Newlon, Harold Rugg and George Counts (Cremin, 1954, 45-48; Gutek, 1983; Karier, 1986). However much John Dewey was an educational philosopher his primary commitment at Columbia was "always 'across the street', in the Department of Philosophy at Columbia University" (Lagemann, 1989, 202). It was Dewey's colleagues at Teachers College who would bring their version of his work to professional educators.

Dewey wrote for the academic press and the intellectual establishment. On matters of social and political affairs he mostly wrote for the *New Republic* (Mills, 1964, 317). The academic journals he wrote for indicate the audience he addressed. He published in *The Journal of Philosophy*, *The Philosophical Review*, *International Journal of Ethics*, *Mind*, *The University of California Chronicle*, and the *Journal of Speculative Philosophy* (Mills 1964, 347). In education he published his writings in the *Journal of Education*, *School Review*, *Kindergarten Magazine*, *Educational Review*, *Proceedings of the NEA*, *Elementary School Teacher*, *American Teacher*, *Progressive Education*, *School and Society*, and *The Social Frontier* (Mills, 1964, 332-333). Dewey wrote for selective audiences, audiences that were largely professional and intellectual. Dewey's prolific writing disseminated his ideas among the literati, but it was his colleagues and students who would broadcast them farther afield. Dewey did not write for the popular press (Mill, 1964, 325).

The significant focus in all of this is the question of social allegiance. If we follow Mills's analysis, it would seem that Dewey wrote for the middle class, not for the man in the street (Mills, 1964, 320). Mills is probably correct in this conclusion. But he is most certainly incorrect in the collateral implication that somehow this fact is a demonstration of "bad faith" with the working class. Dewey mostly wrote for Croly's *New Republic*, which under editors Croly and Lippman was a bastion of America's social democratic politics. Dewey did not speak to the man in the street but he did speak for and to America's radical politics and social conscience. If he did not write to the people, he certainly wrote on their behalf.

Dewey's choice of professional educational affiliation shows his loyalty to the man on the street. Dewey joined the American Federation of Teachers, not the National Education Association. To Dewey and other Progressives the AFT was a real union that addressed working-class issues in union terms: working conditions, salaries, and hours. The stance of the AFT was more consistent with their sympathies for the common man and their Progressive back-to-the-people philosophy (cf. Feuer, 1959) than the NEA stance, which was firmly aligned with the establishment. Unlike the NEA, the AFT's premise was that the reconstruction of education as a profession would follow a reconstruction of the menial conditions of labor under which most teachers worked.

Dewey was active organizing teachers and university professors alike. In 1915, after preliminary meetings at Johns Hopkins University, Dewey called a meeting at the Chemists' Club in New York City that resulted in the formation of the American Association of University

Professors (Dykhuizen, 1973, 170). Dewey was the AAUP's first president. And when the New York Teachers Union joined the American Federation of Labor identified as Local No. 5, Dewey was a charter member and its first vice-president (Dykhuizen, 1973, 170). In both cases Dewey's activism was about the issues of social and industrial solidarity.

The Dewey society became educational philosophy's avenue for "rational" political action. As Anderson noted,

As the full name of the organization implies, as one of its official publications explicitly states, The John Dewey Society was established to foster the study of democratic education in its relationship with the culture, and to promote thorough and systematic inquiry and investigation in the social foundations of education. (A. Anderson, 1959, 17)

The notion that there is an intimate interrelationship between school and society was not new in 1935. Nevertheless, the creation of an organization specifically devoted to studying education's interaction with the culture was a pioneering venture. There was an insistent need for the development of a more adequate and effective conception of this relationship, a conception that could emerge only through realistic and rigorous study of the critical problems that actually confronted both school and society. A John Dewey Society yearbook series began in 1937 with a volume edited by Kilpatrick entitled *The teacher and society*. The yearbook series was the official voice of the society. But year by year, the society retreated from the task it had set for itself, finding the partisan philosophy evident in the first yearbook less and less palatable. By 1939, World War II was immanent and the era of social and educational criticism came to a close as the demands of social solidarity in the face of the Axis war machine preempted the luxury of social and educational criticism. Brameld's *Workers' education in the United States* (1941) was a fading effort to bring serious social and educational criticism back to the Dewey society's yearbooks. The society never really returned to partisan philosophy. When the war was finally brought to a close in 1945, the society found the study of "educational theory," more or less in the abstract, far more attractive than a return to partisan philosophy. The Dewey society yearbooks published in the closing days and after the war, *The Public schools and spiritual values* (Brubacher, 1944), *The American high school* (Caswell, 1946), *Intercultural attitudes in the making* (Kilpatrick, 1947), and *Democracy in the administration of higher education* (Benjamin, 1950) reflect the society's taste for safe topics and projects.[6] Although the content of these yearbooks was not without social comment, it certainly was not the stuff of *The Social Frontier*.

## PHILOSOPHY OF EDUCATION SOCIETY

Raup recalls a first meeting in Philadelphia in 1940 (Raup, 1966), but on 24 February 1941 in Atlantic City, New Jersey, the Philosophy of Education Society was formally inaugurated. The Philosophy of Education Society (PES) inherited the Dewey Society's intellectual legacy. Although both societies continue to exist the Philosophy of Education Society soon eclipsed the John Dewey Society. The membership of the Dewey society became for all intents and purposes, coextensive with the membership of PES. After World War II it fell to PES to elaborate and intellectually redirect what the Dewey society had begun.

By 1938 the context of the Dewey society's investigations ceased to incorporate those urgent socioeconomic problems that had once enforced the social relevance of its investigations (Johnson, 1977, 74). But it had set in place the social and intellectual infrastructure that would in time and history come to be identified and known as philosophy of education after World War II. The success of the Dewey society in developing the pool of talent and identifying a reservoir of academic questions unaddressed by "pure" philosophy, social science, or professional educators created the conditions necessary for the institutionalization of philosophy of education. The failure of Dewey society's attempt at partisan politics ensured that the new discipline's modern institutional form would abandon its social reform stance and adopt a standard of professional practice that was thoroughly academic and socially disinterested.

Unable to come to terms with partisan philosophy, ultraliberals, moderates, and conservatives turned to a more academic version of philosophy of education, an idea that had been around at least since the turn of the century and perhaps since the early 1800s (see Chambliss 1968). But in the United States it was not until the Philosophy of Education Society was organized that a suitable infrastructure for an academic version of philosophy of education was in place.

A substantial segment of the society's membership, led by R. Bruce, Raup: turned their hands to a largely academic version of philosophy of education. On 4 November 1940, Raup wrote to "several acquaintances" suggesting the "desirability of forming a national group of those directly devoted to the teaching or other pursuit of philosophy of education." This group, at least initially, would be those who were "philosophers of education in a technical sense" (Raup, 1940, 1; cf. Raup, 1966, side 2, tm 76). The purpose of this organization would be:

a. the promotion of the fundamental philosophic treatment of the problems of education; b. the cultivation of fruitful relationships between workers in general philosophy and workers in philosophy of education; c. the encouragement of promising young students in the field of philosophy of education; d. the extension and improvement of teaching in the philosophy of education in schools for the education of teachers and in other educational institutions; and e. indirectly, philosophic leavening of the whole educational program and enterprise. (Raup, 1940, 1)

Bruce Raup, Teachers College, Columbia University, was elected president; Theodore Brameld became secretary-treasurer; and an executive committee was appointed comprised of Lawrence Thomas, Stanford University; Gordon Hullfish, Ohio State University; and John Brubacher, Yale University. The list of executive officers is interesting not so much for who it contains as much as for who is absent—neither John L. Childs nor George Counts, the leaders of the philosophical Left was elected. Although Counts was consulted and took part in initial deliberations he was not part of the society's directorate. Brameld is the only representative of the Left and he is quite probably best categorized as a safe member of the academic Left. George Axtelle recalls that it was John Brubacher and Theodore Brameld who held the society together during the war years (Axtelle, 1965, tm 45). Nevertheless, the point remains that the executive was representative of a "new academic start" for philosophy of education.

Unlike the Dewey society, which had initially dedicated itself to an investigation of the role of schooling in the social and economic reconstruction of society, the proposed association was an academic enterprise. This was an organization devoted to a specialized function and that function was philosophizing (Raup, 1940, par. 1–2). Raup saw no purpose in the construction of another general society (Raup, 1966, tm 770) just as he had little sympathy for an "applied" discipline (Raup, 1966, tm 820). As Kenneth Benne, a charter member of the society so gently put it, "Our society would not be an action organization for partisan positions except where the discipline and the teaching of philosophy of education were involved" (Benne, 1966, tm 51).

## THE SOCIAL FRONTIER

The "public" voice of the society was *The Social Frontier* even if, tacitly, the Dewey society and *The Social Frontier* were entirely separate organizations. Harrison Elliott, Sidney Hook, Alvin Johnson,

E. L. Lindeman, Harry A. Overstreet and V. T. Thayer, all members of
*The Social Frontier's* original board of directors, were involved one way
or another in the Dewey society's founding (Johnson, 1977, 70). The
society and *The Social Frontier* were tightly linked in the public mind
by the interlocking directorate of the two organizations, as well as by
the common interest of John Dewey himself, who acted as a director of
*The Social Frontier*, the namesake of the society, and as a contributor of
material to both *The Social Frontier* and the yearbooks.

The John Dewey Society began at about the same point in time as *The
Social Frontier*. The subtle difference between the two was a matter of
emphasis. It was the difference between Counts's "Beardian-
Veblenesque/Marxism" and Dewey's "experimental/pragmatism." For
Dewey democratic cooperation and the resolution of social and economic
questions through intelligent inquiry was central to the idea of social
reconstruction and the creation of the "just" society. The idea of
indoctrination, coercion, and class war as a necessary expedient for rid-
ding America of economic/business superstructure and liberating the
school for the task of "real" education seemed to Boyd, Raup, Rugg, and
the Dewey faction as jeopardizing the possibility of the creation of a
democratic society.

The idea for *The Social Frontier* was advanced by Mordecai Grossman
and Norman Woelfel, two graduate students at Teachers College,
Columbia (Cremin, 1961, 231). It was George Counts, Grossman, and
Woelfel who really controlled the editorial policy of the *Frontier*. The
first issue appeared in October 1934, preceding the incorporation of the
John Dewey Society by some months. The proclaimed task of the journal
was to galvanize classroom teachers into an evangelical elite for the
reconstruction of a new society (Bowers, 1969a, 96). In the initial year of
publication the *Frontier* explored social reconstruction within the terms
of Dewey's ideas of "experimentalism" and small l liberal social
philosophy, but this editorial policy did not last. As the editors and
significant members of the Dewey society became further and further
alienated from Roosevelt's New Deal, Marxism came to be a more
important element in editorial policy and comment.

The board of directors of *The Social Frontier* read like a Who's Who
of Left and ultraliberal thought. The most eminent member of the board
was, arguably, Sidney Hook, but Harrison Elliott, Alvin Johnson, E. L.
Lindeman, Harry A. Overstreet, and V. T. Thayer all played an
important role in support of George Counts, the journal's first editor.
The journal also attracted manuscripts from individuals of all
intellectual persuasions. George Counts acted as editor and contributed
various manuscripts, John Dewey contributed a regular page, Earl
Browder leader of the American Communist Party contributed to the

journal as did Lawrence Dennis leader of the American fascist party, William H. Kilpatrick, John Childs, Boyd H. Bode, Theodore Brameld and other established academics also wrote material for the *Frontier*. Finding little in common with messianic figures like Huey Long or Father Couglin, the board of directors preached the virtues of economic collectivism and the immoral and miseducative effects of capitalism. The board hoped this message would appeal to uncommitted educators and educational theorists (Bowers, 1969a, 91-96). The initial editorial message of *The Social Frontier* found a receptive audience. At the end of the first year of publication it had six thousand subscribers (Graham, 1967, 71).

George S. Counts was the journal's first and foremost editor. Among academic educators, no one advanced Beard's critique of the domination of the American educational establishment by business any more insistently or effectively than Counts (Dennis and Eaton, 1980; Dennis, 1989). He argued that it was ludicrous to believe that the schools could liberate intelligence or engage in the process of social reform until the dead hand of business was removed from the schools (Cremin 1961, 225). In his 1932 speech "Dare progressive education be progressive?" to the Progressive Education Association convention, he electrified the meeting when he censured progressive education's tie to business and the ruling class (Graham, 1967, 65). And again in his monograph *Dare the school build a new social order?* (Counts, 1932), after a caustic attack upon the existing social and economic order, he suggested a more direct role for the school in social reform and the replacement of the present form of national government (Graham, 1967, 70). Counts's critique of American education and its political institutions was too strong for the Progressive Education Association.

When the association failed to respond to his more radical suggestions Counts sought more sympathetic compatriots. He found them in Kilpatrick's discussion group. This was a small group of academic New Yorkers who had begun meeting in 1928 to discuss social and economic questions. Among the members of this group were Edmund des Brunner, John L. Childs, John Dewey, William Heard Kilpatrick, Edward C. Lindeman, Lois Hayden Meek, Jesse H. Newlon, Harry Overstreet, Sidney Hook, Harold Rugg, and Goodwin Watson. The group supported a majority of Counts's proposals (Graham, 1967, 70). In this period social radicalism was in vogue. Glenn E. Plumb constructed a proposal for the nationalization of America's railroads, the American Federation of Labor voted to extend Plumb's proposal to other industries, and the United Mine Workers voted to have the government take over the mines (Schlesinger, [1957] 1988, 41). The Kilpatrick discussion group was an educational expression of a national condition—an economically terrified and socially concerned middle class.

The depression, of course, brought radical issues to a fine focus. The social conditions generated by the depression brought America's implicit assumptions into question.

The nation staggered into the second winter of the depression . . . The cold was bitter in unheated tenements, in the flophouses smelling of sweat and Lysol, in the parks, in empty freight cars, along the windy waterfronts. With no money left for rent, unemployed men and their entire families began to build shacks where they could find unoccupied land . . . These communities quickly received their sardonic name: they were called Hoovervilles.
At the breadlines and soup kitchens, hours of waiting would produce a bowl of mush, often without milk or sugar, and a tin cup of coffee . . . Citizens of Chicago, in this second winter, could be seen digging into heaps of refuse with sticks and hands as soon as the garbage trucks pulled out . . . Clarence Pickett of the Friends found schools where 85, 90, even 99 per cent of the children were underweight, and, in consequence, drowsy and lethargic. (Schlesinger, [1957] 1988, 171)

By October of 1935 the economy appeared to be in free fall and the political atmosphere had turned ominous. Members of the group were finally moved to something more than discussion. The Kilpatrick group provided initial support for *The Social Frontier*, generating the board of directors, and selecting George Counts to be editor and Woelfel and Grossman as associate editors. In 1934 when the first issue of *The Social Frontier* appeared the depression seemed to be beyond the control of Roosevelt and the New Deal. The national mood had moved from a feeling of helplessness to despair, then to anger. The conservatives were angry with Roosevelt's tampering with the economic system, and the liberals were irate with the president's failure to dismantle the system of capitalistic exploitation that appeared to them to be the cause of the nation's difficulties (Bowers, 1969a, 91).

Social conditions did not improve:

The fog of despair hung over the land. One out of every four American workers lacked a good job. Factories that had once darkened the skies with smoke stood ghostly and silent, like extinct volcanoes. Families slept in tarpaper shacks and tin-lined caves and scavenged like dogs for food in the city dump. In October the New York City Health Department had reported that over one-fifth of the pupils in public schools were suffering from malnutrition. Thousands of vagabond children were roaming the land, wild boys of the road. Hunger marchers, pinched and bitter, were parading cold streets in New York and Chicago. On the country side unrest had already flared into violence. Farmers stopped milk trucks along Iowa roads and poured the milk into the ditch. Mobs halted mortgage sales, ran men from the banks and insurance companies out of town, intimidated courts and judges, demanded a moratorium on debts. (Schlesinger, [1957] 1988, 3)

Deteriorating social conditions tempered the editorial policy of the *Frontier*. The editorial policy was Deweyan and Beardian in the first issue, but by the second year of publication, the *Frontier* had turned decidedly Marxist. For Counts, Woelfel, and Grossman the time had come for direct action to replace the social and economic order. In an article entitled "Teachers and Labor" (1935), the editors acknowledged that their proposals implied an advocacy of class struggle. They also acknowledged that their proposals mortgaged social and political evolution to violence—if not to class war.

In 1935 the journal adopted a decidedly Marxist tone. *The Social Frontier* engaged in mercurial rhetoric and the issue of manifestos for the "reconstruction" of capitalist society. Exemplary of this position was an article published in January 1935. The article "1,105,921," argued that although they numbered in the millions, teachers were essentially part of the underprivileged and dispossessed elements of society whose "real" interests would be served by transforming the schools into powerful institutions of social reform. It is interesting to note that the journal's subscription list generated some belief in a general political mandate for a socialist—if not communist—politics. This misinterpretation demonstrated the editorial staff's isolation from the political realities of the day. Perhaps the only equivalent act among the ultraliberals was Dewey's Christmas letter (23 December 1930) to Senator Norris urging him to withdraw from the Democratic party and lead a Progressive ticket against Roosevelt—an act that would probably have cost the nation the REA (Rural Electrification Administration) and the TVA (Tennessee Valley Authority) relief projects that Norris was shepherding through Congress (see Dykhuizen, 1973, 252; Morison, 1965, 960, 965). Norris wisely suggested that he would remain a more effective voice for the common man by retaining his seat in the Democratic party. His decision lost him Dewey's esteem but allowed him to retain an influential place in the Roosevelt administration.

The editors' offer to direct America's revolution did not strike a responsive cord with ultraliberals, American labor, the socialist Left, or the American Communist party. Ultraliberals would not be associated with class war. American labor was not interested in destroying capitalism. Norman Thomas's socialist Left was unwilling to participate in a dictatorship of the proletariat—one dictatorship was no better than another as far as they were concerned. The communists did not believe the schools could be effectively used for revolutionary purposes (Bowers, 1969a, 144–145). And, perhaps more important, *The Social Frontier's* editorial policy did not find support among the rank and file of American educators. Subscriptions fell by thousands after the editors' radical proposals reached the journal's readership. By 1937 the *Frontier* had lost half of its subscribers

(Bowers, 1969a, 164; cf. Graham, 1967, 71), and in a short time the journal was no longer financially viable (Bowers, 1969a, 162). *The Social Frontier* stumbled on for some years, saved first by the John Dewey Society and then by the Progressive Education Association, who rechristened it the *Frontiers of Democracy*. As *Frontiers of Democracy* the journal continued to publish until 1944 (Potter, 1967, 459), but for all intents and purposes as an authentic voice of radical, liberal, progressive, social, and educational reform it passed into history toward the end of 1938.

Liberal thinkers were just unable to come to terms with the demands of social activism. In "Class Struggle and the Democratic Way," (May 1936) Dewey rebuked the attempted synthesis of Marxism and experimentalism. But Dewey could not find an active place for philosophy in social change. Or perhaps it is more correct to say that the role he saw for philosophy in social change was outside of the realm of partisan policy. The role Dewey advocated was philosophy's traditional role—the role of enlightenment. If philosophy had a role to play in social change, it was to assist men to choose wisely in the reconstruction of their society.

When Dewey withdrew his active support for *The Social Frontier* he made one more attempt to discuss the relationship between education and social change in "Education and social change" (1937). He acknowledged that he had no new ideas, but he could not abandon his conviction that educators might play a decisive role in the social reconstruction of society. Education was his theory of action; his Calvinist ethos could not stretch to Marxist theories of direct action and violent revolution. In reaffirming his position he wrote the following: "If a sufficient number of educators devote themselves to striving courageously and with full sincerity to find the answer to the concrete questions which the (democratic) idea and aim put to us, I believe that the question of the relation of schools to direction of social change will cease to be a question and will become a moving answer in action" (Dewey, 1937, 238). At this point Dewey withdrew to write *Logic: The theory of inquiry* ([1938] 1982), leaving his acolytes to pursue the mission he had set (Bowers, 1969a, 171-198).

Finding the social radicalism of *The Social Frontier* incompatible with their experimentalist proclivities the ultraliberals embraced the yearbooks of the John Dewey Society as the device for the expression of their intellectual ambitions. Those ambitions remained what they were in 1928—the social and economic reconstruction of society. What was different was that from now on philosophy would be divorced from partisan politics. Philosophy was no longer to be directed to the cause of social revolution; the role of philosophy would be to clarify the social issues of the day and challenge educators, as the architects of social reconstruction, to articulate their social convictions and rebuild society from their classrooms in light of those convictions.

The naïveté of such a program seems monumental in retrospect. Nevertheless, educators took up the task with great seriousness. For example, the chairman of the editorial board of *Building America* magazine: Paul R. Hanna, Stanford University, brought social conditions generated by the depression directly to the attention of educators and their students through the *Building America* magazine. Unlike the editors of *The Social Frontier*, the editors of *Building America* presented powerful pictorial messages on topics such as housing, transportation, and power and left individual readers to draw their own conclusions about the state of the nation and the need for socioeconomic reform. The editorial board of *Building America*, Paul R. Hanna, Stanford University; C. L. Cushman, Denver Public Schools; Edgar Dale, Ohio State University; William Gray, University of Chicago; Harold Hand, Stanford University; Jesse H. Newlon, Teachers College, Columbia University; and Claire Zyve, Scarsdale Public Schools, collectively, could not bring themselves to the *Frontier's* rhetoric: they were appalled by what was going on in America, but they could not adopt Count's socialist discourse.

The intellectual stance of the John Dewey Society is indicative of the inability of liberal philosophical thought to come to terms with partisan philosophy and social activism. Partisan philosophy at least demands that philosophers begin their investigations in good faith and in reference to warranted versions of existence as it is being lived. The inability of liberal philosophical thought to come to terms with the partisan philosophy is nowhere so graphically displayed as in the inability of those ultraliberals to contribute to the ongoing dialogue of social reform being conducted by the Roosevelt administration. Locked in polemical debate over the function of class war in the reconstruction of a doomed society, they failed to notice the social impact of the Wagner Act, the Social Security Act, and the Banking Act, not to mention the lift the economy. Far from being doomed, America was launched upon a form of social and economic reform that had found the confidence of the American people—even if it had not fired the imagination of reconstructionist educators preoccupied by academic debate (Bowers, 1969a, 158).

In a sense, Dewey and his colleagues were transfixed by the "iron-syllogism." Convinced of the purity of their cause, the persuasiveness of ultraliberal logic, and the example of the Russian Revolution, they assumed that America would follow their lead. They imagined a social disaffection and an impotent political establishment that had lost the loyalty of its constituency. In fact, they were faced with a potent political system and one of America's most powerful presidents, a president who was unconcerned about their debate. In the matrix of dissent and opposition, the Democratic party and the Roosevelt administration ascribed little importance to a group judged by many to be academic dilettantes. Dewey and his colleagues did not understand that the politicians of the day operated in a different milieu of pressing concerns. Their approach stymied their original intent to contribute in the political arena, and they ignored the disintegration of whatever political support they had achieved. The debate over the social and educational purposes of class war left ultraliberal educators in disarray and on the defensive.

By the time the John Dewey Society had published its first yearbook in 1937 (*The teacher and society*) *The Social Frontier* was a spent force. The journal, for all intents and purposes, was in receivership. George Counts had resigned his editorship to lead the fight against the communist takeover of the New York Teachers Union (Bowers, 1969a, 166). Disgusted with the conservative political vision of the board of directors, Woelfel and Grossman had resigned in June of 1937 (Bowers, 1969a, 167). The moderate social reconstructionists had abandoned *The Social Frontier* and given their allegiance to the John Dewey Society. But perhaps most important for philosophy of education, liberal thought had lost its taste for partisan philosophy and social activism.

The history of *The Social Frontier* is filled with irony. It was the voice of liberal reform and yet it had even less effect upon the educational policies of the New Deal than did the National Educational Association (Cremin, 1961, 233). Its most ironic contribution to the history of education appears to be the effect it had upon philosophy of education. In the public mind, the journal painted social reconstructionism and many important ultraliberal philosophers of education as seditious intellectuals using their position in the educational establishment to subvert the American way of life (Cremin, 1961, 234). This was an image that almost all members of the society and most contributors to *The Social Frontier* could not bear. They were passionately devoted to America. If partisan philosophy meant sedition—being linked with the Stalinist left and Earl Browder—they would have none of it.

Americans of social democratic persuasion such as Sidney Hook, John Dewey, George Counts, Harold Rugg, and Theodore Brameld all responded to the critique of the American Communist party at one time or another. In the end the champions of pragmatism abandoned the leftist critique that they had precariously built during the depression and held during the scalding politics of the Moscow show trials and

World War II. The Left's challenge to pragmatism did not survive cold war politics. Of course, neither did pragmatism's romance with Marxism.

The rough and tumble of social activism was no longer deemed to be the proper realm for philosophy. In 1936, just a few years after Counts introduced the idea of class struggle, R. Bruce Raup was denouncing the class dynamic (see Raup, 1936b). In May of 1936 on his editorial page of the *Frontier* John Dewey urged teachers to be neutral (Dewey, 1936). And in June of 1936 Kilpatrick urged teachers to reject high Marxism (Kilpatrick, 1936). The issue of philosophical participation in social activism was symbolically settled in May of 1937 when Dewey wrote his last article in *The Social Frontier* and quietly withdrew to work full time on *Logic* ([1938] 1982). The ultraliberals who had originally supported and contributed their work to *The Social Frontier* withdrew one by one. Even Theodore Brameld who claimed Marx as a spiritual guide in *A philosophic approach to communism* (1933), mellowed in the *Social Frontier* article "Karl Marx and the American teacher" (1935) and eventually abandoned his hard-line views in *Toward a reconstructed philosophy of education* (1956). Cremin (1988, 194-195) notes that after Brameld's defection to the liberal camp only John DeBoer at the University of Illinois remained as a lonely Marxist sentinel.

The collapse of professional support for the social activism of educational philosophy was a stinging rebuke. After World War II philosophy of education would address its comments to the realm of philosophy and leave social activism to the unions or anyone else who was willing to take it up—until the sixties would change all that. From this moment on philosophy of education would launch itself upon the task of professionalization, judging its activities and investigations upon the subtlety of its arguments and the incisiveness of its critiques. Philosophy of education had begun in 1935 as a partisan activity, but by the early 1940s it was a matter of subtle argument and the production of books and articles for the academic press.

## EDUCATIONAL THEORY

The Philosophy of Education Society did not meet during and right after the war years (1942–1947), but the members of the society were active during the war: George Axtelle recalls meetings that took place at Columbia (1965, tm 16). In the post–war years the absence of a journal dedicated to publishing the results of philosophical investigations of education was only too evident.

The journal that consolidated the various initiatives into an academic version of philosophy of education was to come from a collaborative effort on the part of the John Dewey Society, the Philosophy of Education Society, and the University of Illinois. When the university foresaw the postwar academic boom and the tremendous demand for university-level education in all areas it conducted a thoroughgoing review of its programs and services. As part of that review the College of Education decided to devote personnel, time, and research facilities to the study of the more fundamental educational questions. The specific result of that reallocation was "the establishment of a Division of Psychological Foundations; the establishment of a Division of Historical, Comparative, Philosophical and Social Foundations of Education; and the expansion of the Bureau of Educational Research" (Anderson, 1951, 14). The College of Education was also aware of the fact that although they considered the investigation of fundamental nonempirical questions pertaining to education to be of the utmost importance, the opportunity for the publication of the results of these studies was extremely limited. With the establishment of *The History of Education Journal* in 1949 a small beginning had been made. But an outlet for the publication of studies in the philosophical and social foundations was still to be found. That outlet was generated when, in response to a new policy regarding university support for scholarly journals, the John Dewey Society proposed that the society and the College of Education at the University of Illinois sponsor such a journal (Anderson, 1951, 14-16). The result of this collaborative initiative was *Educational Theory*.

With the launching of *Educational Theory* in 1951 the last element needed to realize a thoroughly professional version of philosophy of education was in place. From this time on philosophy of education would be concerned with philosophizing. Despite disclaimers to the contrary (see Anderson, 1951, 18-21), philosophy of education largely abandoned its concern for socioeconomic reform and concerned itself with the task of book making characteristic of the academic enterprise. Kenneth Benne and Theodore Brameld attempted to keep the fire of social reform alive, but their efforts received diminishing support. In the postWar period philosophy of education was rehearsing the ideas of John Dewey and defending pragmatism from intellectual conservatives. The decision to philosophize directed philosophy of education away from the concerns of its natural audience (the profession of education) and toward the less and less "real" conversations of "academic" philosophy.

## STUDIES IN PHILOSOPHY AND EDUCATION

A few years later in 1960 Francis Villemain produced another journal called *Studies in Philosophy and Education*. Its connection with *Educational Theory* was strong. Villemain recounts that a conscious effort was made to avoid any conflict of interest between *Educational Theory* and his journal. Archibald Anderson, *Educational Theory*'s representative, sat at the yearly board meetings of *Studies in Philosophy and Education* for that explicit purpose, among others. Villemain's journal was intended to relate the issues of philosophy to education. In a way his editorial policy was to be even more philosophical than educational theory. On the other hand, the content of *Educational Theory* and *Studies in Philosophy and Education*, at least in retrospect, seem very similar. The journal was largely Villemain's initiative. As such, it never received the solid institutional support that *Educational Theory* received from the University of Illinois. The journal's point of production followed Villemain's career. After a long period of suspension the journal is back in production under the editorship of David P. Ericson at the Graduate School of Education, University of California, Los Angeles. Ericson is attempting to reestablish the journal and return it to its original mission.

## NOTES

1. The Progressive Education Association changed its name to the American Education Fellowship in 1944.

2. What was radical and new in the days of the prehistory of educational philosophy was not new methodological or intellectual gambits—which were radical enough by the philosophical standards of the time—but the political ethics and social radicalism that allied the nascent discipline with the complex forces of social reform that were emerging as America entered the twentieth century (cf. Feuer, 1959, 545).

3. It must be remembered that Dilling's book was relatively indiscriminate in labeling communists. It listed hundreds of organizations and thousands of individuals among whom John Dewey, George S. Counts, Goodwin Watson, and William H. Kilpatrick, appeared prominently (see Eaton, 1975, 96-97; Bowers, 1969a, 34). In Dilling's book it would appear that Karl Marx and Groucho Marx were equally suspect!

4. Even more intensely intellectual socialists steeped in the European heritage like Sidney Hook would in the last analysis construct his version of socialism with reference to his New York ghetto childhood and leaven it with an intense American patriotism (Hook, 1987).

5. It never seemed to occur to them that there might be social questions that were not amenable to rational solution. This fact of course was the appeal of Marxist thought. Intensely intellectual Marxist theory acknowledged the roll of intellect and *revolution* in the "rational" solution of unjust social and economic privilege.

6. The production of the National Society for the Study of Education yearbooks dedicated to philosophy of education was managed by authoritative members of PES. Like the Dewey society's yearbooks they provide another unobtrusive indicator of educational philosophy's academic disposition.

The 1942 yearbook of the National Society for the Study of Education and the 1955 yearbook of the society, both presented an academic version of educational philosophy. (The 1952 yearbook dedicated to "General Education" outlines a place for the study of philosophy and education but it seems more in tune with the original purposes of the Dewey society.) The influence of philosophy of science and analysis on the philosophical study of education is evident in "Philosophical redirection of educational research" the 1972 yearbook of the National Society for the Study of Education. The academic mood remained evident in the the 1981 yearbook of the National Society for the Study of Education, also dedicated to philosophy of education.

The 1942 and 1955 yearbooks followed the manner in which philosophy was presented in many American universities. It was a period that marked the final florescence of philosophical systems. Common to many departments was the belief that each philosophical system (idealism, realism, Marxism, pragmatism, and so on) held a well formed system of epistemology, metaphysics, and ethics that would ground beliefs about the "good" and the "true" and would provide rational guidance for life and therein education (Broudy, [1979] 1981, 8). The yearbooks do not suggest the power of the analytic movement in philosophy that would soon dominate both philosophy and philosophy of education, but they did foreshadow the commitment of educational philosophy to academic versions of educational philosophy. In a sense, the organization of the 1942 and 1955 yearbooks was a way of suggesting that philosophy of education really was about philosophy. The 1955 yearbook is the most interesting of the two in that the commitment to philosophizing reaches its logical conclusion when the yearbook committee turned the writing of the chapters over to "real" philosophers. In the words of the committee, "In the field of general philosophy there are not only more varieties of opinion than in the more limited field of education, but there are also a number of prominent philosophers whose views on education, if once worked out from their author's philosophical premises, may very well provide fresh insights into educational problems" (Brubacher, 1955, 1).

# 4

# Philosophy of Education
# After 1945

In the 1950s educational philosophy's research agendas were directed toward diversifying the curriculum, humanizing school practices, and perfecting the school as a device of social mobility. Educational philosophy's role in all of this revolved around rehearsing the agendas originally defined by the Progressives in the 1930s and 1940s. For a short period after the war American's educational philosophers were allowed the luxury of realizing the intellectual agendas of pragmatism. The core of this ideology was concerned with the establishment of the public high school.[1] Pragmatism argued for the diversification and reorganization of the curriculum: It maintained that there was more to school than the classics and the Bible. It argued for an extension of training in the "practical" arts (commerce, agriculture, home economics, art, physical education, and so on) on the grounds that there were many Americans who were not bound for college and they, too, deserved an education that would allow them to escape from the circumstances of their birth. On the other hand, no one was raising the social issues in the manner in which educational philosophers did in the 1930s (Axtelle, 1965, tm 360).[2]

At the beginning of the postwar period philosophy and philosophy of education enjoyed a demographically driven renaissance as postsecondary enrollments exploded under the impact of returning GI's lured to colleges and universities by the benefits of the GI Bill. Nevertheless after World War II educational philosophy was faced with the transcendence of science and technology on all fronts and the consequences of the discipline's political indiscretions during the depression. Educational philosophy adopted an apologist stance for its preWar politics on the one hand and for its lack of science on the other.

Most American philosophers and philosophers of education abandoned any political economy that traced its genealogy back to Marx (Cremin, 1988, 194-195). The "Red Scare" had taught and McCarthyism reminded professors of philosophy and philosophy of education to leave anarchism, Marx, and the rest of the Left alone (Zinn, 1980, 420-428). Kenneth Benne was written into the *Congressional record* for things that he had written, Brameld's books were burned, and the FBI kept a file on John Dewey. The threat was more than hypothetical. Arguably the most important example of its political apologetics is Theodore Brameld's *Toward a reconstructed philosophy of education* (1956). During the depression Brameld had supported the social reconstruction group advocating that teachers must drop their political neutrality if they were to serve their clientele honorably. In expressing this opinion he had written *A philosophic approach to communism* (1933). He suggested that Marx and Engels might have a viable social critique. But after the war, in the shadow of the Moscow show trials of 1936 and 1937, the explosion of the Russian atom bomb, the 1939 Nazi-Soviet nonaggression pact, the invasion of Korea, and McCarthyism, Brameld recanted. In *Toward a reconstructed philosophy of education* (1956) Brameld carefully distanced himself from Marxist politics. Brameld wrote: "We wish to emphasize that, despite the enormous influence of Marxism upon contemporary utopian thought, it is thoroughly unsatisfactory in various respects to anyone who might properly be considered a reconstructionist" (1956, 31). In this reconstruction Marx and Engels are marginalized. Like Sidney Hook, Brameld was not so sure about the moral superiority or epistemological privilege of the Marxists any more.

After World War II educational philosophy also found a answer for its lack of science. To answer for its lack of science educational philosophy responded with analysis. If educational philosophy could not share in the ethos of experimentalism, it could be clear. If educational philosophy did not lend itself to statistics and mathematics, it could be logical. If it could no longer lay claim to the most powerful, interesting, and explanatory paradigm of systematic study of the natural world and human experience, comparatively speaking, then it would demonstrate its central role in clarifying the "undifferentiated mush" written-up in the guise of educational theory.[3]

## AMERICAN PHILOSOPHICAL ASSOCIATION

Ten years after the founding of the John Dewey Society, the American Philosophical Association started to consider the role of "philosophy in American education" in a book by the same title (see Blanshard, Ducasse, Hendel, Murphy, and Otto 1945). And even then members of the philosophical society were more interested in discovering or inventing a role for philosophy in a world that had taken science and the scientist as its cultural heroes than in applying the tools of philosophy to the problems of schooling (see Beck, 1965; Broudy, 1987; Macmillan, 1991, 279). As Macmillan (1991, 279) noted, there "didn't seem to be any sustained philosophical discussion of educational questions in that academic field." Murphy, a contributor to *Philosophy in American education* (1945), wrote: "The subordination of philosophy to extra philosophical interests in such a way that, having no longer its own distinctive work to do, it can serve as everybody's little helper is something different and undesirable. The confusion of the latter of these proposals with the former is not a contribution to the cause of philosophy, of clear thinking, or of liberal education" (1945, 251). Clearly there was little interest in becoming education's "little helper." But, of course, it must be remembered that this attitude was part of philosophy's defensive reaction to the reformulation of the idea of the university and the evolution of science and social science out of philosophy. In the 1940s and 1950s philosophy was no more happier to work with education than it was with any of the sciences or social sciences. The establishment of science and social science within the structure of the university was part of the academic marginalization of philosophy per se.

America's philosophers were interested in schooling only insofar as it might contribute to their then seemingly dubious tenure in American universities (see Blanshard et al., 1945). Externally, the market for philosophical celebrations of American democracy, naturalism, and social reconstruction was exhausted (Rorty, [1976] 1982b, 63). Internally, the American philosophic establishment's traditional internal enemies (the idealists, the subjectivists, and the transcendentalists) had been exorcised and not even fellow members of the philosophic establishment were terribly interested in hearing them criticized (Rorty, [1976] 1982b, 64). And science was immune to philosophical criticism. An interest in education, it seemed (in the mid-1940s), might provide some relief from the intractable siege of science and social science. Philosophy became, largely, a defensive enterprise. It believed philosophy's renaissance was a matter of demonstrating the low level of argumentation among its academic competitors (Rorty, [1976] 1982b, 62).

The American Philosophical Association was willing to grant that (from their perspective) the "intellectual problem" in philosophy of education was not attributable to professors of education alone. Blanshard and Ducasse indicated that part of the problem was that philosophers were just not "conversant with the concrete and practical issues which concern those who have committed themselves to the profession of teaching" (1945, 243). It was a problem that went without remedy. Although John Dewey, the preeminent philosopher of American philosophy's heroic period, was interested in schooling and education, the country's philosophic establishment was not. When philosophy per se finally did address itself to the questions of schooling or education it often produced tired little "rags"—little "scholasticisms"—or complete irrelevancies. Philosophy's work on education was little better or perhaps worse than the work of professors of education that the philosophical establishment so ardently criticized (e.g., Brubacher, 1955b). And yet it must be admitted that philosophers like Sidney Hook (1956), Susanne Langer (1956), and Abraham Edel (1956) made a serious attempt to show philosophy's relation to education. Nevertheless, their seriousness was not shared by philosophy as a whole.

In the period following World War II the association had little time for philosophy of education. But relations between the American Philosophical Association and the Philosophy of Education Society warmed somewhat over the years. The association held a few seminars and symposia on educational questions in the period after 1945 (see Macmillan, 1991, 279-284), and philosophical journals started to publish special issues on the concerns of philosophy and education. An education special interest group led by Harvey Siegel and Sophie Haroutunian-Gordon met at the American Philosophical Association meetings in the late 1980s and early 1990s (Macmillan, 1991, 283).

Be that as it may, philosophy's lack of interest in education and the defensive posture of philosophy within the university structure at least partially explains the antagonistic relationship that developed between philosophy and philosophy of education. The antagonism reflects the new discipline's inception among professional educators and its strong ties with social science; as far as professors of philosophy were concerned, like science and social science, education was just another competitor for the apparently ever-diminishing pool of academic resources residual to the humanities in a scientific world. Influential professors of philosophy believed philosophy of education was a tangible threat to their own interests and the interests of philosophy in general. From the perspective of "siege-weary" philosophers, philosophy of education was just another example of the "anarchic" profusion of intellectual disciplines that universities had been forced to endure since the end of World War I.

## CONSERVATIVE OPPONENTS

The period marked by the beginning of World War II was a time of desperate intellectual defense for Progressive education in general and educational philosophy in particular, despite a radical increase in the number of educational philosophers in the nation's colleges and universities. War had inhibited social criticism and the socialist critiques of educational philosophy that had not been popular with the establishment prior to the war and were even less so after its conclusion. The conservative critique of American schools led by Mortimer Adler, Arthur Bestor, and Robert M. Hutchins received a sympathetic hearing. Bestor's *Educational wastelands* ([1953] 1985) gave a scathing critique of American schools and mooted the disenfranchisement of professors of education. Influential and articulate conservative critics voiced their concerns about the radical politics and consequentialist ethics of pragmatism and progressive education. William C. Bagley and Isaac L. Kandel at Teachers College, Columbia University, and John D. Redden and Francis A. Ryan at Fordham University were all significant enemies of pragmatism and progressive education (Cremin, 1988, 230). All members of this group had reference to José Ortega y Gasset's *Revolt of the masses* (1932). In this book Ortega y Gasset expressed the fear of all conservatives:

There is one fact which, whether for good or ill, is of utmost importance in the public life of Europe at the present moment. This fact is the accession of the masses to complete social power. As the masses, by definition, neither should nor can direct their own personal existence, and still less rule society in general, this fact means that actually Europe is suffering from the greatest crisis that can afflict peoples, nations, and civilisation . . .

Europe has been left without a moral code. It is not that the mass-man has thrown over an antiquated one in exchange for a new one, but that at the centre of his scheme of life there is precisely the aspiration to live without conforming to any moral code. (1932, 11, 201)

The group deplored the advent of modern culture with its slick and superficial values as did Ortega y Gasset. To their mind modern man did not appreciate the vital system of ideas that the Western tradition had produced—the best that has been thought and said—and the role that system of ideas must play in the development of civilization. To their minds Charlie Chaplin's movie *Modern Times* was not a statement about the situation of America's industrial classes as much as it was a demonstration of the vacuity of their dreams. They did not share the pragmatist's faith in democracy. As far as the conservatives were concerned modern man in general and the pragmatists in particular had nothing to offer as a substitute. Pragmatism's legitimation of progressive education's extension of the school curriculum into the trades, commerce, agriculture, home economics, physical education, and the arts nominalized the school's role in liberal education and reduced schooling to the lowest common denominator. Conservatives stilled discourse about social justice in the name of social order. In this version of things intellectual excellence was the handmaiden of social order.

The conservative cultural politics of classical and Victorian thought was an important and irreducible part of the postwar ethos. And, of course, the 1990s neoconservative's social, political, and educational stance was largely a restatement of the conservatism of the 1950s (cf. Jacoby, 1987, 77). This conservative stance is, essentially, the same stance that Arthur Bestor presented in *Educational wastelands* (1953) and Alan Bloom continued in the 1980s in *The closing of the American mind* (1987). In the period following World War II, Ortega y Gasset's concerns are nicely echoed by Bestor who wrote:

The issue in American education today is not drawn between those who believe in scholarship but are indifferent to good teaching, and those who believe in good teaching but are indifferent to scholarship. The issue is drawn between those who believe that good teaching should be directed to sound intellectual ends, and those who are content to dethrone intellectual values and cultivate the techniques of teaching for their own sake, in an intellectual and cultural vacuum. (1953, 11)

In the moral absolution of the postWar period the conservative critique came to dominate educational thought in the 1950s and early 1960s.

The conservatives' emphasis upon authoritative moral standards, intellectual excellence, and social virtue followed sentiments about education similar to those found in Plato's *Republic* and Aristotle's *Politics*. Classical and Victorian thought continued to have a powerful and socially attractive, if socially elite, ideology of its own. It was an ideology that was consistent with the ethos of Victorian America and its echo—to which the well-to-do continued to pay homage. It is a powerful critique that Progressivism never silenced. Begun at the turn of the century, it has extended into the 1990s.

Among liberals and radicals New Yorkers were at the pinnacle of America's intellectual elite just as the *New Yorker* was the nation's pivotal literary magazine (Mills, 1964, 313-314; Jacoby, 1987, 72-111; see Hook, 1987). John Dewey in the last years of his life as well as Sidney Hook, Lionel Trilling, Richard Hofstadter, and C. Wright Mills shared membership in the city's intellectual fellowship. They were still deeply committed to one version or another of ultraliberal or socialist politics. They were true members of the new class.[4] Nevertheless, the 1950s was a period of academic retreat and professional entrenchment for liberal and socialist thinkers. Liberal and socialist discourse was marginalized. Ultraliberalism and socialism faded rapidly as the excesses of Stalinism and the moral absolution of the Allies' victory in World War II became part of the public domain.

The counterculture and the New Left stilled the conservative critique for a period of time during the war in Vietnam. But the conservative critique survived the war. After the United States withdrew from Vietnam—and the New Left and the counterculture collapsed—the conservative critique reasserted itself in the work of Alan Bloom (1987) and E. D. Hirsch (1987), to cite only the most notable examples. Their target was a poverty stricken American culture with its glib and superficial values. To their mind pragmatism's opened America to all the excesses of tolerance and the effete liberalism that philosophical naturalism inspired. It had confused books with comics, music with rock and roll, sex with love, and drugs with with almost everything. In addition, conservative detractors claimed that pragmatism unfairly judged America by its realities while judging America's competitors and enemies by their aspirations and not the realities of their history, politics, or practices. Unlike the former charges, this one was a telling rebuke.

Sidney Hook (1987) noted in his autobiography that the conservative challenges in the 1930s and 1940s to pragmatism and therein progressive education were mounted almost as quickly as pragmatism's success was noticed:

The educational philosophy of Hutchins and Adler was an attempt to justify a counterreformation in American education. They had an easy time deriding some of the principles and practices of some progressive educators, who were more enthusiastic than intelligent about the ideas of John Dewey. But their target was not so much the principles of progressive education—some of whose practices as embodied in the techniques of activity programs they were prepared to accept—but the philosophy of naturalism. This, they alleged, was the source of what was wrong in American schooling and of what was evil in American life.

In place of naturalism, they urged a philosophy that would radically reform both American schools and the culture of which they were a part. Education was to be desecularized; metaphysics and theology were to be instated as prescribed courses in the curriculum of institutions of higher learning. The controlling values and objectives of the lower school were to rest upon the truths of metaphysics and religion, which were declared "superior" to all other truths, particularly those reached by the scientific method. To implement the required educational reform, the state must abandon its neutrality in religion. (1987, 341)

The counterreformation of the 1980s and early 1990s differed little from the counterreformation of the late 1930s, 1940s, and 1950s (e.g., Bestor, [1953] 1985; Bloom, 1987). To Hutchins, Adler, and Bestor; pragmatism was the cause of the anti-intellectualism that they believed was pandemic in educational thought (Karier, [1967] 1986, 314). To Bestor's mind it was a separate program of teacher education outside of the traditional disciplines of the arts and sciences incapable of separating the issues of instructional method and content that was at fault. But more to the point, the conservative critique counseled the abandonment of the social issues of poverty and deprivation during the delivery of educational services in the name of standards and excellence.

Of course, the conservative counterreformation of the 1980s and 1990s was conducted for almost identical reasons and for very similar purposes and goals of the conservative counterreformation of the 1950s. The social agendas of the sixties were unacceptable to the conservative reestablishment of the late 1980s and the 1990s. Alan Bloom's *Closing of the American mind* (1987), like Adler's Great Books program that preceded it, is essentially an indicator of yet one more attempt to dissolve the logic of pragmatism, which stands at the core of one robust version of what we can say and discursively think about education.[5] Education was to be redefined in terms of the demands of excellence and standards of academic excellence. Real education was training that could protect America from the economic success of the Japanese and the Germans. Real education was socially conservative and intellectually selective. According to them schools would be better off if they were out of the social welfare business. Bloom and Hirsch shared these views.

## EXISTENTIALISM

Existentialism engaged the American literati and the public in the late 1950s and became part of the intellectual establishment Jean-Paul Sartre and Albert Camus became intellectual culture heroes of that period (Jacoby, 1987, 114; Gitlin, 1987; Caute, 1988, 24-36). But existentialism was morally suspect and too intellectually messy and individualistic for American taste (cf. Tice and Slavens, 1983). Its German prose and syntax was tainted with fascism (Tice and Slavens, 1983, 262-264). Its French counterpart was too full of self-indulgence and eroticism (cf. Tice and Slavens, 1983). The heroism of existentialism was commendable, but the war was over, and issues beyond heroism were gaining philosophical attention. Existentialism maintained a certain presence in philosophy but it was relegated to the discipline's margins. Philosophy assigned it the task of protecting the discipline's analytic reorganization in the 1950s. It was philosophy's rear guard.

Nevertheless, existentialism and its bohemian matrix went mainstream in American culture (Jacoby, 1987, 39). Allen Ginsberg's *Howl* ([1956] 1986) and Jack Kerouac's *On the road* (1957) pointed the way toward an American version of bohemian life that was realized first in Greenwich Village and San Francisco and then in the backyards of suburbia.

> The beats seemed designed to humble cultural commentators. Sermons bemoaning conformity did not allude to the living refutation, the beats; and lectures about juvenile delinquency failed to mention this greater danger. Few knew about the beats until the second half of the fifties. When they finally captured the public imagination, spurred by Allen Ginsberg's *Howl* (1956) and Kerouac's *On the Road* (1957), their finest hours were fading. Though no one knew it at the time, the public fascination with the beats announced a zig in the zeitgeist.
> The beats, however, are more than a lesson in the risks of cultural forecasting. They are the last bohemians, and the first of the 1960s counterculturalists . . . They carried bohemia into the age of suburbia where it spread and disappeared. If bohemia died of success, the beats both administered the last rites and invented a new popular version. Accounts of the sixties give a nod toward the beats, but more than a nod is required. Not the revived Marxism or Maoism but the sexuality, drugs, mysticism, and madness of the sixties owe much to the beats. (Jacoby, 1987, 65)

Existentialism's fate in educational philosophy mirrored its fate in philosophy. Ably championed by Maxine Greene, Donald Vandenberg, David Denton, Leroy Troutner, George Kneller, Clive Beck, and many others, it attracted a quite reasonable amount of attention in the sixties and early-1970s.[6] But its success was relatively short-lived. The core elements of tragedy in existentialism—Eros and Thanatos—never inspired American educators (cf. Nietzsche. [1872] 1968, 17-144). Its phenomenological aspect foundering on the problem of intersubjectivity, it remained an interesting aside in the romantic literature of the counterculture and a soft alternative to the technical literature of analysis.[7] It inspired educators to order their professional experience, by way of leading themselves and others to consider cultural, social, and political dissent (cf. Kaufmann [1956] 1968, 11-12).

Existentialists in the education establishment were in the embarrassing position of being unable to find a counterculture voice. In the early 1970s they seemed to pick up the existential humanism that had earlier emanated from places like Paris and Greenwich Village, and in a more contemporary fashion from America's own "sixties" experience. It was a position that emphasized humanism, individualism, and personal autonomy in an attempt to transcend nihilism. But educational existentialists were never able to import the outrageous and irreverent voices of Kurt Vonnegut, Jr., Tom Robbins,

Hunter S. Thompson, or Tom Wolfe into their work. They were too middle class, too reserved, too respectful, and too academic. They never found a way to be barefoot in the park or to wear a flower in their hair. The "folk" and "hip" movement embodied the existential ethos, and Abbie Hoffman stole its word—"Free!" (1968). What was left of educational existentialism was taken by minority activists, feminists, freedom marchers, and the students from Kent State. In comparison with the ideology of the counterculture educational existentialism's answers were too like vanilla. Educational philosophers did not speak to existentialism's usual audience: people who were in the world but not worldly, people who had "respectable lives" but were crushed by them, people who were trying to "make up" or save their own lives, and those who claimed some kinship with Nietzsche on the one hand or Hermann Hesse on the other. They just were not in touch with Jefferson Airplane or Crosby, Stills, Nash, and Young in the way that the counterculture was.

## PHILOSOPHY OF SCIENCE

In the preceding period, beginning between the great wars, the "idea of the university" had radically evolved in response to the social, political, and intellectual movements of the period. The "classicist" university was faced with a demand for new faculties in science, social science, and the professional schools. The Victorian university negotiated an uneasy truce in which it agreed to open its doors to the natural and social sciences—physics, chemistry, biology, geology, astronomy, economics, economic history, politics, sociology, anthropology, and psychology; as well as the professional schools of agriculture, business, engineering, medicine, pharmacy, social work, and education—in return for a letter of safe conduct and the promise of continued, if diminished, tenure for the various departments of arts and letters still resident within the university.

The "hard" sciences like physics, chemistry, and biology had achieved pride of place in the university as they quietly and not so quietly penetrated the surface appearances of the world, dissolved its conundrums, and made the world "ready to hand"—usable for human purpose. The sciences had a powerful if erratic heritage going back to the Greeks and a powerful paternity in the culture heroes of the Renaissance. Further, in the hard sciences it was easy to identify a discipline with the results of its endeavors. Tight lineages and algebras of intellectual inheritance were constructed. The evolution of each discipline's explanatory structures and the internal logic that drove each on to its contemporary form was carefully sketched by historians and later, when it was safe, argued over by philosophers of science. In science the genealogy moved from Animaxus and Aristarchus, to Ptolemy; from Ptolemy, to Copernicus and Galileo; from Galileo, to Newton; and from Newton to his modern contemporaries. It was relatively easy to point out how and where in space and time this and that element or elements of the puzzle fell—or were pushed—together (Koestler, 1959; Ronan, 1983).[8] And this narrative could be extended to collateral players in the culture of science, technology, and medicine (see, Durbin, 1980). In short order, science became society's focus and the scientist its culture hero. "Big science" became the driving force of the university (Price, 1961; [1963] 1986; 1965).

Armed with powerful explanatory and instrumental systems the graduates of business, engineering, and medicine built (or saved) economic dynasties, spanned great rivers, and ameliorated the ravages of age, accident, and disease. These accomplishments soon attracted powerful patrons, extravagant endowments, and research grants to schools of business, engineering, and medicine. Whatever pride of place was denied them by the more traditional members of the university community they obtained in the same manner as did the nouveau riche in the broader society. Part of their elevated social position they earned by brilliance and hard work, and that portion of their place that was withheld by Victorian snobbery alone, they bought.

But not all of the new residents of the university were able to command the same level of acceptance or demonstrate the same level of explanatory or instrumental power. Sociology and political science followed economics as new and less prestigious residents of the university. In the semisciences, disciplines such as optometry and nursing lagged badly behind medicine. Education in the company of the "other" social welfare departments was acknowledged to be a large and putatively important area of study. But it was also deemed to be instrumentally and technologically primitive—if not almost bankrupt. Compared to nuclear physics, astronomy, and neurosurgery the technical armory of the social sciences in general and education in particular seemed relatively modest. The awesome power of science's esoteric technique and technological mysteries diminished the accomplishments of professional educators.

In some sense, philosophy decided that if science and social science could not be beaten in the lists, perhaps they could be domesticated—for philosophical purposes. Philosophy had become an academic occupation under scientific siege. It was obvious that Hegelian idealism or Marxism would not hold back the impact of science and social science. Philosophy of science and analytic philosophy, which presented themselves in the post–World War II period, provided or at least seemed to provide a means to return to the battle with science and social science. Philosophy of science and analytic philosophy contributed a rationale for a reconstruction of epistemology and metaphysics—traditional tasks of philosophy. Their classical form had been superseded by science, which had effectively appropriated both areas of study. Philosophy of science and analytic philosophy gave philosophy's traditional tasks a plausible modern form. Philosophy redefined itself in terms of mathematics and the natural sciences (Rorty, [1976] 1982b, 61); if it could not be the queen of sciences, it would be, at least, its tutor—or so philosophers argued.[9] Philosophy of education followed suit.

The classic example of this attempt to tutor science (in education) is *Philosophy of educational research* (1973). Edited by Harry S. Broudy, Robert H. Ennis, and Leonard I. Krimerman, it represented not only one of the most successful alliances of philosophers and philosophers of education but one of the most significant attempt to tutor education's venture into experimental design. Unfortunately the experimentalists greeted the attempt with a rather icy-silence by.  In the end, the attempt to be the arbiter of educational theory collapsed for a lack of interest, outside of philosophy and philosophy of education. The experimentalists did not believe they required philosophy's assistance.

## ANALYSIS

The alliance of analysis with the Vienna Circle and therein science found a grudging acceptance within the university community and presented a politics that was untouched by the social democratic ideology of pragmatism. In the 1950s and early 1960s philosophy and philosophy of education turned their attention to analysis and the "newly" discovered philosophy of science that was written by Russell and Moore in concert with the great émigrés Rudolf Carnap, Carl Gustav Hempel, Herbert Feigl, Hans Reichenbach, Alfred Tarski, and Ludwig Wittgenstein. The epistemology of Wittgenstein's *Tractatus* ([1921] 1974) became the order of the day. The analysts saw their work as a "refreshingly technical and philosophically interesting" version of educational philosophy capable of delivering an objective understanding of "education" to a profession that was being "whipsawed" by contrary demands of the counterculture and the social establishment. Moreover, philosophical analysis generated the academic respect that philosophy desperately required. The academic establishment required that anything that called itself philosophy must do "analysis."

Israel Scheffler (1960) and Jonas Soltis (1971) among others demonstrated that educational philosophy could play its part in the analytic tradition. Of course, it was George Kneller's *Introduction to the philosophy of education* (1964) and *Logic and the language of education* (1966) that "spelled it all out." *Logic and the language of education* arguably was the most powerful and interesting contribution to education's analytic tradition. In the postWar world educational philosophy became analysis. The significance of this new vector for educational philosophy was large. Caught up in achieving academic legitimacy, in aspiring to the academic requirements that its place in the university required, and in defending itself from its competitors in philosophy and the social sciences, educational philosophy turned to analysis to provide the means to accomplish all of these ends. Harvard, Stanford, Illinois, and Columbia were committed to the "new wave." Although they prepared only a tiny fraction of the nation's educators, their enormous influence confirmed educational philosophy's commitment to analysis.

At the 1971 meeting of the Philosophy of Education Society, Soltis declared that "We are all analytic philosophers," and no one laughed (Soltis, 1971).[10] This mode of philosophical investigation did not acknowledge the agendas of pragmatism.[11] Its intellectual loyalties were to analysis's European intellectual heritage—to the Vienna Circle. The problem in all of this, of course, was that it largely ignored the topic of poverty and deprivation, the new topics of empirical and historical educational research. Neither existential nor concerned with social philosophy, analysis slipped past the issues of class, gender, race, poverty, and the role of the curriculum, and therein the role of the school in perpetuating social inequality. In the name of epistemology and metaphysics analysis served as the discipline's badge of academic respectability. It was undoubtedly the most effective means of satisfying the academic expectations of their university colleagues (cf. Clifford and Guthrie, 1988, 3-4) and distancing educational philosophy's endeavors from previous generations' work (Benne, 1966).

But in avoiding the concerns of the counterculture and the "silent majority," analysis continued to rehearse the topics of Progressivism when it was not concerned with metaphysics and epistemology. It was "old stuff." Its philosophical content was a matter of rehearsing the concerns of the Vienna Circle in educational dress in an academic world that was rapidly giving more credence to materialist and consensual versions of philosophy of science. The penalty was irrelevance in both education and academic philosophy and, eventually, academic disfavor in the competition for educational resources (see Sammons, 1981).

But by the early 1980s it was beginning to be evident that educational philosophy's had "caught up with a stalled train" (Giarelli and Chambliss, 1991, 273). Its "attempt to ground the disciplinary distinctiveness, epistemic authority, and professional legitimacy of philosophy of education through an appeal to a privileged access foundation puts philosophy of education squarely at odds with at least one important trend in contemporary philosophical thought . . . In short, it seems that philosophy of education finally reached a point when it could claim to call itself professional vis-à-vis 'real' philosophy, just at the time when 'real' philosophy was in the process of declaring professional philosophy dead" (1991, 273). Obsessed with the drive to find foundational elements with which to direct educational theory and therein practice, it lost touch with some central elements of philosophy with which it was tightly allied, similarly obsessed with sophisticated elements of technical philosophy it largely gave up its place in the public education conversation (1991, 273). By the early 1980s educational philosophy's analytic research agendas dissolved.

## THE NEW LEFT AND THE COUNTERCULTURE

Its new research agendas would come from the New Left—the alternative voice of educational theory in the sixties (see Gitlin, 1987)—and a resurgent romantic humanism. Research moved from questionnaires to ethnography, and the explanation of research results was transformed from psychometrics to qualitative sociology, political economy, "hegemony," and Marxist or Left historiography. Peter Winch's *Idea of social science and its relation to philosophy* (1958) paved the way for the new social awareness in the social sciences and the Left social critique did the rest. Pragmatism and analysis fled the stage pursued by civil rights protesters, antiwar activists, feminists, and hermeneuticists of all descriptions. Raymond Williams's *Culture and society* (1958) and Richard Hoggart's *Uses of literacy* (1957) paved the way for the hermeneutic revolution. Jürgen Habermas's *Knowledge and human interests* (1971) became the darling of the "middleway" between sociology and philosophy. The hermeneutic circle would find its way back into both philosophy and social science. In philosophy the circle would generate an interest in Hans George Gadamer, Michael Foucault, Jacques Derrida, and the other philosophical heroes of the modern period (see Dallmayer and McCarthy, 1977; Giarelli and

Chambliss, 1991, 273). It was an interest that educational philosophers learned to share.

Herbert Marcuse's *Eros and civilization* (1955) and *One dimensional man* (1964) were central to the Frankfurt School's entry into American social and political consciousness. In social science and the humanities Michael Harrington's book *Other America* (1962) charmed Jack Kennedy and connected the discovery of poverty in the sixties with America's New Left and old Left. American radical humanism was, perhaps, best represented by Paul Goodman (1960), who seemed in touch with the system's contradictions and absurdities. In the new version of educational research the emphasis upon delinquency, disadvantage, and educational handicaps was reformed in the language of poverty, deprivation, oppression, subordination, and resistance (Silver, 1990, 167). Redefined and refocused educational research moved on to new concerns, especially to the war on poverty.[12] Class, gender, race, poverty, and the role of the curriculum and therein the school in perpetuating social inequality became the preoccupations of the day. The dominant voice of protest in the sixties was that of the coiunterculture, New Left, and the civil rights movement, and its vocabulary was derived from Marxists, neo-Marxists, anarchists, romantics, and radical humanists (Gitlin, 1987; Silver, 1990, 166-188). The dominant voice of educational social comment in the sixties and 1970s would find its home in history, sociology, economics, comparative education, curriculum, and then only collaterally and tentatively would enter the world of American educational philosophy.

The 1950s were self-satisfied and comfortable years (Gitlin, 1987, 11-15). But the sixties were as unsettled as the 1950s were pacific (Gitlin 1987, 11-12). A collection of "hippies," psychedelic songsters, black civil rights activists, feminists, and antiwar protesters challenged society and its cultural agendas. The songsters were connected to the ld Left—the political Left of Woody, not Arlo Guthrie. They sang the tunes of Woody Guthrie, Bob Dylan, and Janis Joplin, and played the guitar like Jimmy Hendrix. The 1950s' well-fed sons and daughters of America knew in their hearts that it was their fathers and mothers who had vanquished evil, it was their parents who had had all the good causes, and it was their parents who had robbed them of the opportunity of doing anything worthwhile with their lives (Gitlin, 1987; cf. Keniston 1965). They were in rebellion against their own biography and the world in general. Marlon Brando spoke for them in the classic film *The wild one*. To the reasonable question of every parent of the 1950s, What are you rebelling against? Brando's answer summed it all up: "Whadda ya got?" In a different world they might have grown up moving from summers on the beach to winters on the ski slopes, oblivious to the social and political questions around them, but in the world of the sixties they would move to political commitment in the realization that the self-satisfied values of their parents were less than perfect. And they were outraged to discover what the civil rights movement and Vietnam would teach them: the affluent Republic had feet of clay.

The New Left created a "children's crusade," It was social action by, for, and of the young. The comparison to the actors of the Progressive period is obvious and compelling. The Progressive movement was led by young people: In 1900 Robert M. La Follette was forty-five, Woodrow Wilson and Louis D. Brandeis were forty-four, Roosevelt forty-two, Hiram Johnson thirty-four, Joseph W. Folk thirty-one, Lincoln Steffens thirty-four, David Graham Phillips thirty-three, Ray Stannard Baker thirty, Walter Weyl twenty-seven, and Upton Sinclair only twenty-two (Hofstadter, 1963, 7). In the sixties Todd Gitlin and Tom Hayden were attending university, Bob Dylan and Janis Joplin were not only young but also legends in their own time. Arlo Guthrie was dodging the draft in *Alice's restaurant*, and Abbie Hoffman was running with the street kids of New York even though he was the old man of the movement.

The Vietnam War and the civil rights movement were the focus and the glue of their crusade. Some, like Abbie Hoffman, "dropped out"; some, like Todd Gitlin and Tom Hayden, "dropped in"; but all of them were out to save America. Tom Wolfe, Bob Dylan, Martin Luther King, Jr., Malcolm X, Todd Gitlin, Abbie Hoffman, and Angela Davis— all of them had lessons for America and America's youth. Herbert Marcuse wrote the lesson down in the turgid German prose of *Eros and civilization* (1955) and *One dimensional man* (1964), and Arlo Guthrie's movie *Alice's restaurant* (1969) delivered the message to mass culture just as Lôuis Buñuel's movie *Discreet charm of the bourgeoisie* (1972) served notice of the nation's moral and political decadence to a more sophisticated audience. Not only did the sixties transform whatever was left of Victorian morality, the decade was also busy constructing a new moral code. The code the movement sought to construct would eschew double standards and moral duplicity. The new morality was measured against human need, not objective ethics. The revision was soft and romantic. The new code found its expression in civil disobedience, antiwar protest, feminism, nudity, smoking dope, and easy sex. As Mick Jagger knew, there was money to be had in being bad and lots of money in being (morally) outrageous (Gitlin, 1987, 199). The various manifestations of the sixties were part of the cannibalization, reformation, and reconstruction of America's Victorian morality. Being bad and being outrageous were all part of constructing a new moral ethos. Of course, it was also part of smoking the old man's cigars (cf. Caute, 1988, 23).

In March 1968 Naomi Jaffe and Bernardine Dohrn published "The look is you" in *New Left Notes* and tied women's oppression both to a sexual politics and to capitalist economics (Caute, 1988, 237). Nineteen sixty-nine saw the publication in the *New American Review* of Kate Millett's "Sexual politics" (1969), it was a short element of what was later published in its entirety by Doubleday under the same title (1970). Millet's work in particular was a core element in feminist efforts to rewrite America's social compact.

At about this same point in time women started to take a significant place in educational philosophy, a male-dominated discipline. Maxine Greene, Jane Roland Martin, Mary Ann Raywid, Jo Ann Boydston, Barbara Arnstine, Elizabeth Steiner Maccia, Betty Sichel, and Nel Noddings opened the way.

In 1972 a PES symposium composed of Barbara Arnstine, Maxine Greene and Elizabeth Steiner Maccia was devoted to education and women's liberation. This seems to be the first "official" recognition, at least on the national program, that there had been since the early 1960s in the United States, a broad social/political movement affecting many mostly white, middle class women's ideas of themselves and their lives. That year also marked the beginning of more participation by women on the program. Nine of them acted publicly at that meeting, a number exceeding the total of the three previous years combined. This "flurry" of activity waxed and waned until 1980, a banner year for participation with a total of sixteen women acting in some overt capacity. (Leach, 1991, 289-290)

In the late 1960s sociologists, economists, historians, social critics, and the players of the street reminded educational philosophers, by example, of the academic role in social reform that the discipline readdressed the issues that they had abandoned in the late 1930s. In the 1950s and early 1960s democratic socialism was deemed by educational philosophers to be too dangerous for academic consumption and it all but disappeared from educational philosophy (cf. Cremin, 1988, 194-195). But poverty, deprivation, and some versions of social democratic thought were rediscovered in the 1960s (Sizer, 1970) after being forgotten in the growth of consumption that followed World War II. Social class had been an issue in the 1950s. Evan Hunter's *Blackboard jungle* (1954) is just one example of the ethos that made its way into popular culture. But class—and therein poverty, deprivation, and various versions of social democratic cum socialist thought—was ignored until revived by academics of the New Left such as Michael B. Katz, Samuel Bowles, Herbert Gintis, Martin Carnoy, Michael W. Apple, Henry Giroux, and S. Aronowitz. Their critique of educational philosophy was simple and straightforward. It was bourgeois and establishment.

The American New Left was not deeply connected to Europe's intensely intellectual Left. And although the New Left found it necessary to rediscover Marx, they were much more comfortable with the young Marx. When it came to revolutions it was much more interested in revolutions in the postcolonial worlds of Africa and Asia than in revolution in America. The War of Independence began in 1775 and ended in 1783, and that was that as far as the New Left was concerned. It was a stance that was more than evident in the constitutional document of the New Left, the *Port Huron statement*.

The New Left radicals of America, Britain, and Europe hop-hopped to the chant of "Ho-Ho-Ho Chi Minh! We will fight, we will win!" but they were hopping and bopping, however similarly, to different drummers (Gitlin, 1987, 134-135; Caute, 1988, 71-72). New Left politics was dependent upon the clean cut liberal tradition of American college students for numbers. The New Left was a small minority even during the peak of its popularity. Herbert Marcuse was as close to the European Left as most American intellectuals would ever get.[13]

Of course, students and intellectuals are not identical; yet campus politics of the sixties cannot be disassociated from books, ideas, or intellectuals, all of which suffuse a student universe.

Who were the sixties intellectuals? Probably most were not American: Jean-Paul Sartre, Albert Camus, Frantz Fanon, Herbert Marcuse, Isaac Deutscher, Wilhelm Reich. Students did not necessarily grasp, even read, Sartre's *Being and nothingness* or Marcuse's *One dimensional man*, but these individuals and their writings glowed with protest, revolution, and morality that sharply broke with American liberalism . . .

Some American intellectuals played small roles in the sixties, but then fell away; others played roles despite themselves: Paul Goodman, Norman Mailer, Michael Harrington, William H. Whyte, Rachel Carson, John Kenneth Galbraith, [and] Betty Friedan. (Jacoby, 1987, 114-115)

Socially radical versions of educational philosophy found inspiration in a post-Vietnam amalgam of the old and New Left. The hermeneutics and softer social criticism of Habermas, Gadamer, Foucault, and Derrida remained popular through the late 1980s. But after the Berlin Wall came down in 1989, so did the Left's social and educational critique. After the Soviet Union and Eastern Europe held an informal plebiscite on Marxism and almost immediately and unanimously passed a vote of "no confidence" the academic Left found itself intellectually disenfranchised and dispossessed of its social base. The Left retreated into what has been described as "The Great Silence."

Most American educational philosophers found more sympathy with C. Wright Mills or Paul Goodman than Gramsci, Althusser, or the Frankfurt School. Radical American thought was fractured as its European counterpart. It was divided between its intense intellectuals who traced their loyalty to Europe's intellectuals and those members of the counterculture committed to romanticism's excesses: instinct and feeling (Caute, 1988, 23). New York's Living Theater, San Francisco's anarchist and est-minded poets, jazz connoisseurs, readers of *The Village Voice* and *Evergreen Review* were in common league and at odds with the serious New Left. Tom Hayden, Jane Fonda, and Todd Gitlin had a common cause, Abbie Hoffman had a great time. Mao and Che were their heroes but the counterculture was their worldview. Goodman's *Growing up absurd* (1960) is probably the best example of educational thought from this fractured radical perspective. In the end America's educational philosophers were better liberals than Leftists.

## NOTES

1. Like all ideologies, the discourse of educational philosophy (prag-matism and therein various versions of progressive education) operated transparently and resolved the educational world in its terms.

2. Pragmatism was dismissed in the late 1950s. What remained of pragmatism's politics or political economy was found to be insufficiently radical for existentialism, the New Left, and insufficiently technical for the analysts. As Rorty notes, the pragmatists kept trying to make anti-Philosophical points in nonphilosophical language (Rorty, 1982, xiii-xlvii). In the post-1945 world pragmatism was accused of not being philosophy—of being something else (i.e. literature, history, or education). It was philosophically dismissed. Pragmatism's nonphilosophical social language was abandoned in a frenzy of patriotism and analysis. Its anti-Philosophical points were neglected in professional philosophy's attempt to ground philosophy in some metaphysical or methodological foundation. Educational philosophy like academic philosophy in the guise of analysis abandoned or ignored pragmatism's epistemology because it was insufficiently precise and rigorous (Rorty, 1982, xvii; Rorty, 1980).

In the shadow of the collapse of the counterculture and the New Left pragmatism is experiencing something of a revival. To argue that pragmatism's original program of research was spent (as above) is not the same, of course, as arguing that pragmatism as a philosophical stance is spent. Some of the attempts to reconstruct pragmatism à la Rorty's philosophical suggestions are among the most interesting contemporary gambits in educational philosophy. At the moment versions of neopragmatism hold the field, if only by default.

3. This last comment, of course, paraphrases Brian Simon's description of the stance of the English philosophical analyst R. S. Peters (Simon 1991, 376). But Simon's description of the central intellectual elements of philosophical analysis are consistent with the ethos of English and American versions of that endeavor.

4. The new class refers to the subset of professional intellectuals who emerged during the industrial period. Unlike their predecessors they tend to make their living through artistic, technical, or hermeneutic manipulation of symbols. They are profoundly separated from moneyed and working classes by their de facto possession of the means of production and their commitment to their own intellectual fetishes. Alvin Gouldner discusses this class at length in *The future of intellectual and the rise of the new class* (1979).

5. It is the fashion among philosophers of education to blame analytic philosophy for the contemporary intellectual malaise. Analysis was, in one sense, a method of endeavor, not the endeavor itself. Analysis had two virtues for educational philosophy: (1) it was the P/philosophical style of the postwar period that gave its advocates a certain default prestige, and (2) it gave educational philosophers the tools to refine meticulously and repeatedly the reservoir of questions and answers that were constitutive of Progressive education. There was more than analysis to blame, the contemporary malaise was a failure of intellectual nerve—the inability of existentialism, analysis, and the New Left to transcend pragmatism's old research agenda.

6. Clive Beck of course is a Canadian resident, but his tight connections with American existentialists makes it seem appropriate to include him in this group.

7. Despite efforts to use "ordinary discourse" to solve the problem of intersubjectivity (see Vandenberg, 1987), the vast majority of scholars remained unconvinced that any promising solution to the question had been found. The

phenomenologists were forced to psychologize without psychology. And without a resolution of the Husserlian problem the gambit worked itself into a cul de sac.

8. Similar narratives about the evolution of marginal or high-risk versions of science are available (e.g. Zukav, [1979] 1986).

9. It must be admitted that both of the former provided a rich endowment of hints and assembled reminders that were heavily suggestive to postwar philosophers.

10. Macmillan points out that while this phrase does not appear in the text of this article, it was "said aloud at the meeting" (Macmillan, 1991, 284, f. 49).

11. In a very real sense, philosophical analysis's dismissal of the research agendas of pragmatism is—to answer Joe R. Burnett's rhetorical article in *Philosophy of education since mid-century* ([1979] 1981)—"Whatever happened to John Dewey?"

12. In 1964 the Economic Opportunity Act authorized federal economic commitments to an assortment of purposes connected with poverty, education and educational research among them.

13. A few radicals would consider radical tracts such as Ted Honderich's *Violence for equality* ([1976] 1980). But individuals like Honderich never appealed to liberals or to the counterculture.

# 5

# Conclusion: The United States

In the end the civil rights movement would be "won" and the war lost. But in between a lot of things would change. The American federal government would discover that the Vietnam War was not politics by another means. The middle class would discover a moral obligation to the poor and the disadvantaged. Black Americans would discover their political power, and the country would disestablish the legal legitimation of segregation. Feminists would create an ideology that claimed a new place for American women in the social order of things. And the New Left would implode, taking the counterculture with it. Free schools and a concern for equality of educational opportunity would be transformed into a new conservative emphasis upon basics, excellence, and advanced placement.

If one attempts to understand why postwar philosophers of education in the United States asked certain questions, used certain philosophical methods, and accepted the research program that they did, it is necessary to place all of these questions in their historic and academic contexts. Many of the early European professorships of philosophy since Kant were chairs of philosophy and pedagogy. But chairs of philosophy and pedagogy were not about schooling; their aim was the dissemination of philosophical wisdom to groups who were, apparently, fairly resistant or indifferent to philosophy. They were concerned with philosophy first and pedagogy second—very much second. Philosophy largely ignored many of the questions of education and almost all, if not all, of the questions of schooling. Even though some executive members of the discipline during the profession's early years were professional philosophers, philosophy (the discipline) was indifferent at best and most of the time was openly hostile to questions about education. In most instances individuals who would become significant individuals in the profession came to philosophy of education from the education industry, not from philosophy. Usually they had initially trained as teachers and in many cases completed their education in schools of education. The exceptions were trained wholly or partially within departments of philosophy and/or were supervised or heavily influenced by professors of philosophy.

It must also be remembered that Progressive education, the project of educational philosophy at the turn of the century, suffered from a certain general popularity. It became the conventional wisdom of the day and lost its intellectual power. Even worse, it generated a failure of imagination among educational philosophers. It was not that all the goals of an equitable and egalitarian system of education had been accomplished, it was just that they had become invisible—lost amidst the florescence of the educational system in the postwar period.

In its historical context educational philosophy has played an important part in the establishment of a universal, comprehensive, and compulsory system of public education. It was the philosophy and rhetoric of Dewey, Counts, Rugg, Kilpatrick, and others plus the influence of the philosophers of education in the graduate schools of Stanford, Berkeley, Ohio State, Illinois, Minnesota, Harvard, Yale, and Chicago that provided the intellectual power to establish "progressive education" as the common form of American schooling. From the beginning philosophy of education has been limited by the modest nature of its means (rational argument) and its conservative agenda of ends (social reconstruction through education). On the other hand, the discipline has undoubtedly been immensely successful.

Public education has been cynically described as a charity institution conducted on the cheap for the benefit of those who can not afford better. Teaching has been depicted as labor intensive, technically mundane, and, except for its philosophy and psychology, theoretically unsophisticated. Further, education as a university discipline has been hampered by the inability of educators to produce an instrumental technology. Be that as it may, America's professional schools of education established themselves as influential elements of American society and important long-term determinants of educational policy. They revolutionized the schools for which they inherited responsibility and saw to the establishment of the common school. They trained millions of licensed professionals to staff the schools; removed the conduct of education from the hands of charlatans, quacks, and untrained novices; established a directorate of administrative professionals, necessary and constitutive of the infrastructure of all professions; and developed a research base for the controlled evolution of the institution. Schools of education in general and educational philosophy in particular have been influential in the reform and extension of an institution that was intellectually moribund, elitist, discriminatory, and racist. Educational philosophy provided educators' work with its fundamental justification and legitimation. It provided the common school with its ideology.

The central core of John Dewey's work in philosophy and education was always social reform coupled with a systematic resistance to the political, social, and economic transgressions of America's ruling class in general and the democratization of education in particular. The central concern of educational philosophy since the turn of the century was social reconstruction through the common school. As Dewey wrote in a closing section of *Democracy and education* ([1916] 1966),

The reconstruction of philosophy, of education, and of social ideals and methods thus go hand in hand . . . Such practical changes cannot take place without demanding an educational reformation to meet them, and without leading men to ask what ideas and ideals are implicit in these social changes, and what revision they require of the ideas and ideals which are inherited from older and unlike cultures. (331)

Like various members of the American Social Science Association, progressive educators were convinced of the centrality of education in social reform. And if Dewey and other intellectuals were unsuccessful in their more grandiose utopian plans, they were successful in generating a version of schools that displaced more patrician versions of education. Even in the period of greatest acceptance Progressive versions of schooling were not without intellectual opposition, but "Dewey provided the educational reformers with intellectual respectability; he gave them a philosophical lineage; he could assure them that what they were doing had the sanction of the most scientific logic and a rigorous theory of knowledge; he gave them an ideology" (Feuer, 1959, 563).

Educational philosophy also continued and institutionalized the moral and social critique of education begun by various Enlightenment thinkers. They tied education to the idea of social reform and social responsibility—a gambit begun by the American Social Science Association in the mid-1800s. This mission was revived by the New Left, and for a short time educational philosophy sponsored a certain unconventional social ethics and political radicalism. The radicalism disappeared for a short period during the moral absolution generated after World War II, but it but reappeared in the context of the 1960s civil rights movement and the Vietnam War.

When assessing the contribution of educational philosophy to the practice of schooling the usual conclusion is that it simply has been finessed by unimaginative men (cf. Cremin, 1961). Although the more substantial political roles that educational philosophers aspired to before or after World War II did not eventuate, they captured the language and ideology of education; that is, while the practitioner and the technician influenced daily practice, the language and ideology of progressivism effectively controlled what could be said and discursively thought about education. Progressivism was the American language of education, and pragmatism was its ideology.

# Part II

# Philosophy of Education
in Great Britain

# 6

# Genesis

Philosophy of education as it arose in Britain reflects that country's social and intellectual history, the biographies of the individuals who helped to construct that history, the discipline's unique establishment within the university community, the careers of L. A. Reid and R. S. Peters, and the professional society that gave it an intellectual and professional identity.

In Britain the antecedents of educational philosophy can be traced to myriad individual biographies and intellectual movements. Perhaps the most important beginning can be found in the Scottish Enlightenment (see Sloan, 1971). The Scottish Enlightenment was but one aspect of the eighteenth-century Enlightenment, but its emphasis upon education, its Presbyterian system of kirks, the little schools they supported, and the universities that stood as the keystone of that system were unique. Education was widely available in a manner that it was not in England during that same period. And the universities were central to Scotland's intellectual establishment. Even David Hume, who was the most prominent of all Scottish intellectuals of the period, sought appointment to the Chair of Moral Philosophy in Edinburgh. He also sought appointment to the Chair of Logic in Glasgow (Sloan, 1971, 14-15). He failed to achieve either, but Hume's quest is silent testament to the centrality of the university to Scottish intellectual life. The leaders of the Enlightenment in Scotland were intimately involved in university affairs, unlike their English counterparts who were to be found in the learned societies and associations of London (Sloan, 1971, 14).

The character of the Scottish universities was quite different from their English equivalents. The Scottish Reformation placed new instructions and demanding standards upon the five universities of Scotland in the eighteenth century. The *First book of discipline* (1560) composed by John Knox and fellow reformers formulated a policy for the practice of church and state and proposed a national plan for education. Ambitious in its scope, it proposed a plan to "instill wisdom, learning, and virtue into the youth of the country and thus provide both church and state with qualified leaders" (Sloan, 1971, 16). Although never formally adopted by Parliament, its ideals were never forgotten. It required a form of elementary school in every kirk, a grammar school in every town, and a college in every city. The universities' charters obligated them to serve all classes of society on at least, putatively, an egalitarian basis. The Scottish universities were not the private reserve of the privileged—at least not in the same way as they were in England.

The first chairs of education were established in Scottish universities in the late 1870s. These were the closing days of the Enlightenment's influence, and the chairs were largely devoted to the task of finding and preparing teachers for the schools of Scotland. But as time passed, the Scottish universities did take up the academic study of education and often were almost free from the responsibility of basic teacher education. It was to these Scottish universities that English educators commonly referred when they sought a model for university participation in the study of education (Simon, 1983).

What was common in the eighteenth century both to Scots and to the English was a simple faith in the idea of human progress and a fundamental faith in the efficacy of reason in the resolution of human difficulties—weather and circumstances permitting (Hughes, 1958, 27-28). The domestic study of education was consistent with this intellectual predicate.

Philosophy of education in Great Britain has important antecedents in the work of intellectuals from both Scotland and England. John Locke, Jeremy Bentham, James Mill, and John Stuart Mill were important contributors to what one day would be an academic discipline established in the nation's colleges and universities. Insofar as the study of education was philosophical its first important English representatives were John Locke's early essays. The earliest of these essays for the literature of education are *Thoughts concerning education* ([1695] 1978) and his *Letter concerning toleration* ([1690] 1977). Locke's political philosophy was brought to the industrial world on its own merit and so was his educational thought.

Locke's *Thoughts concerning education* ([1695] 1978), is one of a few English philosophical texts of the period that has retained some intellectual importance well into the modern period. This work was not central to his philosophical work; Locke was immersed in the politics and political philosophy of the time. Although most of the currency of his work for education is now past and his recommendations seem almost trite, Locke's thought is one of English philosophy's major contributions to the antecedents of educational philosophy.[1]

In the period between the Scottish Enlightenment and turn of the century it was philosophy (to repeat a point made earlier in the American section) that provided the most thorough intellectual interrogation of "human nature, social forces, progress, marriage and family relationships, economic process, maintenance of government, international relations, elementary jurisprudence, primitive customs, history of institutions, religion, ethics, aesthetics—all topics of import in the social sciences of our day" (Bryson, 1932b, 304)—education and schooling, of course, were not excluded from this list. The political and social philosophy of Jeremy Bentham, James Mill, and John Stuart Mill was the transitional link between the development of serious philosophical considerations of education and the appropriation of the systematic study of education by social science. Between the middle of the nineteenth century and the Great War many of these topics were appropriated by social science.

If there was a single important domestic figure in all of this it was probably Jeremy Bentham. Bentham's work was as fragmented as it was seminal. Although his work on education was largely confined to pamphlets, it was an important inspiration for more systematic work by both of the Mills. James Mill's article "Education" (1815) in the *Encyclopedia Britannica* and his essay "Schools for all" were important contributions to the liberal crusade for universal elementary education. James Mill was a tireless educational reformer who—more than aware of the widespread provision of elementary education in almost every parish of Scotland—ceaselessly urged some form of education for all the children of England (Burston, 1969, 25). John Stuart Mill's *Principles of political economy* ([1848] 1891) argued for a system of primary education as a means to accomplishing a more republican form of democracy. Collaterally, he saw education (i.e. rationality) as a decisive means of reducing civil disorder and a critical element in the moral instruction of the poor.

John Stuart Mill's life paralleled the period in which the basic elements of a national system of elementary education were conceived and eventually established. In 1806, the year of Mill's birth, the English government did not believe that it had a significant role to play in the education of the public at large. But by the year of his death, 1873, a national system had been undertaken—although not accomplished—by the passage of the 1870 Education Act (Seaman, 1985, 189-190). In both *Principles of political economy* [1848] 1891) and *On liberty* ([1859] 1947) it was clear that for Mill elementary education was a constitutive element of any real democracy. Mill's numerous comments certainly contributed to the social pressures that finally established Britain's system of elementary education for all (Garforth, 1979, 9, 24). But he never wrote extensively on education, nor did he ever claim to be an expert on pedagogy (Garforth, 1979, 85). His comments on education, although reasonably extensive, are scattered through his works and letters and were never systematically developed.

Nevertheless, Mill's work did foreshadow the idea of pubic responsibility for mass education. For example, he wrote in his *Principles of political economy:*

The uncultivated cannot be competent judges of cultivation. Those who most need to be made wiser and better, usually desire it least, and if they desired it, would be incapable of finding the way to it by their own lights . . . Now any well-intentioned and tolerably civilized government may think without presumption that it does or ought to possess a degree of cultivation above the average of the community which it rules, and that it should therefore be capable of offering better education and better instruction to the people, than the greater number of them would spontaneously demand. Education, therefore, is one of those things which it is admissible in principle that a government should provide for the people. ([1848] 1891, vol. 2., 573-574)

It was a minimal version of education that opted for a social responsibility for those things that people who would not out of ignorance, or of a breach of duty, or could not as a consequence of penury, provide for themselves. This obligation only extended to those elements of education that would cause the community to suffer from the consequences of ignorance, that is, it only extended to elementary education (Mill, [1848] 1891, vol., 2. 573-576).

Mill's work mirrored the attempt of Victorian intellectuals and members of the middle class to come to terms with the idea of mass education. It was a point at which England's educational establishment was just beginning to grapple with understanding the place of science in the university and the role of mass education in industrial society. Collaterally, it should be remembered that the devolution of these issues was only partial because the English universities still were primarily medieval institutions in concept and practice. The humanities and philosophy conformed to the university ethos in a way that science and social science did not (cf. Abrams, 1968, 148).

Mill's most systematic treatment of higher education is found in his Inaugural address at St. Andrews University" (1867). In this address he is a good friend of the classics and is largely concerned with retaining a place for the humanities in the university. In Mill's view there was a place for science insofar as it supported philosophy and logic and the attendant and collateral classics. To his mind the place of philosophy and the classics in the university was quite obvious. They made prudent the practice of the various professions (Mill, [1867] 1985). The place of the professions themselves in the university was more dubious in Mill's mind.

## RADICAL UTILITARIANS

There was, of course, a body of work concerning the idea of education to which the British establishment made direct reference. It was a Victorian literature that noted Rousseau and the continentals. But it was John Locke, Jeremy Bentham, and James and John Stuart Mill who were at the center of their faith in the power of education. And insofar as the establishment was interested in continentals their reference was primarily to Comte's *Positive philosophy* ([1830-1842] 1893) and Rousseau's *Social contract* [1762] 1987). Their arguments concerning the obligation of the state for public education had the same continental points of reference. Their interest in Rousseau's *Emile* ([1762] 1907) and *Sophie* ([1762] 1907) was directly related to the implications of the books' social philosophy for republican politics and only collaterally related to their radical humanism. The connection between Rousseau's *Emile* and *Sophie* and his *Social contract* ([1762] 1987) is obvious. The citizens who are the elements and beneficiaries of the general will are a collection of Emiles and Sophies (Gay, 1987, 9).[2] They are citizens capable of making decisions that impinge upon the public in terms of the common good, citizens who have been able to transcend the advice of self-interest. John Stuart Mill commended Rousseau in *On liberty* ([1859] 1947, 46) but he was always worried with the central and powerful role that Rousseau defined for the state. In *Social contract* the state has a monopoly of the means of force and may compel citizens to abide by the general will (see Rousseau, [1762] 1987). The powerful role that both Comte and Rousseau outlined for the state was quite unacceptable to the Victorian mind. To the English Victorian it was the case that the state had jurisdiction over acts prejudicial to others but that was all (J. S. Mill, [1859] 1947, 75). The Victorians were only too aware of the potential for the state to play the role of the tyrant. Mill wrote:

A general State education is a mere contrivance for molding people to be exactly like one another: and as the mold in which it casts them is that which pleases the predominant power in the government, whether this be a monarch, a priesthood, an aristocracy, or the majority of the existing generation in proportion as it is efficient and successful, it establishes a despotism over the mind, leading by natural tendency to one over the body. An education established and controlled by the State should only exist, if it exist at all, for the purpose of example and stimulus, to keep the others up to a certain standard of excellence. ([1859] 1947, 108)

Mill's rather unsystematic but powerful comments upon education were part of what the Victorian sensitivity viewed to be a philosophical literature appropriate to educational discourse. Mill's thought was a powerful antidote to the "despotism of society over the individual" evident in Comte's and Rousseau's thought (see J. S. Mill, [1859] 1947, 13). To Mill's mind education was a privilege of individuals and families and not, beyond certain minimums, a concern of the state ([1859] 1947, 107).

All of the radical utilitarians were semimodern figures attempting heroically, if unsuccessfully, to come to terms with the idea of mass education and social reform. Jeremy Bentham, James Mill and John Stuart Mill marked a transition between the classical and modern period. They moved away from metaphysical vagaries, argued specific cases, subordinated the law to humanity, rather than vice versa, and promoted issues of social reform. But their focus never was able to transcend the fixed and final supreme end—property. Nevertheless, the contribution of philosophy to education and therein educational philosophy in Britain was distinct. The radical utilitarians joined the issues of social reform and education. The joining made social reform and education into social, economic, political, and philosophical issues.


EDUCATIONAL CRITICS

In this history educational philosophy is a modern phenomenon (cf. Snook, 1969). Nevertheless, it makes significant reference to the nineteenth century. The work of the radical utilitarians can lay some claim to the paternity of educational philosophy's modern form. But if there is one intellectual that is more or less central to the discipline's nineteenth-century origins, it is to be found in the work of Herbert Spencer. Spencer's was able to crystallize the social and educational debate in terms of a conservative Victorian political economy. It made his educational thought distinctively modern and distinctively British. It is to the work of Spencer that philosophical debates about education in the early part of the twentieth century refer. Its modern form is a debate over the provision of mass education—elementary and secondary—and its efficacy or lack of efficacy in social reform.

The crystallization begins with the publication of Herbert Spencer's *Education: Intellectual, moral, and physical* ([1861] 1897),[3] which articulated the debate between classicism and science. His book *The study of sociology* ([1873] 1904) confronted the issues of poverty and deprivation in industrial Victorian society. The two texts cast the educational debate of the Victorian period into sharp relief. Spencer's primitive philosophical polemics about schools and education were largely by-products of debates about the social order and its justification on the one hand, and discussions about the amelioration of the most egregious excesses of the new industrial order on the other. Spencer's writings and the debates they generated rested on the belief that English society was fundamentally in good order, and whatever evils existed could be remedied with relatively moderate and topical social therapies (Abrams, 1968, 48). The desirability of industrialism; or the social order was never at issue.

The Victorian establishment was not monolithic in its analysis of England's educational system. It had its modest critics like Henry Sidgwick and its radical critics like Spencer. Sidgwick had qualms over particular elements of the curriculum, particularly in regard to the question of modern languages. Spencer had qualms about it all. In Spencer's words,

It is one thing to admit that aesthetic culture is in a high degree conducive to human happiness; and another thing to admit that it is a fundamental requisite to human happiness ...
And here we see most distinctly the vice of our educational system. It neglects the plant for the sake of the flower. In anxiety for elegance, it forgets substance. While it gives no knowledge conducive to self-preservation—while of knowledge that facilitates gaining a livelihood it gives but the rudiments, and leaves the greater part to be picked up any how in after life—while for the discharge of parental functions it makes not the slightest provision—and while for the duties of citizenship it prepares by imparting a mass of facts, most of which are irrelevant, and the rest without a key; it is diligent in teaching every thing that adds to refinement, polish, éclat. ([1861] 1897, 72-74)

Herbert Spencer assaulted educational classicism (Jack Kaminsky, 1967, 527). He did not share the belief that education should be based upon the *quadrivium*: arithmetic, geometry, astronomy, and music; and the *trivium*: grammar, rhetoric, and logic commonly presented in English and elite American schools as a liberal education. Spencer wrote that this educational classicism contributed little to the struggle for existence and whatever merit it had was confined to the social distinction it provided and the comedy of manners it authored.

*Education* ([1861] 1897) was an extension of his general and systematic doctrine of evolution to education. Spencer's utilitarianism and his emphasis upon the struggles of industrialized society and caustic criticism of classical education endeared him to the age (Carneiro, 1967; Kennedy, 1978). His work seemed to fit nicely within Britain's industrial ethos. Even more important, his attack on classics was part of the ceaseless war he waged against the state per se, against free libraries and free education (particularly secondary). He opposed the extension of government into the entire realm of social welfare. His thought was consistent with the Victorian worldview (see Spencer, [1892] 1940, 39-40). To his mind social reform versions of schooling contributed little to the struggle for existence (Spencer, [1861] 1897). While Spencer argued that elementary education for all was a necessary requirement for a lower class in which people knew their station, the provision of further education extending into the esoteric air of secondary education or the provision of free libraries was unnecessary and, perhaps, dangerous. The provision of anything more than elementary education would only fan the socialist ideas of the dangerous classes (Spencer, [1892] 1940, 39-40). His work provided a rough-and-ready rationale for abandoning the dangerous classes to their own devices—educational and otherwise. Spencer's stance was radically removed from the classicism of Arnoldian culture. Victorian England was forced at least to consider Spencer's attack upon classical education in his *Education* ([1861] 1897) if for no other reason than the provocative intellectual impact his essays on evolution had, published under the title *First principles* ([1862] 1880).

Spencer wrote extensively on education but only as an adjunct to his philosophical investigations of evolution (Royce, 1904, 127; Carneiro, 1967, xvi). Spencer's advice fell on rocky ground in Britain. His argument for science as the basis of education, his opposition to the National Association for the Promotion of Social Science, and his distaste for what he perceived to be the maudlin versions of welfare promoted by the association disconnected social science as Spencer understood it from any establishment power base that might support it.[4] The establishment was firmly connected to the association. Spencer's caustic comments upon the work of the society cast him in the place of the not-so-loyal opposition. His suggestions for education were as controversial as they were unacceptable to the Victorian social reform movement (Silver, 1983, 93). Insofar as he received popular approbation, it was in terms of his defense of individualism. His popularity among the Victorian elite rested upon his intellectual justification of opposition to the interference of the state in the affairs of individuals. His opposition to the interference of the state in personal affairs is outlined in *The man versus the state* (Spencer, [1892] 1940). The book was enormously popular (Low-Beer, 1969, 26). Victorian adulation of his criticism of the growing paternalism of the Victorian state did not extend, however, to his anticlassical stand on education.

In time the intellectual impact of Spencer's work would be far more important in America than in Britain. Well before the turn of the century the intellectual stance he adopted was critiqued by Henry Sidgwick in *The methods of ethics* ([1874] 1962) and *Outlines of the history of ethics for English readers* ([1886] 1892). Sidgwick found Spencer's sociological ethics empirically and philosophically defective. Sidgwick disputed as a matter of empirical fact Spencer's claim that pleasure and (its obverse) pain were motivating forces in human affairs. The eminent Sidgwick wrote, "It still does not seem to me that I judge pleasures to be greater and less exactly in proportion as they stimulate the will to actions tending to sustain them" ([1874] 1962, 126). For Sidgwick, volition was an irreducible factor in the character of human affairs and their empirical description, just as the question of whether or not we could, in fact, achieve the greatest pleasure (good) through some scientific hedonistic calculus ([1874] 1962, 129-130) was dubious to him. Philosophically speaking, he argued that it was impossible to resolve practical questions by using Spencer's gambit of referring ethical questions to the final and perfect form of society—a voluntary organization in which constraints upon individuals were wherever possible absent and within which the voluntary actions of all individuals create pleasure unmarginalized by pain—for adjudication (Sidgwick, [1874] 1962, 470).

In *Outlines of the history of ethics for English readers* ([1886] 1892, 256), Sidgwick commented: "I am not aware that any other writer on Ethics, from the 'evolution point of view,' has adopted Mr. Spencer's doctrine as to the relations of Absolute and Relative Ethics." He then dismissed Spencer from the ranks of serious philosophy with a sniff and a footnote—as did the English philosophical establishment. Academic philosophers in Britain also followed Sidgwick's lead. The popularity of Spencer's work plummeted after his death, despite being nominated for the Noble Prize for Literature in 1902 (Kennedy 1978, 12). After his death he was not considered to be a serious or important philosopher by the academic establishment.

Although Spencer maintained philosophical legitimacy only in America he was the intellectual force with which social reformers in both countries had to contend. Far from being an absurd and marginal figure out of step with his time and history (contra Silver, 1983, 93), Spencer captured and spoke for the sentiment of privilege and power as well as for the middle classes. The privileged and powerful found

England's underclass a very suspect commodity with dubious social and political qualities. The middle classes saw the underclass as a social force that might destroy the newly found comfort and ease that had been created in the industrial revolution. The lower orders did not seem very receptive to devices (books, concerts, or lectures) or institutions (schools, libraries, and museums) that constituted patrician versions of social welfare. As far as the establishment was concerned the most likely effect of universal mass education would be to make a suspect and unruly lot even more intractable.

But if Spencer was suspicious of the role education could play in social reform he had no doubt of the place of science in "real" education. Real education was a scientific education. Both Spencer, ([1861] 1897) and Huxley ([1880] 1888) struggled to launch science in its own right as part of the university curriculum. In Huxley's inaugural lecture upon his assumption of the chair at St. Andrews once held by John Stuart Mill, Huxley doubted that his argument for the central role that science might play in the university would have been shared by his predecessor. Putting the case as strongly as he could, Huxley argued:

Neither the discipline nor the subject-matter of classical education is of such direct value to the student of physical science as to justify the expenditure of valuable time upon either; and the second is that for the purpose of attaining real culture, an exclusively scientific education is at least as effectual as an exclusively literary education ...

[Nevertheless, to the mind of intellectual conservatives] culture is obtainable only by a liberal education; and a liberal education is synonymous, not merely with education and instruction in literature, but in one particular form of literature, namely, that of Greek and Roman antiquity. They hold that the man who has learned Latin and Greek, however little, is educated; while he who is versed in other branches of knowledge, however deeply, is a more or less respectable specialist, not admissible into the cultured caste. The stamp of the educated man, the University degree is not for him. ([1880] 1888, 7-8)

Huxley was not sanguine about the chances of placing science within the university curriculum. He stated this on 1 October 1880 in an address delivered at the opening of Sir Josiah Mason's Science College:

How often have we not been told that the study of physical science is incompetent to confer culture; that it touches none of the higher problems of life; and, what is worse, that the continual devotion to scientific studies tends to generate a narrow and bigoted belief in the applicability of scientific methods to the search after truth of all kinds. How frequently one has reason to observe that no reply to a troublesome argument tells so well as calling its author a "mere scientific specialist." ([1880] 1888, 6-7)

As Huxley noticed Victorian science was not particularly respected among the literati.

Despite the case made by Huxley and others, science continued to be conducted in English universities largely on an amateur basis until after the end of World War II (Seaman, [1973] 1985, 273; Williams, 1982, 2-3). Universities remained the domain of a liberal education until after the war. The impact of the work of Huxley and Spencer—if Spencer's work can be separated from its odious social ethic—can best be characterized by its impact upon various attempts of the Education Department to expand the curriculum of the elementary schools (see Hadow, 1926, 16). The work of both men was important and provocative, but it never displaced Britain's simple faith in the humanities and the centrality of the humanities to all wisdom. This simple but powerful faith was central to standard versions of educational philosophy in the period following World War II.

## UTOPIANS, FABIANS, AND LIBERALS

In the Victorian period the general social sentiment and pragmatic assessment was that if the underclasses were pushed too far there would be trouble—trouble that might be avoided by a modest and Christian charity for the situation of the dispossessed. The source of this assessment was, largely, the product of the English intellectual establishment—socialist, liberal, and conservative. The difference between them was a matter of how modest that charity was to be and whether or not the state would be intimately involved in the extension of that charity.

Fabians,[5] Utopians, and liberals were all part of the reform establishment. They were morally united, distressed by the condition of England's underclasses. But they were divided by their politics. Liberals hoped to legislate away the difficulties of England's. The liberal version of social reform hoped to improve the conditions of the lower orders from a decent distance. Utopians and Fabians argued that disinterested social reform was stillborn. Utopians such as Robert Owen acted directly to ameliorate the conditions of industrial labor, education, and domestic life as a matter of personal conscience. Fabians on the other hand were moved to direct action by the social and economic plight of industrial workers. The Fabians organized, agitated, and participated in a modest form of direct action. The fact was that, generally speaking, the Fabians were as lower class as the public schools were public. They plotted the economic reorganization of the establishment from the glittering cafés of the Strand, but the venue and their economic situation compromised their credibility among many elements of the dispossessed. This same fact, of course, meant that the Fabians' socialist foibles were both understood and tolerated by the establishment in a manner that would never be extended to the nation's communist or anarchist counterpart. The establishment noticed but was not particularly disturbed by the comments and essays of members of their class. George Bernard Shaw's caustic wit and the activist political discourse of Sidney and Beatrice Webb were as amusing as they were disturbing.

The Fabian Parliamentary League in the flush of its first success delivered a manifesto for social reform. In the manuscript entitled *The true radical programme* were demands for adult suffrage, salaries for Parliamentarians, a progressive tax system, land reform, and a system of state education that both educated and fed the underclasses (Pugh, 1984). The work of Sidney and Beatrice Webb was exemplified by specific critiques of the abuses of power and privilege. But their emphasis upon direct action and indifference to theory left them outside of the revolution going on in social science (Soffer, 1978, 21).

Both the Fabians and utopians were reformers rather than revolutionaries, although some Fabians liked to fancy themselves as revolutionaries. They were concerned with finding a Victorian path to socialism (Pugh, 1984, 14). Their *modus operandi* was at one with Victorian society. Humanitarian or utilitarian, benevolent or heartless, sentimental or pornographic, religious or irreligious, evangelical or high church, Malthusians or Fabians, little Englanders or imperialists, they all acted out of an elevated sense of moral responsibility (Seaman, [1973] 1985, 6). This elevated moral responsibility was the enduring characteristic of the age and made them at one with Victorian society. Their loyalty to Victorian society determined that they would never be "real" revolutionaries.

The utopians ensured that Victorian society would pay attention to social reform. Robert Owen's utopian experiments in New Lanark in Britain and New Harmony in the United States were first steps in the revitalization of the labor movement as well as a practical demonstration of social reform. Not only did he fundamentally alter the organization of work in the New Lanark Mills, but also he initiated a system of infant education in a nation that was reluctant to extend education to the sons and daughters of those who toiled in the New Lanark Mills or anywhere else in England for that matter (Silver, 1969). His utopian reforms delivered to him an international reputation and inspired hundreds of Owenite communities. Robert Owen's widely influential utopian tract *A new view of society* (1818), drew its inspiration his own conscience and from the work of Claude-Adrién Helvétius.[6] Owen's work challenged the establishment to provide education for all of the nation's children, rich and poor alike. Like the chorus in Greek tragedies it was one of the mirror images against which modern educational philosophy contemplated itself.

## LIBERAL ESTABLISHMENT

Liberals had slightly different agendas. John Ruskin was largely exemplary of English liberals and their schizophrenic attitude toward the working class. He was appalled at the condition of the working class but was unsure about what could be done for them without disturbing the natural order of things.

His attitude toward the provision of mass education spanned the range of passionate advocacy to diffident action. As an articulate spokesperson for the oppressed, he demanded social and economic relief for the poor and the provision of educational opportunity in particular. Education in the minds of many Victorians had been prostituted to the demands of new wealth, particularly to the new wealth of the industrial middle classes who did not have a proper appreciation of the idea of "social station" ([1865] 1905, third lecture). There was a place for education and liberation of the underclass as long as it supported social order, justice, and peace (Ruskin, [1865] 1905).

Ruskin's early 1870s Hincksey Road project, perhaps the most quixotic project generated by an interlocking directorate of social reformers, was an object lesson in the dignified "athleticism" of manual labor for the aristocracy. An effete attack upon laissez-faire capitalism and its industrial order, the project assumed a reorganization of the industrial order from the top down by an enlightened aristocracy that had been educated in the nobility of manual labor (Lawson, 1984). Ruskin believed that the aristocracy would gain a certain respect for those who labored by doing manual work themselves, and the lower classes in turn would find a new affection for the aristocracy. Before the project was abandoned, the enterprise attracted the casual and occasional labor of Oxford University students, many of them undergraduates of Balliol College.

Nevertheless Ruskin's plan did not extend to a strictly egalitarian version of society. The educational system planned for turn of the century England and described in the 1870 Education Act was a system designed to fit poor children for their station in life, not to raise them above it (Seaman, [1973] 1985, 198). In Ruskin's words,

There is no honest desire for the thing [education] itself. The cry for it among the lower orders is because they think that, when once they have it, they must become upper orders. There is a strange notion in the mob's mind, now-a-days (including popular economists and educators, as we most justly may, under that brief term "mob"), that *everybody* can be uppermost; or at least, that a state of general scramble, in which everybody in his turn should come to the top, is a proper Utopian constitution; and that once given every lad a good education, and he cannot but come to ride in his carriage (the methods of supply of coachmen and footmen not being contemplated). And very sternly I say to you—and say from sure knowledge—that a man had better not know how to read or write, than receive education on such terms.

The first condition under which it can be given usefully is, that it should be clearly understood to be no means of getting on in the world, but a means of staying pleasantly in your place. ([1867] 1905a, 396-397)

John Ruskin's work, of course, was the classic example of the Victorian liberal's attempt to come to terms with the underclasses, the "dangerous classes," and those who worked in the factories. Ruskin's essays and letters on social questions, work, and education added to the demand for a progressive system of education for all and social reform— just as they added to the middle class's wariness of those who would, those who could not, and those who would not work.[7] Ruskin may have been a social subversive (Lawson, 1984) but certainly not in any modern sense of subversive. He was an advocate of the working man whose exploitation was only too obvious (Lawson, 1984, 30-33). Yet education for the masses was a matter of gently showing them the wisdom of their place as much as it was a matter of freeing them from their ignorance and the oppression of their situation. Ruskin was committed to the liberation of the lower orders as long as that liberation was accomplished within a reform version of the existing state of affairs.[8] Ruskin's stance was elaborate and reflected the complexities and confusions evident in the period. They were the same complexities and confusions evident in the trade union movement. Ruskin's stance was the predicate for extending education to classes in which the "haves" had little faith.

Ruskin in "The harmful effect of servile employment" ([1867] 1905c) presents the intellectual establishment's stance in its most pleasant, hopeful, and socially conscious form. He writes:

I know, as well as he does, the unconquerable differences in the clay of the human creature; and I know that, in the outset, whatever system of education you adopted, a large number of children could be made nothing of, and would necessarily fall out of the ranks, and supply candidates enough for degradation to common mechanical business: but this enormous difference in bodily and mental capacity has been mainly brought about by difference in occupation, and by direct mal-treatment; and in a few generations, if the poor were cared for, their marriages looked after, and sanitary law enforced, a beautiful type of face and form, and a high intelligence, would become all but universal in a climate like this of England. Even as it is, the marvel is always to me how the race resists, at least in its childhood, influences of ill-regulated birth, poisoned food, poisoned air, and soul neglect ...

Yes, very solemnly I repeat to you that in those worst treated children of the English race, I yet see the making of gentlemen and gentlewomen—not the making of dog-stealers and gin-drinkers, such as their parents were; and the child of the average English tradesman or peasant, even at this day, well schooled, shows no innate disposition such as must fetter him for ever to the clod or the counter. (405, 406)

Ruskin's social and educational demands contained a commitment to the social and intellectual liberation of the working man just as they contained a commitment to science and technical education. The core of Ruskin's thought revolved around issues of social reform and the salvation of the "worst treated children of the English race".[9]

Nevertheless, it was a prescription that was not without personal and social impact. Ruskin could command an audience of thousands of men and women. Individuals working under brutal conditions of labor as far away as Australia would "weep for joy" after reading *Sesame and lillies* ([1865] 1905), a tract that rehearsed the economic, social, and political writings of his earlier works (Lawson, 1984, 26-28). This of course did not make Ruskin a socialist or a capitalist. Ruskin, like Rousseau, desired to return to a a simpler medieval world in which the profound questions of the urbanized industrial world would just dissolve (cf. Lawson, 1984, 33). In a sense, he was a primitivist and an agriculturalist, or perhaps a Victorian is a better characterization. Like Owen's work, Ruskin's thought was one of the mirror images against which modern educational philosophy contemplated itself.

## CONSERVATIVE ESTABLISHMENT

Conservatives shared at least one view with liberals: Members of the dangerous classes were in their place because of personal failings. And that was that. But unlike the liberals the conservatives were dubious about the lower classes' redemption. Radicals believed that society had to be changed to accomplish social reform, liberals believed that social reform could be accomplished by making people aware of the suffering of those who labored in the factories of industrial Britain. Conservatives, at one with Herbert Spencer, believed that either remedy would cause more harm than good. Conservatives were convinced of the salutary effect of studying the classics. Books such as Plato's *Republic* reminded individuals of the importance of station in the maintenance of social order and justified an aristocratic order that they found quite natural.

Conservatives were suspicious of the "dangerous classes" and by the same token committed to their redemption. This schizophrenic Victorian stance finds a familiar reiteration in F. H. Bradley's skirmishes with the utilitarians in *Ethical studies* ([1876] 1927); that is, Bradley (the Victorian conservative) was obsessed with "station" and the problem of inveigling the "lower orders" (a group of which he, like most Victorians, was profoundly wary) to act in a manner that was beyond, and not expected, of their social situation.

Alexander Bain's *Education as a science* (1889) was a widely distributed and influential philosophical tract.[10] It was a mild mixture of pedagogical suggestions and social comment with a philosophical stance representative of the aristocratic politics of the period. In his book the Scottish professor reminded the monied classes of Locke and suggested to them that the thought of philosophers such as Henry Sidgwick and the autodidact Herbert Spencer, while interesting, was unimportant for the conduct of educational work (Bain, 1889, 3). Bain, and men of similar intellectual commitments, asserted the centrality of the classics for true education and defended them from the philosophical forays of men such as Sidgwick. Sidgwick would have replaced the study of the classical languages of Greek and Latin with modern languages such as French, and pseudophilosophers such as Herbert Spencer who would have done away with traditional concepts of the curriculum altogether (Bain, 1889).[11] Bain reminded the Victorians of the common belief in the salutary intellectual effects of studying Greek and Latin. He reminded Victorians of the "proper" role of primary education. Like many conservatives he was quite sure that secondary education would be wasted on all but the few. In the words of this professor of logic at the University of Aberdeen, "The primary school begins and ends the education of the masses" (Bain, 1889, 437). Like Plato's *Republic*, Bain's *Education as a science* saw no reason to waste education on those who could not appreciate or accomplish it. It was a stance that conservative Victorians found comforting and consistent.

Conservatives were dubious about the educability of the masses and hoped for their redemption through some "trickle-down" effect. If conservative thinkers had an educational focus it was not on the working classes, but on the middle classes. In the end, even Matthew Arnold, probably the most egalitarian of the establishment's conservative "schoolies," believed that the salvation of the working classes was in a great democratic reform: the establishment of public schools for the middle classes (Connell, 1950, 266-268). In Arnold's scheme of things real education was beyond the reach of the lower classes. If the upper classes were lost in materialism and the lower classes vulgarized, then it was only through the good offices of the middle classes that the civilization and the amelioration of the conditions of Britain's lower classes would be possible (Connell, 1950,

266-268). Thus, insofar as Arnold was committed to the civilizing effect of a "liberal education"—an introduction to "the best that has been thought and said," a curriculum that militated against civil anarchy and commended personal altruism particularly in matters of the public welfare (Rothblatt, 1976, 149–150)—he was opposed to the unalloyed versions of technical education that were becoming increasingly popular (Connell, 1950, 267–268). If Fabians and utopians cast mirrors against which modern philosophy of education contemplated itself, conservatives provided that contemplation with a sobriquet, liberal education.

## INTELLECTUAL ESTABLISHMENT

The source of educational thought in the Victorian period was largely the product of the intellectual establishment—liberal, conservative, Fabian, and utopian. John Stuart Mill's *Principles of political economy* ([1848] 1891) argued for a system of primary education as a means to reducing civil disorder and the moral instruction of the poor just as it argued for the centrality of education in the modern state. Ruskin's essays and letters on social questions ([1865] 1905; [1866] 1905a; 1907)—education, of course, among them ([1865] 1905; [1852] 1904)—also added to the demand for a progressive system of education for all. Education for the masses was a matter of gently showing them the wisdom of their place while demanding that their betters dissolve the permanent underclass that industrialism seemed to have created (Ruskin, [1867] 1905a, 394 -401). Utopians such as Owen, of course, were largely concerned with constructing a tolerable industrial environment in which all could share in the rewards of industrial modes of production. Owen assumed that a decent respect for the situation of the industrial classes would consolidate the virtues of Victorian culture and extend them to all. In Owen's world utopianism was a matter of extending to the industrial workers of Britain at least a small portion of what the middle classes already enjoyed. Owen's version of education was "on the side" of the workers, just as it was "on the side" of the Victorian world and the "sensibilities" that it represented. Conservatives merely demanded that whatever occurred in the name of education did not disturb the social order or their position of privilege.

## SOCIAL SCIENCE

So far it is social science that is the missing element in this rendering of educational philosophy's history.[12] If one nominates a predicate for social science it is enough to trace it back to the work of the philosophic radicals. Jeremy Bentham, James Mill, and his son John Stuart Mill were particularly central to the idea of social science. Among the philosophical radicals it is John Stuart Mill who is central to our concerns. He fashioned a version of social science suitable for English readers and extended philosophical investigations of social science into the realm of political and social philosophy and therein education.

The idea of a social science certainly did not originate with John Stuart Mill, and it is more accurate to cite the origin of social science among the French than the English (Senn, 1958, 568-570; Burns, 1959, 431-432). Comte used the idea as early as the 1820s (Burns, 1959, 432). Mill brought the idea home to England halfway through the nineteenth century (Abrams, 1968, 53-57; Sidgwick, [1886] 1892, 268). Comte's version of social science assumed a central role for the state that the English found quite unpalatable. The English embraced an idea of social science that was mixed with Mill's laissez-faire political economy. Without the central role Comte assumed for the state, it proved to be more acceptable to the English. Mill's *System of logic* ([1843] 1884) provided just that. When coupled with his *Principles of political economy* ([1848] 1891), a work that formally outlined a role for government that did not interfere with personal liberty and privilege, social science became a more acceptable undertaking.

The implication of large scale government and government intervention in civil society implicit in Comte's positive sociology appalled Victorian sensibilities. The Victorians were much more comfortable with Mill's political economy with its nominalist version of government and Spencer's sociology. Following Mill's lead the British were unanimous in their opinion that good government was government that governed least. Mill's ameliorative social science appealed. The Victorians were not concerned with social reorganization as much as they were concerned with "toning down" social problems in the "best of all possible worlds."

## MORAL PHILOSOPHY

Until the advent of social science the study of human affairs was the monopoly of moral philosophy. As was previously noted, in the period prior to the Great War it was philosophy that provided the most thorough intellectual interrogation of education and schooling just as it provided the most interesting discussions of "human nature, social forces, progress, marriage and family relationships, economic process, maintenance of government, international relations, elementary jurisprudence, primitive customs, history of institutions, religion, ethics, aesthetics—all topics of import in the social sciences of our day" (Bryson, 1932b, 304). At Oxford and Cambridge in the nineteenth century matters pertaining to the systematic study of society were called moral philosophy. As the study of the human condition became more sophisticated and complex, some moral philosophers apportioned a larger segment of their time to the study of "social issues." In this context a social philosopher came to mean a moral philosopher concerned with society working in an essentially classical tradition (Abrams, 1968, 5). But eventually, social science (in the singular) and then the social sciences (in the plural), as one after the other of the social sciences evolved out of moral philosophy, appropriated a logical if not chronologically prior claim to the study of society. Initially psychologists, sociologists, political scientists, economists, anthropologists, and educators were moral philosophers with interests "as wide as the customs and institutions of man" (Bryson, 1932b, 19).[13] The traditional questions of social philosophy devolved into the hands of the social sciences and literature (Hughes, 1958, 25). Mill's idea of a social science helped separate social philosophy into statistics, economics, sociology, education, social welfare, and all of the other disciplines that were to evolve out of the obvious need to control the social conditions that urbanization and the industrial revolution had generated.

It should be remembered that during this period social science was primitive and educational theory was still in the process of being invented. Social science would not take its first tentative steps until 1856 when the National Association for the Promotion of Social Science was established. Herbert Spencer's version of social science was still in the offing and its final form would not be available until *The study of sociology* was published in 1873. It would, of course, add to the confusion. It was a version of social science dedicated to explanation and theory, it was radically at odds with the social reform version of social science adopted by the National Association for the Promotion of Social Science. Not only was it dedicated to the production of theory and explanation but it was—as a matter of scientific principle— indifferent to the individuals it professed to study.

The idea of a professionalized version of social science and therein education, with specialized subdisciplines, a systematic program of organized research, objective standards, and an organized group of investigators proctoring each others' research and transmitting that research to the offices of government and the profession was, at this time, still unrealized. The version of social science presented to the world by the association (social science's dominant form in Great Britain) was primordial and ill-formed compared to its modern form. It was largely romantic, dedicated to social reform, and unable to articulate the difference between systematic study and science. It occupied a place halfway between the humanities and science. Primarily theory-free, it devoted itself to commending various nostrums. The study of education was excluded from the university environment and was still fairly amateurish. In social science there was no systematic graduate training, and professional organizations to proctor and direct research were still in the wings (Soffer, 1978, 37). Methods for the selection of social problems and the analysis of and verification of data were still wanting (Soffer, 1978, 37).

For the most part statistical information about the schools was only just beginning to be gathered. Discussions of education centered on political and social philosophy. The thrust of intellectual debate was about the social order and the role of the school in the justification of privilege or the amelioration of deprivation. It was a debate conducted, at least partially, in the threatening shadow of socialist, Fabian, or Marxist polemics about a new social order. In this milieu education was not an object of investigation in its own right. It was worthy of attention, largely because of the common belief that education was instrumental to social reform—that is, the pacification and salvation of the underclasses' children. This dialogue was not driven by a quest for knowledge but by the common Victorian fear of social disorder. Victorian society was afraid that industrialism had or was creating an explosive situation between "haves" and "have-nots." The idea of a permanent unruly, defiant, and perhaps even rebellious working class was an unsettling prospect.

William James provided an additional impetus for the socially conscious revolution in social science. James was a frequent visitor to Oxford, Cambridge, and London. During his several visits to England over of three decades he became an influential collaborator in the intellectual spirit of the period (Soffer, 1978, 35). Witty, charming, and intellectually courageous, he was at least as influential in England as he was in his native United States.[14] It was James who reinforced scholars efforts to apply social science to the problems that industrialism had created and was unable to solve. He argued that "in principal" social reform could be accomplished with a method that used both experience and theory to resolve desperate social conditions (Soffer, 1978, 15-45). Through his analysis of the psychological origins of consciousness and behavior, he demonstrated that a social science capable of direct intervention in human affairs was possible. James work was a powerful antidote to the fatalism of Spencer's version of social science.

By mid-century social science had started its evolution out of social philosophy. Eventually it evolved into the numerous disciplines we now recognize as constitutive elements of the social sciences. By the mid-twentieth century, political science, sociology, anthropology, psychology, education, and other disciplines had introduced themselves to—but had not established themselves within—the British academic establishment (Soffer, 1978). Of course, the journals followed suit. *Mind* is an excellent example of the kind of journal that bridged the transition of philosophy into social science. "*Mind* became, to mix a metaphor, the heart of British and American psychology" (Soffer, 1978, 130). It offered a place of publication to philosophers and psychologists alike. Philosophers such as William James and John Dewey, and psychologists like James McKeen Cattell, preferred to publish in *Mind*. Nevertheless, purist psychologists such as G. Stanley Hall would begin their own journal (*The Journal of Psychology* [1888]) to eliminate the interminable debate over "philosophical" questions. *The Journal of Psychology* found no place for the work of William James or John Dewey or for the theoretical work of social psychologists such as James Mark Baldwin (Soffer, 1978, 130). The change in editorial policy and the establishment of new journals, however, merely shadowed the evolution of social science away from social philosophy.

It was only after social and political philosophy had evolved out of moral philosophy that there would be a place for educational philosophy in social science's new establishment. But educational philosophy would not unfold while its role was being played out by some combination of social philosophers, statisticians, economists, and sociologists. Pride of place in the social sciences would fall to those Victorian disciplines more directly concerned with facts and their quantification (Abrams, 1968, 8-30). Gathering data was one way of displacing the evil of industrial society but it also had the advantage of assuring that monies devoted to philanthropy were well spent— social science and effective philanthropy went hand in hand (Abrams 1968, 32, 36). Statistics was a discipline that appealed to the countinghouse morality of Victorian England.

By the end of the century social positivism as presented in the works of Jeremy Bentham, and James Mill, and most significantly in John Stuart Mill's *System of logic* ([1843] 1884) was a dying tradition in the social sciences (Soffer, 1978, 32). But it was steadily becoming the dominant tradition in philosophy. Mathematics and statistics were paving the way for positivist science and positivist philosophy. Soffer (1978, 30) that reports Raphael Meldola could claim in the Herbert Spencer Lecture of 1910 that through the powerful device of mathematics veridical explanations could now be made by men who had never conducted an experiment. Mathematics or statistics would not, at this point in time, provide an epistemology or general method for the social sciences but it would provide a paradigm of rational explanation (Soffer, 1978, 27). Philosophy's romance with a unified science would wait for Wittgenstein's Vienna. The critical positivism of Ernst Mach and Richard Avenarius propelled science into a positivist phase. And Karl Pearson in *The grammar of science* ([1892] 1900) successfully argued the case of scientific laws as descriptive, not causal. In so doing Pearson removed the concept of physical necessity from philosophy and science and endowed it with logical necessity. Pearson's work lacked—but fitted nicely within—the stress on language and logic that was characteristic of Russell's work on mathematical logic and Wittgenstein's deliberations. The divergent directions of social science and philosophy foreshadowed the different paths that education as social science and education as philosophy would follow. Except for L. A. Reid's attempt to keep educational philosophy in touch with its literary predicate, philosophy of education followed philosophy's obsessive positivist concern for logic, epistemology, clarity, and precision.

## THE NATIONAL ASSOCIATION FOR THE PROMOTION OF SOCIAL SCIENCE

Social science was created to debate and investigate a residue of questions left unattended by academic moral and social philosophy. It responded to the demand by the middle classes for social and economic reform in a society that was beginning to question the idea that private charity was capable of dealing with the pauperism, filth, crime, drunkenness, and ignorance that appeared as a primary legacy of industrialism. These questions seemed ill-fitting in universities dedicated to the pursuit of wisdom.

The study of education as a *corporate* enterprise established itself outside of the university environment in England. Initially, education was the concern of a vast array of social reformers, social philosophers, socialists, and utopians of various descriptions who belonged to various associations where education was deemed to be a key instrumental device for social reform. It was a device for the moral reform of individual wickedness, the social pacification of the hooligan underclass, the reclamation of their children, and the amelioration of industrialism's worst excesses. Social investigations of education were conducted by a number of voluntary bodies concerned with the moral improvement of society and were conducted and consolidated under the auspices of the National Association for the Promotion of Social Science.

The association was an umbrella organization—a coalition of reform groups (Abrams, 1968, 39-40). The members of the association were amateur reformers drawn together out of a mutual concern for the alarming social conditions of industrial England (Furner, 1975, 11). Radical utilitarians, utopians, chartists, Fabians, and socialists of all descriptions joined the National Association for the Promotion of Social Science, as did members of the establishment. The association was concerned largely with freeing the underclass from ignorance, poverty, and moral depravity in all its forms. It promoted the study of education as part of its charter for social reform (Silver, 1983, 100-131).

Founded in 1857, the association collected social facts and statistics with the ambition of crafting of social legislation. As Mr. Gradgrind pointed out in Dickens's *Hard times* (1854] 1931), education was about facts. To the Victorian mind it was the facts that would specify the political action or social legislation necessary to reform society. Education in a society that traced poverty and deprivation to individual moral failings, was, of course, a central and manipulable device that could be pressed into the service of social reform.

Education was an active and important department of the National Association for the Promotion of Social Science (Silver, 1983, 100-131). The association worked to generate rationality (a democratic politics), philanthropy (social reform), and moral reform (thrift and temperance). In other words, it was dedicated to social reform as well as the production of data, facts, and information. Both concerns were major elements of this anti-Spencerian version of social science. It represented an amateur version of investigation similar to the belief of earlier Baconians that science was merely the knowledge of many facts. It assumed that huge masses of data would reveal the real causes of industrialism's under-class. Social data would show them how to live and suggest a means to democratic social reform.

The association promoted the study of education while it simultaneously and unfortunately tainted the discipline with the brush of amateurism, if not incompetence (Silver, 1983, 100-131). But, as Tholfsen notes,

The bourgeoisie took up the mission of "elevating the masses" with their wonted earnestness. This meant transmitting appropriate traits and habits to the upper strata of the working classes. The capitalist virtues of thrift and diligence—redefined in the gospel of work—were singled out for special attention. Morality and intelligence were to be fostered in a context of deference and respectability. To accomplish these ends existing institutions were expanded and new ones constructed. (1961, 229)

"Sunday Schools, Ragged and Industrial Schools, National Schools, British Schools, Mechanics Institutes, Working Men's Colleges, Working Men's Reading Rooms, Mutual Improvement Societies, and libraries" were all part of a a Byzantine effort to encourage the working class to aspire beyond their station while maintaining the proper attitude of deference and acquiescence to wealth and the aristocracy (Tholfsen, 1961, 228, 233).

Under the charter of the association various academic dilettantes, social reformers, and professional educators began an unsystematic and haphazard study of schooling. The image of social science outside of the ambit of systematic and theoretical studies was authenticated by practice, not theory. Thus, from the beginning educational studies were alienated from England's universities. The university did not enter into the intellectual investigations of poverty, deprivation, education, and schools. These topics were part of the domain of unionists, Fabians, and Owenites: reformers, not the stuffy and aristocratic dons of the university establishment who had neither the interest nor the inclination for the field. Education was part of the social reform movement, not the university.[15] Of course, social science's initial establishment in the societies and associations of the city of London helped delay the commencement of the university study of education and therein educational philosophy until after World War II.

The early voice of the association was *Meliora: A quarterly review of social science.* It achieved a subscription of over seven thousand in its first year of publication (Abrams, 1968, 39). Like the association, *Meliora* was dedicated to eliminating an array of social problems (Abrams, 1968, 39). The association's publication *Transactions* followed a similar theme. Suffused with moral judgements, *Transactions* concerned itself with the state and individual freedom, the individual and the individual's moral development, and class and social stability. Both *Meliora* and *Transactions* were representative of the middle-class's social concern. Christian, middle class, and prescriptive, both journals were concerned with "elevating" the lower classes. Little was said about the excesses of wealth and privilege. The journals were judgmental, and the judgments ran in one direction. Social criticism and social thought ran down the social scale, not up.

In the end, the National Association for the Promotion of Social Science dissolved into the various social sciences—education among them. During its existence it established "philosophical" questions about education in the realm of public administration (a social science and civil service), social science, and the public domain. Philosophical questions were rehearsed in innumerable governmental reports and pressed into the service of social reform or privilege—depending upon one's point of view. From the beginning of the 1900s to the mid-sixties philosophical questions about education remained the province of public administrators and English intellectuals. In addition, the great intellectual families of England adopted the issue of education, among others, as their own. The Balfours, Beveridges, Sidgwicks, Haldanes, James Wards, Keyneses, Marshalls, and Toynbees were all deeply concerned with the idea and practice of education. In many instances they left the university in order to establish important roles in the world of public policy (Soffer, 1978, 7). They were key educational reformers. The evolution of educational thought and institutions depended, largely, on the hard work and systematic thought of these families. "This relatively small group, unique in the scope and vigor of its activity, altered the whole direction of science, education, letters, and government" (Soffer, 1978, 7). It is perhaps not surprising, then, that the *Balfour* Act of 1902 initiated the period of educational reform in the twentieth century and the *Beveridge* Report foreshadowed the 1944 Education Act and brought the period of Victorian initiatives to a close, that is, even after the close of World War II the great families were still important players in the evolution of educational thought and practice.

## SOCIAL SCIENCE, THE CIVIL SERVICE, THE GREAT FAMILIES, AND EDUCATIONAL PHILOSOPHY

In Great Britain the National Association for the Promotion of Social Science (NAPSS) tied both social science and the social reform movement to the systematic study of education and thereby appropriated fundamental educational questions to social science. It was obvious to many members of the establishment that the academic reputation of education could be enhanced if the discipline could at least partially be reclaimed from the issues of social welfare. The simple idea was that education was an intellectual enterprise, not a matter of social welfare. The problem with government schools was that they were more closely attached to social welfare than they were to intellectual achievement. The establishment's solution was to staff the government schools with intellectuals not caregivers and rededicate the institution to intellectual achievement.

Many years later when Peters took up the chair of education at the London Institute of Education he believed like other members of the university establishment, however subliminally, that it would be necessary to bring teacher education and fundamental educational questions back into the realm of philosophy and to segregate them from issues of social science and therein the social welfare if either was to achieve academic or professional respectability.

The appropriation of education's fundamental questions by social science, the civil service, and the great families gave the systematic study of education's fundamental questions to groups outside of the university. Upon their appointment to the chair of education at the London Institute of Education both Reid and Peters faced the task of reclaiming the central position of philosophy in the study of education from social science, the civil service, and the great families. Success eluded Reid, but Peters accomplished many of these tasks.

## THE 1890S SOCIAL REFORM MOVEMENT

At the turn of the nineteenth century there was little public demand for education. The creation of the British and Foreign Schools Society in 1807, a charitable nondenominational organization, was largely responsible for initiating a demand and agitating for a national system of elementary education (Seaman, [1973] 1985, 190). But public recognition is not the same as the realization of an ideal, educational or otherwise. In practical terms the period from 1800 to almost the turn of the century did little more than suggest the possibility of universal and free education.

Meager governmental contributions for the support of education of any variety, the abysmal condition of day schools, and the presence of a corps of educators who could only be given the title "teacher" as a courtesy encouraged the privileged to establish a system of private education for themselves. While it is pleasant to imagine a system of "public education" that can trace its heritage back to ancient institutions—medieval craft guilds and city companies, "the public school system," intimately tied into the boarding school, was an invention of the latter half of the 1800s (Tawney, [1918] 1964b, 52).

The flood of new wealth generated by the industrial revolution; the demand for educated executives, managers, clerks and employees generated by the expansion and consolidation of the empire; reform and professionalization of the civil service; and the growth of the professions, medicine, law, and the church combined to create a powerful new economic demand for an educated ruling class and a new class: an industrial intelligentsia (Tawney, [1918] 1964b, 53). In this context the privileged and articulate were more than willing to pay for a system of schools that would ensure their children access to the elite social and economic positions. They were not interested in extending those same advantages to the children of the working classes.

"The public school system" and the examination system both reflected deep social divisions that were beyond the reach of normal political redress. Largely unlettered and untutored, London's working class had access to a quality of education that was no better than the exploited condition of their lives:

Since the middle classes allow the workers only a bare minimum standard of living, it is not surprising that they receive only as much education as will serve the interests of their masters, which in fact amounts to very little. In relation to the size of the population the educational facilities in England are negligible. There are a very limited number of day schools available to working class children; they are of a poor standard and attract only a very few scholars. The teachers are retired workers or other unsuitable persons who, unable to earn a living in any other way, have turned to teaching as a last resort. The vast majority of these "teachers" are themselves virtually uneducated and lack the moral qualities essential in a teacher. Moreover, they are under no sort of public control. In education, as in everything else, free competition is the rule, and as usual the wealthy derive all the advantages from this arrangement. The poor on the other hand, have to put up with all its disadvantages, because for them the competition is not really free at all, as they have not the necessary knowledge to make for themselves any judgement [about the quality of schooling offered]. There is no compulsory education in England. In the factories . . . compulsory education exists only in name. (Engels, [1845] 1958, 124)

By the early 1900s the English economy had largely recovered from the depression of the 1890s. But vast economic and social anomalies remained. While the wealthy lived in luxury alongside the long shadows of the Victorian empire, many others lived in desperate poverty. Despite great mechanical and material achievements, "poverty was neither exceptional nor cyclic; by any acceptable twentieth-century standard it was normal" (Seaman, [1973] 1985, 27).

Although they invested heavily overseas, the Victorians found no need, it would seem, to invest in Britain's domestic establishment. They obstinately resisted investing in public health, housing, or education (Seaman, [1973] 1985, 39). As far as they were concerned the solution to shortages of hospitals, homes, and schools was charity. This remedy was never very effective but it had the advantage of offering moral absolution for the politics and economics of greed that had generated the appalling social conditions of London and the industrial Midlands. The unfortunate consequence of all of this was that the moral absolution of charity was so attractive and its economics so nominal that it became "the" solution to questions of public responsibility for "community goods." Thus, the monied classes built private homes, hospitals, and schools for themselves and mostly let members of less fortunate classes take care of themselves. It was better to give than be taxed! These collective social policies left parts of England not merely "an undeveloped estate" but a slum (Seaman, [1973] 1985, 40).

Abject poverty and great wealth made the nation a land of social and economic contradictions. Prostitution was a constitutive element of Victorian life (Mayhew, [1851] 1967 vol. 4, 210-272) while chastity was the icon of feminine virtue. Close to Regent Street and the Strand were the clubs of St. James. The clubs were openly dedicated to white slavery, prostitution and all the attendant excesses of the empire's seemingly endless wealth, all of which grew and prospered almost under the shadow of St. Paul's Cathedral (Chesney, 1970, 11-37). Close to those same places, purveyors to the royal families brought the most luxurious goods of the empire to indulge the exotic tastes of London's privileged few (Chesney, 1970, 11-37). On the other hand, a short walk from the Strand were shops selling adulterated food, passages littered with garbage, feces, and even "uncoffined bodies" (Chesney, 1970, 14).

This was also the England of the Victorian underclass. It was the class of which Engels noted hundreds of thousands grew up "undrained, unpoliced, ungoverned and unschooled" (Engels, [1845] 1958). It was the exciting world of Dickens's *Oliver Twist* ([1837] 1974). The titillation of potentially sharing or being thrust into the appalling conditions of Twist's world, however abstractly, fascinated readers who were safely outside of the empire's underclasses. It was a bitter world that Jack London described in *The people of the abyss* (1903).

## LITERARY DISCOURSE

Literary discourse about society, education, and children was part of an increasing public awareness of the seemingly intractable poverty that followed industrialization. The system was knowingly elitist and class preferential. In this system children of the monied classes, both dim and bright, were Brahmans, and children unlucky enough to be born poor and/or not so bright were Untouchables (Fawcett and Thomas, 1982, 281). Education was a matter of class and secondarily a matter of intelligence.

Ignorance, drunkenness, and crime were interpreted with an eye to poverty, and poverty was interpreted in the Victorian times with an eye to a causal connection between it and individual wickedness or moral turpitude. But at least part of the literati were beginning to question whether or not England's industrial slums and dangerous classes were something other than a function of individual defects or failings. England's literary guild was among the first in the intellectual establishment to take up the issue. And some of the period's best authors featured the question of the schools in their intellectual investigations of the times and its social problems. England's literary guild made the fundamental questions of education a public issue.

The novels of Charles Dickens were the first stories to feature children as central characters and to place their schools under literary scrutiny (Collins, 1964, 1-2). *Oliver Twist* ([1837] 1974), *Nicholas Nickleby* ([1839] 1983), *David Copperfield* ([1849-1850] 1981), and *Great expectations* ([1861] 1931), among others, evoke the world of childhood and feature examples of the thirty-odd schools that appeared in Dickens's novels (Collins, 1964, 1-2). Teachers like Mr. Gradgrind and Mr. M'Choakumchild in *Hard times* ([1854] 1931) became part of the parlance of the day (Collins, 1964, 1-2). Dickens's work, of course, is only illustrative of a vast array of literature that was becoming part of literary culture directed toward the world of childhood. It was a literary culture that was congenial to Dickens's romantic view of childhood and children. William Wordsworth, Thomas Carlyle, and Charles Lamb, to name but the most obvious, all shared Dickens's views to one degree or another.

The schools Charles Dickens described in *Hard times* ([1854] 1931) were joyless, repressive places. The schools for the children of those who would work, those who would not, and those who could not were little better than the conditions of their existence. Classes were held in buildings unfit for teaching and staffed by individuals who were barely better educated than those they served (Engels, [1845] 1958, 124). At best they were institutions that ceaselessly disgorged information and demanded its reiteration (Dickens, [1854] 1931, 1). As Mr. Gradgrind demands,

Now, what I want is facts. Teach these boys and girls nothing but Facts. Facts alone are wanted in life. Plant nothing else, and root out everything else. You can only form the minds of reasoning animals upon Facts: nothing else will ever be of any service to them. This is the principle on which I bring up my own Children, and this is the principle on which I bring up these children. Stick to the Facts, Sir! (Dickens, [1854] 1931, 1)

Schools were warehouselike buildings in which teachers like Mr. M'Choakumchild dolefully taught and children cheerlessly learned (Dickens, [1854] 1931). In them children—more than on occasion—were brutally beaten as well as instructed. They were convinced during the course of their instruction of the importance of obedience, submission, and conformity, and the significance of academic excellence in avoiding the cane.

As in the United States it was the literary guild that brought the issue of education to the attention of the middle class. In this case it was Great Britain's novelists that made education and its fundamental assumptions a public philosophical issue.


## POVERTY AND EDUCATION

In comparison to the countries of the European continent and North America, England was slow to adopt a system of free and compulsory education. Fueled by sectarian bitterness and the general fear that any form of education would render an insubordinate working class even more insubordinate, the debate over elementary education wholly supported by the public purse was slow and protracted (Seaman, [1973] 1985, 189-190). In other words, sectarian competition coupled with the suspicion that elements of Britain's industrial class were a dangerous social quantity prevented the establishment of anything that looked like a national system of state supported elementary education. Fearful that even elementary education might reveal to workers that they were being ill-used and that their labor was being ill-rewarded, the English establishment found little reason to hurry into a program of compulsory and free education for all.

As Henry Mayhew, author of the establishment's chronicle of London's underclass, somewhat disingenuously wrote in his establishment survey of the conditions of the working class, *London labour and the London poor* ([1851] 1967):

*Education*, is as far as I have been able to ascertain, more widely extended among street children than it was twelve or fifteen years ago. The difficulty in arriving at any conclusion on such a subject is owing to the inability to find any one who knew, or could even form a tolerably accurate judgment of what was the state of education among these juveniles even twelve years back.

Perhaps it may be sufficiently correct to say that among a given number of street children, where, a dozen years ago, you met twenty who could read, you will now meet upwards of thirty. Of sixteen children, none apparently fifteen years of age, whom I questioned on the subject, nine admitted that they could not read; the other seven declared that they could, but three annexed to the avowal the qualifying words—"a little.". . .

As to mundane matters, the boy told me that . . . France was a different country to this: he had heard there was no king or queen there, but didn't understand about it. You couldn't go to France by land, no more than you could to Ireland. Didn't know anything of the old times in history; hadn't been told. Had heard of the battle of Waterloo; the English licked. Had heard of the battle of Trafalgar, and of Lord Nelson; didn't know much about him; but there was his pillar at Charing-cross, just by the candlesticks (fountains). (Mayhew, ([1851] 1967), vol. 4, 472-473)

In other words, the extension of education was modest even by the most charitable interpretation. Children of the street were largely unschooled. Their natural cunning kept them alive and their natural intelligence provided for their day-to-day survival. A formal education was reserved for their betters; the lessons of the street, the factory, and the mine were reserved for them.

Prior to the industrial revolution the lot of England's working class was not the difficult existence it was to become. In Engels's words,

In short, the English industrial worker of those days lived very much in that state of seclusion and retirement . . . They were not much troubled with intellectual and spiritual problems and the even tenor of their lives was seldom disturbed. They could seldom read and it was still rare for them to be able to write. They went regularly to Church. They took no interest in politics, never formed secret societies, never concerned themselves about the problems of the day, but rejoiced in healthy outdoor sports and listened devoutly when the Bible was read to them. Their unquestioning humility enabled them to live peacefully side by side with the higher ranks of society. But this meant that they had no intellectual life and were interested solely in their petty private affairs, such as their looms and their gardens. They knew nothing of the great events that were taking place in the outside world. They vegetated happily, and but for the Industrial Revolution would never have left this way of life, which was indeed idyllic. Yet they remained in some respects little better than the beasts of the field. They were not human beings at all, but little more than human machines in the service of a small aristocratic class which had hitherto dominated the life of the country. (Engels, [1845] 1958, 12)

The industrial revolution transformed English society and the situation of its working classes. As Engels noted of the transformation,

London is unique, because it is a city in which one can roam for hours without leaving the built-up area and without seeing the slightest sign of the approach of open country. This enormous agglomeration of population on a single spot has multiplied a hundred-fold the economic strength of the two and a half million inhabitants concentrated there. This great population has made London the commercial capital of the world and has created the gigantic docks in which are assembled the thousands of ships which always cover the Thames . . .
It is only later that the traveller appreciates the human suffering which has made all this possible. ([1845] 1958, 30)

But the industrial revolution had changed all that. If prior to the industrial revolution Britain's industrial workers lived in stoic ignorance they were compensated by a certain pastoral splendor. After the industrial revolution the loss of splendor was not compensated for by a coming to wisdom. In the words of Jack London,

Nowhere in the streets of London may one escape the sight of abject poverty, while five minutes' walk from almost any point will bring one to a slum; but the region my hansom was now penetrating (the East End) was one of unending slum. The streets were filled with a new and different race of people, short of stature, and of wretched or beer-sodden appearance. We rolled along through miles of bricks and squalor, and from each cross street and alley flashed long vistas of bricks and misery. Here and there lurched a drunken man or woman, and the air was obscene with sounds of jangling and squabbling. At a market, tottery old men and women were searching in the garbage thrown in the mud for rotten potatoes, beans, and vegetables, while little children clustered like flies around a festering mass of fruit, thrusting their arms to the shoulders into the liquid corruption, and drawing forth morsels, but partially decayed, which they devoured on the spot. (1903, 8)

Education for the underclasses was a matter of aristocratic self-interest, class snobbery, and feigned Christian charity. Insofar as the bourgeoisie was concerned, human beings had meaning and existence only to the degree that they were part of the process of turning a profit and avoiding a financial loss.[16] This was an attitude that did not go unnoticed in Dickens's Christmas carol ([1843] 1911).

Victorian society created a hyperelitist definition of education that was socially segregated and elitist in its provision and extension, and substantively classical in its content. Social expectations ensured education would remain elitist, and the civil service examination described below, ensured that the definition of an education would remain a liberal education, that is, a classical education. From this point on educational thought would revolve around an adulation of the public school ethos on the one hand and the fairly confused demand of the labor movement for educational opportunity even if it was not quite equal.[17]

Artistocratic elites and the middle classes were not worried about extending educational opportunity, they were worried about creating a pacific populace and an unproblematic industrial work force. It was a complicated task given the fact that domestic developments were encouraging social and economic differences between "public" and government schools. Although the idea of a system of free and compulsory education had an altruistic ring its substance was social and economic self-interest. The consolidation of the socioeconomic differences between "public" and government schools was accomplished by the civil service.

Consolidation of the "public school system" was accomplished by a reform of the civil service—the institution of an examination system. The examination system opened the door to new avenues of employment, avenues which had been controlled by patronage alone, to the middle classes—although, putatively, these avenues were open to all. It must be remembered that in this new world the plan was to professionalize the civil service not to open it to all comers (Seaman, [1973] 1985, 202-203).

The finesse—the exclusion of the underclass from the civil service by a system of examinations that was fair in form but discriminatory in practice—was accomplished by the simple device of basing the examinations on traditional classical and literary subjects. Thus, success in those examinations remained the privilege of those who could afford the expensive curriculum of the "public school system" in general and, preferably, the Greater Public Schools, which had appropriated the traditional classical and literary curriculum as their private preserve.[18] Thus the examination system closed the civil service off to the broader population and created a powerful demand for the expensive product of the "public school system."[19]

The 1918 Education Act did little to change the definition of "an education." Nor did the act substantially alter the extension of education to the "lower classes." As Simon (1974, 297) notes, the entire interwar period was marked by the Geddes syndrome. The Geddes Committee convinced the middle class that the country could not afford a further extension of governmental-supported education. As a result the Labour government's attempt to extend education by raising the leaving age was defeated in the House of Lords in 1931 and the Spens Committee's recommendations to realize the spirit of R. H. Tawney's Labour Party education policy statement, *Secondary education for all* ([1922] 1988), was treated with indifference at best and at worst vilification (Simon, 1974, 296-297).

The commitment to an elitist segregated version of liberal education dating from the late 1920s strengthened the status differential between liberal and technical education and contributed to a proliferation of types of schools, and types of curriculums (Silver, 1983, 169). The English bifurcation of schooling proceeded along two lines: socioeconomic class and liberal versus technical curriculums. Schools of the highest status preserved the grammar school bias; they were socially exclusive and featured a humanist liberal curriculum. Schools of the lowest status were open to all and featured a technical (craft) curriculum. The proliferation of schools was indicative of a failure to respond to demands for more egalitarian versions of education and an inability to appropriate a status equivalent to liberal education for technical areas of study needed in a changing world and by society's new cultural hero, the scientist.

"An education" was and remained a celebration of English culture and Victorian virtues. "An education" was a liberal education. The social debate during and after World War I crystallized a version of liberal education that excluded technical, vocational, and most scientific forms of professional training from the realm of education. Technical education was lower class and menial. It was irrevocably connected to the sooty shops of British industrialism and antithetical to the faith of the establishment and large segments of middle-class society in the humanities. The mythology of the virtue of a liberal education was so well entrenched in British society that requests for technical education generated by reference to the relative decline of English industrialism were usually discounted or ignored even by the captains of British business and industry (Roderick and Stephens, 1981, 3-12; Silver, 1983, 151 172; Rolt, 1980, 148-177). Opposition to scientific or technical education as a matter of principle and adherence to the rightness of this formulation of liberal education would condition the form, conduct, and evolution of English education in the twentieth century (Roderick and Stephens, 1981).

The fact of and belief in a two-class system of education, shaped the fundamental social and intellectual context that foreshadowed the fund of questions and answers that would constitute part of the research agenda of educational philosophy in the 1960s. But more to the point it helped shape educational opinions of philosophers who became significant points of reference for the new discipline. Bertrand Russell, of course, was the most important of these philosophers.

## BERTRAND RUSSELL

The conviction of elitist liberals was that the "greater good," public and private (personal liberty), was served best by reserving "real" education for those who were able to take advantage of what it had to offer. This moral conviction emanated from the aura of Victorian culture. Beatrice and Sidney Webb, Shaw, Wells, Russell, and Whitehead all contributed to this tradition. Russell was especially important in that his books on education translated Victorian elitist liberal versions of educational values into popular and readable prose. In Britain the establishment found the social collectivism of the Webbs or Shaw's egalitarian social stance all a bit much, but they were willing to close one eye and embrace the social and intellectual elitism of Wells, and Russell. Like H. L. Mencken in the United States, elitist liberals of the period ridiculed or were at least suspicious of democracy, and when the opportunity presented itself they adulated an aristocratic version of social conduct, taste, and manners at the expense of individuals who could only aspire to but never achieve such social station.

In the period between the world wars elitist liberals such as Shaw, Wells, Russell, and Whitehead saw both the condition and the behavior of the underclass as a threat to the maintenance and extension of individual liberty, that is, to the new liberties and privileges of the middle class. The dangerous classes were a threat to social order. And a threat to social order was a threat to personal liberty. Russell understood that civil disorder generated state repression and a paternalistic state. Just as he was afraid that the state on the one hand or the collectivists on the other would find means and reason to curtail the personal liberty so laboriously extracted from Victorian authority, he was afraid of government schools that would kill the spark of liberty and genius. The position of elitist liberals is evident in Russell's writings on authority ([1949] 1968) and ethics, sex, and marriage (1987). In respect to education the stance is most obvious in Russell's *On education: Especially in early childhood* (1926).

In an apologetic tone, Russell wrote in his first book on education: "Progress should not be sacrificed to a mechanical equality at the present moment; we must approach educational democracy carefully, so as to destroy in the process as little as possible of the valuable products that happen to have been associated with social injustice" (Russell, 1926, 17). Russell articulated the belief that most of the aristocracy and the middle class felt in their hearts.

Even Russell could not escape the grasp of the commitment to an elitist segregated version of education which was pervasive. Russell turned to education and many other social topics only after his philosophical prowess had been spent in the intellectual labor required by the writing of the *Principia mathematica* ([1910-1913] 1927) (cf. McGinnis, 1988, 71-203). In Russell's books on schooling, *On education Especially in early childhood* (1926) and *Education and the modern world* (1932), he constructed his comments and apologetics about education which were those of a well-educated person remarking upon a less than perfect institution. In the introduction to the first book he went out of his way to point out that he was writing as a parent and not a philosopher. And later in *Education and the modern world*, written in 1932, he wrote:

Every social system has its appropriate educational instrument, which, in the case of the British oligarchy, was the public school—Eton first and foremost, but also, though in a lesser degree, such schools as Harrow, Winchester, and Rugby. Through the operation of these schools, the mentality of the eighteenth century aristocrat remained that of the holders of political power throughout the nineteenth century, in spite of profound changes in the nominal constitution. The public schools still exist, and are still regarded by most well-to-do Englishmen as embodying all that is best in our tradition. It is, therefore, still necessary to discuss their contribution to our national life. (74)

Lest this quotation be misleading, it should be remembered that Russell was one of the first to admit and perhaps require that education be democratic (1926, 16). But the petition was a matter of bad conscience. Similar to other Victorians, he was trapped between England's aristocratic history and his democratic impulses. Like many he was trying to find a way to condone democratic education without embracing its "herdlike" leveling quality. His comments might have been those of any well-educated English person of the time. He could not imagine how to deliver mass education without reducing it to the lowest common, indeed very common, denominator. Russell was committed to mass education, he just did not believe in it. His sentiments were a good deal like those of Harold Wilson who believed that the *intellectual* cost of education for all was just too high if it meant dismantling the public schools.

Russell's book-length comments on education could not be construed as philosophical even by the most charitable interpretation. But the sheer fact of Russell's interest in the topic of education suggested in an enticing manner that it might be suitable stuff for philosophical investigation. It was deemed philosophical by association—in some circles. Unfortunately, his comments did not leave much philosophical capital to draw upon. Moreover, the implication that philosophy and education did not mix, a conclusion easily drawn from Russell's comments in the introduction to *On education* was not lost on the English philosophical establishment.

## NOTES

1. Outside of the radical utilitarians, it was not until Herbert Spencer established education as a philosophical issue in the middle of the nineteenth century would England's intellectual establishment take serious note of domestic educational philosophy. Englishmen like Robert Owen found their inspiration in continentals like Claude-Adrien Helvétius, and later others would find a similar inspiration in the work of Rousseau, Montessori, Herbart, Pestalozzi, and Froebel.

2. The romantic obsession with children and childhood that was central to the Victorian period was not part of their utilitarianism. It certainly must be traced to Rousseau's *Emile* and *Sophie*—a segment of educational thought that was procured on license from the continent. Nevertheless, perhaps equally important domestic contributions were coming from the pens of Dickens, Lamb, and others.

3. Although the first of the essays that make up this book was published in 1854 in the *Westminster Review*, I have selected 1861, the point of their republication in the book *Education*, as the time from which to date educational philosophy's prehistory. It was at that time that the essays on education began to have not only their national but also their international impact.

4. In Spencer's view social science had a remarkably modern form. Social science was a device for the production of theory and explanation not social reform. It was this fundamental difference over the purposes of social science that set him at cross-purposes with the National Association for the Promotion of Social Science that believed it was social reform not the production of theory that was at the core of social science.

5. The Fabian Society was founded in 1883-1884 in London. It was dedicated to the establishment of a socialist and democratic state in Great Britain through education. Although its membership was always small it attracted some of the most important intellectuals of the period. They hoped to solve Great Britain's social difficulties through meetings, lectures, discussion groups, and conferences— that is, primarily through education—although they were not averse to generating and supporting strikes and other forms of direct resistance and social protest. An intellectual movement of the middle class, the Fabian Society frequently gathered in various cafés and private salons in the better parts of London to debate their ideas. Fabian salons became famous as hothouses of radical social thought.

6. Of course, Helvétius's work identifies with Locke's writing as much as it does with the writings of domestic thinkers like Jeremy Bentham and Tom Paine (Silver, 1969, 12-13).

7. John Ruskin, (1907), "Fors Clavigera, " in *The works of Ruskin* (vols. 27-29), eds. E. T. Cook and A. Wedderburn (London: George Allen); ([1852] 1904) "Modern education," *Stones of Venice*, in *The works of Ruskin*, (vol. 11, pp. 258-263); ([1865] 1905), "Sesame and lillies," in *The works of Ruskin* (vol. 18); ([1866] 1905a), "The crown of wild olive," in *The works of Ruskin*. (vol. 18); ([1866] 1905b), "The ethics of the dust," in *The works of Ruskin* (vol. 18); ([1867] 1905a), "Of public education irrespective of class-distinction," *Time and tide*, in *The works of Ruskin* (vol. 17, pp. 394-401); and ([1867] 1905b), and "The relations of education to position of life," Time and tide, in *The works of Ruskin*. (vol. 17, pp. 402-404 ).

8. John Ruskin, ([1867] 1905a), "Of public education irrespective of class-distinction," *Time and tide*, in *The works of Ruskin* (vol. 17, pp. 394-401), eds. E. T. Cook and A. Wedderburn (London: George Allen).

9. Educational theory in Ruskin's world, not surprisingly, reflected the ethos and worldview of Victorian culture. Insofar as it recognized the complexity of living in a rapidly industrializing society it recommended the reading of selected authors such as James and John Stuart Mill for liberals, Rousseau or Ruskin for those with Fabian tendencies, and the work of Herbart, Pestalozzi, and Froebel for those of a more romantic persuasion. It was a superficial prescription for understanding the self and society, and the educational institutions that serviced both.

10. Alexander Bain was professor of logic at the University of Aberdeen.

11. At this point it is particularly interesting to compare Paul Hirst's ([1965] 1974) argument for a "Liberal Education" with Alexander Bain's (1889) concern with the evil of "disproportion" in the curriculum and Mill's commitment to the centrality of philosophy cum humanities in a liberal education ([1867] 1985). Even out of context the arguments are similar; that is, both Bain and Mill present a spirited Victorian defense of a classical curriculum besieged by the continued demand of science and professional schools. Scientific areas of study demanded a larger and larger share of educational resources—largely at the expense of classics. Hirst's stance seems to be a rehearsal of the Victorian stance of Mill and Bain—albeit in the modern dress of analysis. Peters's opposition to technical education in *Ethics in education* (1966) does not read all that differently either.

12. In Great Britain the failure to see educational philosophy—at least in part—as a reaction to social science and the appropriation of educational questions by social science is the missing element in all other histories of the discipline.

13. A. C. Haddon's (1898-1899) Torres Straits Islands expedition foreshadowed the passing of speculative studies of human beings and their institutions.

14. Nevertheless, like many Victorian intellectuals he was a victim of psychosomatic illnesses. He endured suicidal depressions, hysterical blindness, and crippling spinal problems. He found a solution to his psychosis in his strength of character and his voluntaristic psychology. James presented his voluntaristic interpretation of mind in *Principles of psychology* (1890). After the publication of *Principles,* mind was no longer defined as merely a receptacle for the storage of "sensa" but was a mode of coping with the demands of the world.

15. In this Victorian version of things teacher training was relegated to the training colleges. They were poor institutions, and their economic poverty reflected the politically disenfranchised clientele their students served. Thus, both the study and the training of teachers suffered from disregard and neglect. As the McNair Report noted, a "trail of cheapness" marked the history of the training colleges (McNair, 1944, 13). Teacher training did not share the cozy, special relationship with the Treasury that the university establishment did.

16. In this context the term *bourgeoisie* refers both to the British middle class and to the British aristocracy.

17. Labor's confused educational demands, only nascent at this point, would finally be articulated by R. H. Tawney in the labor tract entitled "Secondary education for all," ([1922] 1988) after the turn of the century. Questions of distributive justice in the extension of education to the working class became a central element of the social reform discourse and the reserve of questions that was constitutive of educational philosophy particularly as education's philosophical questions were discussed and argued in the various reports and royal commissions so influential in the evolution of English education after World War II.

18. Moreover, an education beyond the elementary level was, for the most part, closed to the working class, and, to all intents and purposes a tertiary education at Oxford or Cambridge was the private preserve of the establishment (Lawson and Silver, 1973, 314-363).

19. As Simon noted, "No other country in the world paid such close attention at this time to the education of its governing class. Certainly no other country could boast so highly organised and segregated a system of schools in which pupils could be submitted to consistent social and moral as well as intellectual guidance. In the boarding school the total environment could be controlled to produce the desired result" (1965, 108).

# 7

# Education for All

The proliferation of segregated schooling; the inability to locate the whereabouts of frontiers between technical, professional, and liberal education; and Churchill's attempt to redeem his wartime promises on postwar social security in Beveridge's Report confused the issue of educational reform. Although the Beveridge Report paid little or no attention to education, it promised that things were going to be better and it foreshadowed the 1944 Education Act. Postwar educational reform was intended to remove the stigma of "lower-class" education from government schools (Lawson and Silver, 1973, 421). But the form of this "education without stigma" had yet to be determined when the war ended. The Norwood Committee recommended a tripartite education, in essence a "liberal education" for those children interested in learning for its own sake, a "modern" education for those students interested in science or the applied arts, and a "technical" education for those more immediately concerned with concrete things:

For example, English education has in practice recognized the pupil who is interested in learning for its own sake . . .
Such pupils, educated by the curriculum commonly associated with the Grammar School, have entered the learned professions or have taken up higher administrative or business posts . . .
Again, the history of technical education has demonstrated the importance of recognizing the needs of the pupil whose interests and abilities lie markedly in the field of applied science or applied art. The boy in this group has a strong interest in this direction and often the necessary qualities of mind to carry his interest through to make it his life-work at whatever level of achievement. He often has an uncanny insight into the intricacies of mechanism whereas the subtleties of language construction are too delicate for him . . .

The various kinds of technical school were not instituted to satisfy the intellectual needs of an arbitrarily assumed group of children, but to prepare boys and girls for taking up certain crafts—engineering, agriculture and the like . . .

Again, there has of late years been recognition, expressed in the framing of curricula and otherwise, of still another grouping of pupils, and another grouping of occupations. The pupil in this group deals more easily with concrete things than with ideas. He may have much ability, but it will be in the realm of facts. He is interested in things as they are; he finds little attraction in the past or in the slow disentanglement of causes or movements. His mind must turn its knowledge or its curiosity to immediate test; and his test is essentially practical . . .

Within this group fall pupils whose mental make-up does not show at an early stage pronounced leanings in a way comparable with the other groups which we indicated. (Norwood, 1943, 2-3)

The Norwood Committee's distinction were used to interpret, control, and perhaps in some sense defeat the 1944 Education Act's egalitarian tendencies. Like Bertrand Russell, the Norwood Committee recognized the demand for mass public education; they just did not believe in it. To them mass public education was just another well intentioned but misdirected means that would reduce English education to the lowest common denominator. The report disingenuously used the democratic and humanistic language of the New Education Fellowship to serve the purposes of England's public schools. The committee's report would help extend the half-life of elitist and class exclusive versions of schooling until well after the Festival of Britain in 1951. It was not until the 1960s that the promise of comprehensive education for all would be reconsidered. The English aristocracy still had little faith in the educability of those without social standing. A primary purpose of education for the masses was still a matter of instructing them in the natural social order and assisting them in recognizing and accepting that order.

For present purposes it is important to note how philosophical dialogue insofar as it concerned education was dominated by the language, agendas, and reports of the civil service. Even during World War II there was little sign that questions of educational philosophy were being consolidated into a single intellectual enterprise. Immediately after World War II L. A. Reid's work seemed to be running in a restrained fashion, parallel to and with little impact upon the aristocratic monopolies of learning. The success of the civil service in dominating educational language, what could be thought and discursively said about the undertaking, effectively flanked Reid's work. Educational philosophy could not emerge while its tasks were effectively dispersed among England's nascent social sciences, the nation's various great intellectual families, and dominated by the reports and commissions of the civil service.[1]

Nevertheless, the clear implication was that there was no going back to "before the war." There was going to be medical care, proper housing, and wise schooling for everyone, not just for a social elite. It mattered little that there were quiet and not so quiet grumblings in the middle class. The ideology of the Beveridge Report made it clear that if there was going to be social advantage and social discrimination after the war, it was not going to be Victorian. The egalitarianism of the wartime queue was the symbol of the Beveridge Report and the society to which it spoke (Lloyd, [1979] 1989, 246). Postwar Britain meant fair shares and no untoward advantage for the establishment. The ideology and promise of the queue was that if everyone shared equally, and if no one was greedy, tomorrow would be better for everyone (Lloyd, [1979] 1989, 246).

The obsessive preoccupation of the tertiary establishment during the immediate postwar years was the reestablishment of England's university system. With physical plants ravaged by the war (bombed by the Germans and appropriated for the war effort by the armed services), staffs depleted (some staff lost to the war and almost a generation of aspiring academics who had deferred their education), and educational and experimental equipment not replaced since 1939, the first concern of the vice-chancellors was to restore the national and international intellectual preeminence of the nation's universities. Historically universities had had privileged access to the Treasury and a self-justifying amount of prestige, academic success, and international recognition. Unfortunately, in a country almost bankrupt by the war, the tradition of privileged access to the nation's purse was no longer a solution to the universities' difficulties (Stewart, 1989, 71-72; Marwick, [1982] 1988, 23).

The teacher training colleges were another story. After the 1944 Education Act, England's universities could have made a direct contribution to the instruction of teachers (Stewart, 1989, 70-72), but the task of rebuilding Britain's universities was seen as more important than upgrading the colleges of teacher education that had struggled financially since the moment of their inception. In intellectual circles the colleges were eschewed as centers of learning (Stewart, 1989, 69). University staff believed that training-college status had to be raised dramatically if teacher education was to become one of the professional schools of the university. English vice-chancellors were disinclined to take up any suggestion of a direct participation in teacher education at the university level (Stewart, 1989, 70). In Stewart's words:

The familiar university experience created the amateur assumption that no one needed to undertake any preparation as a teacher to enter the university teaching profession. Academic excellence in the discipline was the primary requirement and the basic criterion for esteem in the fraternity of scholars. Any skills necessary for effective undergraduate presentation, any consideration of criteria for the selection of courses and how to construct them were seen as the kind of things which any intelligent man or woman could work out for him/herself. (1989, 71)

The naïveté of the lecture assumption allayed among the academics of the university the further idea that perhaps the lecture was not the most efficient or effective—let alone the only—manner of teaching. It promoted the mischievous idea that primary and secondary teaching was a self-evident activity. It also encouraged the university community to reach the fatuous conclusion that there was nothing to know about education.[2]

England's educators were interested in something else. Closer to "the people" than England's tertiary institutions, the country's educators were busy trying to implement the spirit of the Beveridge Report (1942) and the explicit promises of the 1944 Education Act. Although the Beveridge Report was silent on the mission of England's primary and secondary educational establishment, the 1944 Education Act committed that establishment to eradicating England's most irritating educational inequities. In a very broad sense it was a commitment to realizing the spirit of R. H. Tawney's Labour Party education policy statement, *Secondary education for all* ([1922] 1988). The actual initial redistribution of educational resources in the 1944 Act was extended in the immediate postwar period by the modest determination of Atlee's Labour government to banish an elitist and socially segregated version of liberal education. It was a commitment that both Conservative and Labour governments in years to come would find impossible to abandon and difficult to avoid although they ensured its implementation was anything but rapid. And just as the 1944 Education Act directed educational planning, until the arrival of the Robbins Report (1963) the national economy conditioned what the act promised. England was £3,000 thousand million in debt, stripped of its colonies, and faced with an empire coming apart at the seams. Social and educational reform were conditioned by one fiscal crisis after the other (Marwick, [1982] 1988). Shortages of buildings, equipment, and teachers made the achievement of anything more than a bare implementation of the provisions of the 1944 act impossible (Marwick, [1982] 1988, 60). Nevertheless, there was no going back. The educational system was made more egalitarian, and secondary education for all in one form or another was the order of the day.

After the Robbins Report (1963) a concentration on subspecialization in education research and teaching was possible. The subspecialization signaled the professionalization of the university study of education. The idea of a professionalized version of educational theory, with specialized subdisciplines, a systematic program of organized research, objective standards, and an organized group of investigators proctoring each others' research and transmitting that research to the offices of government and the profession became a reality. Educational history, psychology, sociology, and philosophy all professionalized. The period between 1940 and the mid-1960s brought a new emphasis on psychology and history (Stewart, 1989, 76).

In a sense, educational philosophy remained in the "public" domain in the years immediately following World War II. And, of course, as long as it remained in the public domain there was little reason for either governments or universities to provide some special place for its study. To a large extent the delayed establishment of educational philosophy was a function of the lack of broad support it found in the country's intellectual aristocracy and university establishment.

## POSTWAR PREFACE TO EDUCATIONAL PHILOSOPHY

Philosophy of education was, truly, a new member of the university created by the political whirlwind of the postwar period. It was established by the social, economic, and demographic events of the times as well as by the hopes and expectations of English academic politics in the postwar period (see Simon, 1983; Silver, 1983, 149-278). It was a product of the explosive population increase in the postwar period and the advent of postindustrial society (Simon, 1983, 1). It was the child of industrialization and urbanization and of all the social forces that conjoined to refuse a return to the organization of work that had existed "before the war" (Lloyd, [1979] 1989, 295). Rejected also was a closed social system, a remnant of Victorian society that existed in England between the wars. Unlike other members of England's academic establishment, educational philosophy joined England's sophisticated intellectual establishment in the mid-sixties practically by spontaneous political generation. The invention of educational philosophy was a great deal like the invention of political philosophy; that is, just as political philosophy was a product of political events and a particular historical and socioeconomic situation (cf. Laslett and Cummings, 1967, vol. 6, 370), philosophy of education was generated by the political, historical, socioeconomic, and educational situation of the period following World War II.

All of the "educational foundations" were late appearing on the English scene. What passed for educational philosophy was a grab bag of aphorisms gleaned from individuals important in the intellectual history of the West (Peters, 1983). Psychology focused on the pioneering work of Burt, Spearman, and Godfrey Thompson (Stewart, 1989, 76). Sociology of education did not really appear until after World War II and then it initially was inspired by Karl Mannheim's work (Simon, 1983, 4). English educational history tended to be a rehearsal of the findings and work of various committees and royal commissions (Silver, 1983, 176). Moreover, educational philosophy's establishment as a university subject was largely the result of external social and political pressures rather than the result of any particular academic accomplishment (cf. Simon, 1983, 1).[3]

The 1950s and 1960s brought educational sociology and educational philosophy firmly into the university folds. The establishment of modern versions of the university with a de-emphasis upon philosophy and classics and a new place for science and social science was viewed by the conservative establishment as something more than a slightly suspect phenomenon (Marwick, [1982] 1988, 95). Nevertheless, Raymond Williams's *Culture and society* (1958) and Richard Hoggart's *Uses of literacy* (1957) had paved the way for sociology into the university establishment. Working in the twilight area between literary criticism and sociology, they provided a protocol of academic work familiar to English dons. Their work offered a strong legitimation for social science at the University of London and at totally new universities such as Sussex, York, Kent, Warwick, Lancaster, East Anglia, Essex, and Stirling.

In the late 1950s and early 1960s the sociology of Basil Bernstein and Jean Floud found support in Harold Wilson's Labour politics. Richard Peters's educational philosophy championed the sentiments of the conservative education establishment. This period marked the fruition of the implicit promise evident in the eclectic work of Percy Nunn in the 1920s and Fred Clark's tentative sociological investigations of educational effects.[4] Educational psychology and history made their first serious contributions in the period before World War II. Educational sociology entered the university establishment in the 1940s through the influence of Fred Clark, Director of the London Institute of Education. His book *Education and social change* (1940), launched sociology of education (Simon, 1983, 7; 1991, 376). Of course, the educational studies and presence of Karl Mannheim at the institute during the war years greatly assisted the completion of what Clark had begun. Jean Floud and Basil Bernstein each brought a professionalized version of educational investigation to the educational database that social science had been slowly amassing since the organization of the National Association for the Promotion of Social Science in 1857, and Richard Peters and Paul Hirst brought a similar version of educational investigation to educational philosophy that was promised as early as 1693 in the work of John Locke. Both sociology and educational philosophy brought a professionalized version of investigation to the university study of education.

A place for education was more difficult to establish. Not yet underpinned by any generally accepted theoretical position (Simon, 1983, 7-8), it was established by the vortex of postwar reconstruction. Philosophy was drafted by the academic establishment to provide a general theoretical position for education. The draft was foreshadowed by the appointment of L. A. Reid to the nation's first chair of educational philosophy at the London Institute of Education. But Reid's work did not lend itself to the provision of general theoretical structures; soft and humanist, it did not fit within positivist versions of theory. Reid's successor R. S. Peters provided education with something that looked like a general theoretical base and a plausible legitimation for the university study of education.

In practice the ideals, promises, and committee reports made little difference to the actual process of educating in the 1950s and 1960s. The demand for educational reform remained, the political debate continued, and the resistance to change was undiminished. But in this case, public concern was not pacified by the traditional solution of yet another bifurcation of the existing educational system. Questions about educational opportunity remained matters of strident public discussion. Moreover, government reports demonstrated growing concern about the role of social factors in observable differences in schooling between groups of different socioeconomic class, ethnicity, and gender. Other reports reflected concern about problems of manpower and the adequacy of technical and scientific training. In addition the process of university expansion was already under way. This expansion generated diversified and unconventional university curriculums. New institutions, Sussex University in particular, rapidly established academic reputations of their own and challenged the formerly unrivaled colleges of Cambridge and Oxford, which were forced to modernize their curriculums to meet the challenge of the new universities (Lawson and Silver, 1973, 431-447).

The discussions of education related to social policy and social reform became more strident after the election of the Labour government of Harold Wilson. The cutting edge of this debate revolved around the comprehensive school (Silver, 1983, 265). and pointed away from the contretemps generated about the differences and similarities of technical and liberal education that had dominated educational commissions' reports and debates in the 1920s and 1930s (although there were many similarities). In essence, it followed the general concern of the Beveridge Report and the explicit concerns of the 1944 Education

Act. In educational terms, the debate was concerned with the role of schooling in the delivery of social welfare and social reform and in a sense it was an attempt to address questions raised before the turn of the century by the National Association for the Promotion of Social Science. Obliquely the educational debate addressed the concepts and facts of poverty, social justice, social class, social change, fairness, equality of access and opportunity, streaming, testing, selecting, school use, and success.

## THE TEACHERS COLLEGES

Unarguably, the inception of educational philosophy in Great Britain was more closely related to the fund of questions and answers that constituted philosophy than it was in the United States. But the genesis of educational philosophy in its own name and in its own right in the nation's universities is only partially attributable to philosophy.[5] The prehistory of educational philosophy is closely related to the history of the country's teachers colleges, just as the teachers colleges were tied to the Victorian impulse for social reform. The establishment of educational philosophy was part an attempt to improve the intellectual and academic standing of the colleges. English academics in general and philosophers in particular hoped that a good dose of philosophy might give education—now foisted upon the universities by the Robbins Report (among other things and events)—an intellectual rigor that they were only too sure it did not possess, and like sociology, to their minds, probably could not possess. The elite university establishment expected and demanded that educational philosophy make the study of education academically respectable. The putative grounding of the discipline in the long history of philosophy was expected to legitimize the study of education within the university establishment by setting up terms of reference, pioneering "fundamental" research, and developing a mode of academic discourse recognizable to English dons. In one sense then, philosophy of education was created by the academic expectations of the establishment. Drafted by the establishment to generate a general theoretical position for the university study of education, the new discipline took up its allotted task with great energy (Simon, 1983, 8). While the government was expected to erase the trail of economic destitution that dogged the training colleges from their inception in the 1860s (cf. McNair, 1944, 13-14), educational philosophy was to erase the trail of low expectation and intellectual poverty that had marked the curriculum of teacher training colleges and therein teacher education.

The creation of an academic infrastructure for educational philosophy at the London Institute was an act of faith in the efficacy of humanities in general and philosophy in particular, any explanation of the inclusion of educational philosophy in Britain's tertiary establishment based upon its academic power would be decidedly unconvincing. The academic establishment believed that philosophy could fundamentally alter the study of education and that was that. The disciplines that contributed most to the study of education were philosophy (prior to World War I), psychology, history (between the two World Wars) and sociology (during and directly after World War II). Educational philosophy did not develop a systematic literature until late in the 1960s. But it should be remembered that there was precious little in the way of systematic educational literature extant. What is amazing is the meager supply of educational research. Professors of education were initially caught up in administrative work and there was little time or energy for research (Simon, 1983, 2-3). Education was a "rule of thumb business with a semi-amateur status that traded upon aphoristic accounts of teaching" (Silver, 1983, 177).

Britain always had had a supply of talented philosophers and intellectual tourists who were willing to comment upon education, but there was very little in the way of any systematic educational research or literature. Locke, John Stuart Mill, Ruskin, Spencer, Huxley, and Russell all wrote about education. And, to be sure, there were interlopers—men that never made any pretense about being philosophers, let alone philosophers of education. For example, successful educational administrators like T. Percy Nunn and labor politicians and polemicists like R. H. Tawney were influential individuals who had, respectively, immense impact upon the substance and conduct of education, teacher education, and educational policy.[6]

In its modern founding the discipline was foreshadowed by not much more than Percy T. Nunn's *Education: Its data and first principles* ([1920] 1947). Additional contributions in the years to follow were Bertrand Russell's *On education* (1926), Whitehead's *Aims of education* ([1929] 1957), C. D. Hardie's *Truth and fallacy in educational theory* ([1942] 1962), D. J. O'Connor's *An introduction to the philosophy of education* (1957), and L. A. Reid's *Philosophy of education* (1962). But it was Nunn's book that interested Britain's educators.

Percy Nunn's *Education: Its data and first principles* (1920) was representative of the strange amalgam of philosophy, psychology, sociology and history that marked the transitional period. Percy Nunn, Director of the London Institute of Education, wrote what must have been the most successful text for teacher education in the period between the wars. He insured its success with a profusion of philosophical and literary allusions and appropriate quotations that mightily appealed to educators and dons alike. And while educational philosophy found an impetus in the work of Percy Nunn so did educational psychology— one of educational philosophy's most significant competitors.

Nunn's book was an impressive success. The fact that he was Director of the London Institute of Education must have helped promote the sales of what was, at the time, a very impressive text. *Education* ran through twenty reprintings and two editions by the time World War II fixed the Empire's attention upon the conduct of the war (Simon 1983, 6). The book was a grab bag of psychometrics, classicism, and salon literature. Its faith in psychology was almost quaint and its philosophy was Victorian. The collection of literary allusions to education, schools, students, and teachers was utopian in its perspective. From a modern perspective it was hardly a "shilling shocker" or the hard hitting prose of R. H. Tawney's (1918] 1964a; [1918] 1964b) labour repudiation of the nation's educational policy. But, then again, it was hardly the maudlin prose of *Tom Brown's school days* either. It was one of the first examples of a professional literature for educators. It was also progressive education's most successful British text (Silver 1983, 159). Nunn's book cited, noted, or quoted a host of classical philosophers, literary figures, and social scientists (Aristotle, Alexander, Marcuse Aurelius, Jane Austen, Bosanquet, Browning, Ibsen, Croce, Darwin, Decartes, Dewey, Epictetus, Hegel, Hobbes, James, Kant, Kafka, Piaget, Pascal, Rousseau, Russell, Schiller, Shaw, and Veblen to name only the most recognizable). By implication the text alluded to a potential literature upon which educational philosophy might one day draw. He convinced, at least some, of philosophy's potential to comment upon, guide and, in some cases, suggest solutions to questions of English educational practice.

Prior to Nunn's book educational "knowledge," knowledge of educational techniques, had been, largely, gleaned from European educators such as Friedrich Froebel, Johann Heinrich Pestalozzi, and Johann Friedrich Herbart, (cf. Simon 1983, 4). It was leavened with various versions of Arnoldian culture (Rothblatt, 1974), and given modern dress at a later point in time with the psychology and statistical work of Karl Pearson, Cyril Burt, Charles Spearman, and Godfrey Thompson. Educational theory at this time was dedicated to the humanization of educational practice and the delivery of educational service at an inexpensive price. But it was characterized by the first dim awareness of the importance of learning theory in educational practice and a certain romantic individualism that was infatuated with the natural goodness and innocence of childhood.

R. H. Tawney, the principal author and public advocate for Labour's Consultative Committee on Education wrote powerful tracts on the class segregation of English education. Nunn and R. H. Tawney might have brought some unity to the endeavor. But Nunn was too busy running one of Britain's most important institutions and R. H. Tawney was caught up with direct political action and class politics in the sunset of Victorian England. Nunn's book was indicative of the Victorian educational stance. Insofar as the book was psychological, it was devoted to questions of learning achievement and the measurement of educational effects. And insofar as it was philosophical it was directed toward a democratic ideal (Nunn [1920] 1947, 12-13). Both it and Dewey's *Democracy and education* (1916), were concerned with community and individual excellence. But Nunn's book was safely anchored outside of the issues of social and educational reform and political democracy. An eclectic version of Herbartianism (see Simon 1983, 4) it vacillated between philosophy and social science. In a sense, *Education* followed the classical path that social science had marked years before. With its foundations clearly in philosophy it was quietly moving questions of education out of the realm of philosophy into the realm of education.

Russell's book took a place in the discipline's literature not unlike the place that Margaret Mead's *Coming of age in Samoa* ([1928] 1968) took in the literature of anthropology—a pioneering, interesting, salable, but not very philosophical cameo. Bearing silent witness to the promise of analysis, although strangely outside of the undertaking, was Alfred North Whitehead's *Aims of education* ([1929] 1957). C. D. Hardie's book was largely ignored in Britain and in Australasia where he took up a chair of education at the University of Tasmania in 1946; *Truth and fallacy in educational theory* ([1942] 1962) went out of print without much ado (Hardie 1985). D. J. O'Connor's book attracted more interest in the United States than in Britain, where Israel Scheffler was working along lines similar to those of O'Connor and Hardie. O'Connor's book seems to have been one of the important intellectual constructions that philosophers of education in the United States used to adopt analysis as a central mode of practice in the period following World War II.

And while it must also be admitted that Britain's New Education Fellowship showed a certain interest in Montessori, Herbart, Pestalozzi, and Froebel, in the final analysis their work never became a major consideration in the discipline.[7] If anything the thought of these writers was more a matter of something to be dealt with, that is, something to be marginalized. The ideas of these educators were deemed to be something the teachers colleges could review in the name of intellectual or educational ideas if they were not up to the task of philosophical analysis. Judging pragmatism to be intellectually soft and fatally infected by the Progressive Education Movement, Britain largely ignored the educational philosophy that America generated between the Great Wars (Armytage, 1967, 75). It was something to be transcended, a historical artifact at best. Certainly pragmatism was nothing to be taken too seriously.

Educational philosophy had been announced but what remained to be delivered was the product and the infrastructure necessary for its production. The discipline required recruits. Neophyte staff from philosophy and education had to be enlisted. The academic role of the educational philosopher had to be defined and defended from various academic competitors. The nature of its discourse and the linguistic practices appropriate to its discourse needed to be identified and publicized. The nature of discourse appropriate to the community and the fund of questions that would constitute an academic mandate still needed to be defined. The linguistic protocols of competent practice were yet to be modeled. And social devices to proctor the community had yet to be established. In other words, the work of men like Locke, James and John Stuart Mill, Ruskin, Spencer, Huxley, and Russell announced the possibility of something like educational philosophy and prospectively contributed to the questions and answers that would, one day, constitute educational philosophy's research domain, but their work did not provide the linguistic practices or the literary and social technology necessary to sustain the discipline. Both the work of education's philosophical tourists and academic interlopers would contribute material to the literature of education but neither group would establish the educational philosophy as an academic enterprise—a contribution to a literature or even a literature is not an academic discipline, although it is an important antecedent.

## L. A. REID

Before the work of the discipline's executive scholar R. S. Peters can be discussed later in this chapter, attention needs to be paid to the work of Louis Arnaud Reid the discipline's pioneer. Reid and Peters, both professional philosophers, played an important intellectual and managerial role in establishing the university study of educational philosophy. But their efforts should not be confused with the diffident contribution to the discipline from academic philosophy. As Reid

(1966, 11) noted, his academic colleagues as a whole were not very much interested in education. Both Peters and Reid were drafted from academic philosophy to launch educational philosophy as an academic enterprise. With the appointment of L. A. Reid to the chair of educational philosophy at the Institute of Education, philosophy of education joined the ranks of those elements of the social sciences that were continuing to be segregated out of moral philosophy into academic disciplines in their own right—although not quite "established" in the university system.

Reid came to the Institute's Chair of Educational Philosophy as an established professor of philosophy. Completing his studies he took up a position in 1919 as assistant lecturer in philosophy at the University College, Aberystwyth—a constituent of the University of Wales. Later in his career he would move on to the University of Liverpool, where between the years of 1926 to 1932 he was senior (independent) lecturer, and head of the Department of Ancient Philosophy and Political Philosophy (Reid, n.d., chap 4, 11). From 1932-1947 he was professor of philosophy at Armstrong College (now University of Newcastle upon Tyne). From this secure chair he was appointed to the first chair of educational philosophy at the University of London's Institute of Education.

Philosophy of education played out its first gambits in the educational reconstruction and reform generated by the postwar world. Modest in terms of its establishment, the discipline began as a small academic department headed by L. A. Reid at the London Institute of Education (Peters, 1983, 33). Reid took educational philosophy's first chair in 1947, a point in time that long preceded the dramatic growth during the discipline's adolescence.[8] It fell to Reid to fight the preliminary political battles within the university establishment and recruit the staff that would one day provide his energetic successor, R. S. Peters, with the institutional base from which to establish philosophy of education as an academic enterprise within the English university establishment.

He was appointed largely because he was a "legitimate" philosopher and because he had written several articles concerned with educating. The fact that he was untutored in the study of education was relevant to his selection. It was in fact a major recommendation.[9] Like Peters who was to follow him, it was hoped that Reid would bring the academic sophistication, insight, and intellectual standards of the academic establishment to the world of teacher education. He nursed the discipline through its academic infancy. And it was not a particularly easy infancy. Reid by his own account noted that many of his students and colleagues as well as professional educators found the whole idea of devoting some period of a postprofessional year to the study of educational philosophy—at a time when all and sundry seemed obsessed by the immediate problems of classroom practice—somewhat outrageous (Reid, 1966, 18-19). Reid found himself in a situation in which he was barely tolerated both by the academic establishment and by "schoolies" alike. Development of the institute's new initiative was slow. It is only fair to say that until Peters was appointed in 1962 the discipline was, still, little more than an aspiration of the London Institute.

Prior to and during Reid's appointment, the subject was largely absent from the curriculum of most universities, and at colleges of education it took the form of the "Great Educators" approach. This approach was a guided tour of comments about education from various individuals important in the intellectual or educational history of the West. Divorced, usually, from the historical context that would give meaning to the comments under examination, these courses, like those in the United States, were philosophical only in the most nominal sense of the word and contributed little to the development of a meaningful and interesting form of discourse in the philosophy of education (Peters, 1983, 31). But be that as it may, it was L. A. Reid who first attempted to bring academic philosophy to England's teachers with an eye to the requirements of their work. In the late 1940s Reid was successful in establishing an Easter Conference on philosophy for teachers—a conference that remains an enduring part of the curriculum of the department of philosophy at the London Institute of Education.[10] His personality did not lend itself to the dynamic kind of institution building at which Richard Peters felt so at ease. And yet Reid's solid Calvinism would not let him rest. It fell to Reid to write, not to build. Reid was busy writing the some of the first contributions to the discipline's domestic literature. In the course of his career he wrote, by his own account, nine books and about a hundred papers (Reid, 1966, 3).[11]

It is impossible to understand Reid's work without reference to his literary concerns. After a "preliminary skirmish" with engineering as an undergraduate he became obsessed with the questions of philosophy. He also read fine arts and literature, two areas of study that were enduring intellectual concern. Reid had abandoned engineering for literature, poetry, and philosophy and his philosophy ran quickly back to its aesthetic predicate (see Reid, 1931). His writing was soft and romantic with obvious links to England's and America's literary guild.

In Chapter 3 (entitled "Edinburgh") of his unpublished autobiography Reid recounts his seduction by the humanities:

Laing taught me to love English literature . . . He taught me as much about English composition and the elegance of style as anyone ever has, and through him I got the beginning of an insight into criticism.

Apart from all this, I made a new friend, Alastair Shannon. He was finishing his first year of Philosophy at the University . . . We made acquaintance over a model railway I had constructed in a shed in the garden: this acquaintance was a turning-point in my life. Shannon's interests were in philosophy and literature. He was a disciple of Bergson and introduced me to *Creative Evolution* and *Matter and Memory*. He lent me both of these, saying at the same time "You'll never get through them". But I did. It was at this time that I fell head-over-heels in love with philosophy. And with poetry too . . . I spent a lot of time I ought to have been working at other things, writing and writing, as well as reading all the poets I could get hold of—starting, I think, with Walt Whitman, with, of course, reams and reams of Swinburne which I spouted to myself when out on the solitary walks I have always enjoyed . . . The glowing summer of 1914 was (apart from the examination preparation) a time of glowing intoxication with poetry and philosophy. I lived in a delightful dream, reading and arguing and learning and writing. And, towards the end of the summer I came to the conclusion that philosophy and poetry (with music then as a subsidiary) were *my métier*, and that whilst interests in engineering might remain, they would do so in the background. (n.d., 13-14) [12]

Upon Reid's retirement in the early sixties his work and its aesthetic or literary critique of education was abandoned by the discipline in the name of a more rigorous philosophical fashion: analysis.

## LIONEL ELVIN AND THE INSTITUTE

A central role in the establishment of the discipline was played by members of the London Institute of Education and its director, Lionel Elvin. They prepared the way for the massive postwar expansion of schooling in Britain just as they prepared for a massive expansion of the institutional base for the study of education. That expansion would provide the impetus and organizational infrastructure and educational resources and diversification of educational studies that reached fruition in the 1970s. The expansion made educational philosophy possible (cf. Simon, 1983, 8). It was Lionel Elvin who decided to recruit Richard Peters. Author of the teacher education section of the Robbins Report, Elvin decided on the importance of philosophy for the study of education. In at least a modest sense, the discipline was created by the fiat of the London Institute and Director Elvin's academic preferences. The fact that the institute wanted to maintain a chair of educational philosophy at all was at least partially a function of Elvin's deep and abiding faith in "liberal education" (see Elvin, 1977, 46-61). In Elvin's words, "The London Institute was big enough to have and demand whatever it wanted" (Elvin, 1989). And the institute wanted the leavening effect of philosophy in the institute's teacher education curriculum. As far as Elvin was concerned philosophy was the keystone of a liberal education and it was the keystone of teacher education. The Director appointed Richard Peters.

## R. S. PETERS

Peters, formerly a reader in psychology and philosophy at Birkbeck College, moved to the London Institute early in the 1960s. A philosopher by vocation and training and a philosophical psychologist by occupation, his career aspirations were frustrated at Birkbeck by a department of experimentalists. Although supported by his then head of department, Professor Mace, it was apparent to Peters that the domination of experimentalism would prevent him from ever succeeding Professor Mace to the chair (Elvin, 1989). The frustration of Peters's career ambitions at Birkbeck combined with his collateral interest in education made it possible for Elvin to recruit Peters as successor to the chair of education at the institute. It was still England's only chair of education.

Peters's decision to join the Institute had immense impact. Paul Hirst indicates that the news of Peters's decision to join the Institute was greeted with great excitement (Hirst, 1989). Peters brought a substantial reputation to the chair. He had written a philosophically successful book entitled: *The concept of motivation* (1958) and another successful book with Stanley Benn, *The principles of political thought* ([1959] 1965). Once appointed to the Chair of Educational Philosophy at the University of London, Institute of Education, Peters immediately attempted a task analogous to the one he had taken up in psychology: He had earlier determined to rid psychology of the conceptual confusions and a low level of argumentation that diminished the theoretical power of psychology. Transferring his not inconsiderable energies to the study of education he found a similar intellectual task. He was determined to rid education of the "conceptual mush" that confounded meaningful investigations of the discipline. It was not a long step from the analysis of motivation to the questions of education.[13]

Richard Peters was, largely, responsible for providing the initiative, energy, groundwork, and academic capital necessary for doing what education's philosophical tourists and interlopers had left undone. It was Peters who would provide the literary and social technology to establish the discipline as a member of the university community by initiating the Philosophy of Education Society of Great Britain. It was his energy, talent and drive that set the society in motion and provided the predicate for its organization. Under his leadership educational philosophy would eclipse educational psychology, sociology, and history as the core of educational studies (Simon, 1983, 4). For the duration of Peters's career, Britain's educators looked to educational philosophy for insights into education in a way that they had never done before.

An intellectual discipline is established by its societies. But it is defined by its elites and it was Richard Peters who did just that (Larson, 1977, 227; Toulmin, 1972). It was Peters, the second professor of educational philosophy at the London Institute of Education, who spoke to Britain's academic establishment, the profession, and the public. It was Peters who maintained the image of a unified and scholarly community and who presented the intellectual aspirations of educational philosophy to an England that was busily attempting to construct a more egalitarian version of schooling—an educational system that would provide secondary education for all. Perhaps, most important, it was Peters who was constitutive, at least in the early days, of educational philosophy's "authoritative" reference group. He was the "gatekeeper" of the profession for those constructing their careers, competing for academic recognition, the esteem of their colleagues, and places of honor within educational philosophy and the intellectual establishment.

Public and academic recognition of philosophy of education as a professional discipline within the English academic establishment was, for the most part, a result of the appointment of Peters to the chair at the London Institute in 1962. In his 1963 inaugural lecture, "Education as Initiation," he laid claim to the area of philosophy of education and proclaimed the philosophical analysis of "education" as central to the philosophy of education (Dearden, [1979] 1984, 22–25; Peters, 1983). In England, educational philosophy's first academic success began with analytic philosophy. It was Peters who brought the genius and style of the Oxford  school of philosophy and Wittgenstein's brand of philosophical thought to philosophy of education in Britain.

Like Reid, Peters was directly recruited from philosophy, but unlike his predecessor, Peters was an academic politician. He defined the discipline's professional literature, but also recruited the neophytes necessary to establish the profession, saw to their promotion, and established an institutionalized forum for professional discourse. He modeled and advertised the linguistic protocols of competent practice on the radio and in the United Kingdom's only professional journal (*The Proceedings of the Philosophy of Education Society of Great Britain*). He spoke in the lecture halls of England's universities and teachers colleges and directed the social network that proctored competent practice. By 1970 the discipline had become an academic profession: a chair was established at Kings, more chairs would soon follow in other places, a professional society was launched (*The Philosophy of Education Society of Great Britain*), and its journal was in print.

Following Peters's lead, it was no longer allowable for "real" philosophers of education to be interested in scholasticism for educators, tales about the Great Educators, or stories about the implications of idealism, realism, and so on for schooling; nor was it allowable to be interested in folk wisdom and aphorisms about education enunciated by parents, teachers, and administrators. "Pure" philosophers could no longer address the issue of education *ex cathedra*—although it must be admitted that a certain dispensation was granted to those individuals who could claim membership in the philosopher's guild. Or, more precisely, Peters saw the discipline's task, in the first case, as part of or constitutive of an attempt to tie education to a moral transcendental and thereby remove the discipline from the realm of everyday political discourse. He saw the discipline's second occupation as the attempt to free intelligence from the confusions of language. Third, and analogously, its next occupation was to free education's paradigm from the confusions of its own ill-formed discourse. Last, he thought it was important to reclaim a goodly portion of educational discourse for philosophy. Professional practice was defined (see Peters, 1983, 33; Simon, 1983, 8). From then on there was little or no place left for the work of autodidacts, philosophical tourists, or even quasi-professionals of previous generations—except, perhaps, as they were useful to demonstrate the interesting intellectual curiosities of another time. Amateurism was on the decline and the establishment of a profession was under way.

In a sense, the new discipline followed an academic history that paralleled British philosophy in the twentieth century. Just as British philosophy was mortgaged to the "linguistic turn" (e.g. Ayer, [1936] 1946; Ryle, [1949] 1964)—the triumvirate of epistemology, analysis, and metaphysics (see Rorty, 1967)—educational philosophy in Britain was indebted to some of the same creditors. But the mortgage was not established until well after World War II (Dearden, 1982; Hirst, 1982; Peters, 1983; Tice and Slavens, 1983, 492-493). Foreshadowed by C. D. Hardie's *Truth and fallacy in educational theory* ([1942] 1962) and D. J. O'Connor's *An introduction to the philosophy of education* (1957), analysis became established as the method of educational philosophy with the publication of R. S. Peters's *Ethics and education* (1966).

answers that was constitutive of educational philosophy in the United States found its inspiration in the social reform movement of the 1890s, while the reservoir of questions and answers that was constitutive of educational philosophy in Britain was inspired by philosophy—if not the desire to "cool out" some of the excesses of the educational reform movement inspired by the Robbins (e.g. Wilson, 1979, 15-43) and Plowden Reports (e.g. Dearden, 1976), and social science. Peters tied the discipline he was constructing tightly to ethics and the academic culture of philosophy, a virtue that John Wilson commended in *Preface to the philosophy of education* (1979, ix).

Having established philosophical analysis as central to the philosophy of education and having brought a certain respectability to the new discipline by way of his own personal reputation within "pure" philosophy, Peters then set about establishing the Philosophy of Education Society of Great Britain. The preliminary work for the founding of the society was accomplished in the 1963-1964 academic year (Philosophy of Education Society of Great Britain [PESGB], 1964a, 1964b). After consulting various bodies, a steering committee to "draw up the arrangements for the official founding of the Society" was established: "The Steering Committee was composed of Professor R. S. Peters, Professor L. A. Reid, Mr. C. H. Bailey, Mr. R. F. Dearden, Mr. M. A. B. Degenhardt, Mr. P. H. Hirst, Miss B. H. Hosegood, Mr. T. W. Moore, Mr. K. Neuberg, Dr. L. R. Perry, Mr. H. T. Sockett and Mrs. J. White" (PESGB, 1964). The society held its first annual general meeting on 13 December 1964 (PESGB, 1964b). President: Professor Louis Arnaud Reid; Chairman: Professor R. S. Peters; Secretary: Mr. P. H. Hirst. In 1967 the first volume of the *Proceedings of the Philosophy of Education Society of Great Britain* was published. The steering committee suggested the following officers: L. A. Reid was the first president of the society; Peters was chairman of the society. Paul Hirst took responsibility for the office of secretary, and Mr. K. Neuberg was treasurer (PESGB, 1964b).

The Philosophy of Education Society of Great Britain was modeled on philosophy's Aristotelian Society. The society was predicated upon an ideology of exclusive professionalism. Membership in the society was an necessary condition of participating in the discipline. Moreover, it was an important condition for publication in the society's journal. Neither the public nor educators were encouraged or invited to the "real" discussions of the society—it knowingly excluded educators. Although it was sympathetic and concerned about teachers and the schools, the society understood the academic (university) disdain for "schoolies" and was careful to avoid being associated with them.[14] Its form was designed to gain the approval of philosophy and encourage the participation of academic philosophers.

The difference between philosophy of education in Britain and the Commonwealth and philosophy of education in the United States can be found in the manner in which Dewey departed from metaphysics and Peters did not. Dewey abandoned metaphysics for physics (see Dewey, [1925] 1958). Educational questions in Dewey's scheme of things became materialist, contingent, and "socially aware." Peters, on the other hand, reaffirmed his allegiance to ethics and therein metaphysics, not physics, in the objective morals of *Ethics and education* (1966). The reservoir of questions that would be constitutive of philosophy of education was heavily influenced by metaphysics. In the United States John Dewey based his writing on a theory of experience, therein heavily mortgaging educational philosophy to physics and thereby science and social science. In the American version of the discipline, at least initially, the task of educational philosophy was to "change the world not solve it". In Britain the task was to "solve the world not change it."[15]

Peters's work became an all-pervasive element of professional discourse. His work could not be ignored. Many of the most important people—and people who would become important—concerned with philosophy of education spent a major portion of their time and energy reacting to, defending, or rehearsing Peters's arguments. Despite differences between lecturers within the department, the dominance of Peters's version of analytic philosophy assured that the work of the institute's academic staff and graduates largely would be devoted to developing a rabid antipathy or positive affection for Peters's ideas. And as his ideas reached out to the Commonwealth a similar reaction would occur in Australasia. Thus, reaction and defense became the pervasive style of professional conduct in England and the Commonwealth.

In this analytic version of the discipline the connections between politics, society, and education were eschewed. When John White attempted to sketch such connections in a very preliminary fashion, Peters quickly drew him back into line (White, 1989). Whatever else social and political speculation was, it was not philosophy—not in Peters's department anyway. Even more pointedly, Peters's stance turned its face from some of the more "socially aware" gambits that philosophy itself was starting to play out. Nothing demonstrated English philosophy's new mood more than Peter Winch's *Idea of a social science and its relation to philosophy* (1958). Philosophy was developing a social awareness, if not a conscience. The discipline was discovering social questions that were as important and as compelling as the questions of analysis, epistemology, and metaphysics that had transfixed a previous generation of philosophers. If Winch was right, it would be incumbent upon philosophy to be mindful of the nature of human society first and the technical questions of philosophy second. It was a view that Peters did not share.

Peters and his ex-colleague from Birkbeck, A. Phillip Griffiths, were of the persuasion that certain objective Kant-like transcendentals could be known and thereby could provide fundamental ethical principles for human conduct (Hirst, 1982, 7). Peters developed the position in *Ethics and education* (1966). It was a stance that would attract some favorable philosophical comment in *Philosophers discuss education* (Brown, S. C. 1975). The question of the possibility of Kant-like transcendentals and collateral attempts to spin out the implications of those transcendentals was the central issue of English educational philosophy until well into the 1980s.

## BENN AND PETERS

In the book *The principles of political thought* ([1959] 1965) Benn and Peters explicitly stated the social and political principles necessary for the practice of democracy in an industrial state. Given what Benn and Peters wrote, it is evident that Peters's analysis of education was fixed a long time before the result of his philosophical analysis, reported in *Ethics and education* (1966) was published. In a section discussing education in a democratic state Benn and Peters wrote:

The modern state provides many services, like medical care, poor relief, unemployment insurance, and education, which might still be provided by other associations, as once they were . . .
    In a nation of many millions, a majority came to resent the way in which wealth and opportunity were distributed, the state would be pressed to provide a variety of social services, involving a great extension of its authority. Egalitarians are not satisfied if the state merely guarantees minimum standards: they protest that any special advantage that can be bought, like a public school education, or medical treatment in a private ward or nursing home, is an offence against social justice. Consequently certain activities hitherto undertaken by non-state associations are not merely supplemented by state provision; they are now in danger of total absorption in the quest for uniform standards . . .
    They fear that men become demoralized as they come to depend on the state for more and more of their needs. According to the critics, they no longer bother to provide for old age and sickness, for themselves or their families. They demand ever greater material advantages while seeing no need to exert themselves to get them . . .
    What the critics object to is that the state, in providing such services, has insisted on making them compulsory. Where formerly a responsible person joined with others to safeguard his own interest by deliberate choice, now he pays what is virtually a tax, and receives benefits which do not seem directly related to it, and which he has made no deliberate personal effort to obtain . . .

Of course such criticism presupposes a moral position. They rest like Mill's attack on paternalism, on the belief that individual initiative and personal responsibility are valuable in themselves . . . ([1959] 1965, 340-342)

The position sketched by Benn and Peters is, of course, a position that no responsible Victorian would have rejected (see Peters 1966, 130-143). Fair in form but discriminatory in practice, it reserved special social and educational privilege for the monied classes in the name of preserving the moral character of the working class

Thus, for Benn and Peters the state needed to be quite careful in deciding what role it should have in the delivery of welfare services:

In deciding the part it is to play in providing a service, therefore, a government must consider whether a voluntary association might possibly provide it more efficiently than it can itself, whether it might be more ready to experiment, or more adaptable in meeting varied requirements and changing conditions; or whether the service requires a uniform standard throughout the country. If a minimum (but not a uniform) standard of efficiency will suffice, the best arrangement may be a system of inspection supported by grants-in-aid. There may be grounds for adopting parallel provision, e.g. a system of state and non-state schools existing side by side, the one offering sound and sufficient education on orthodox lines, the other operating, in effect, as a sort of experimental laboratory. But if the state accepts such a partnership, it must see that its partner is not forced out of business. There may be a case for, say, tax remission, to enable experiments to continue. In some cases, the state's part might be to encourage and guide existing organizations, e.g. by subsidies to approved bodies, rather than to supersede them. ([1959] 1965, 343)

An unsuspecting reader must be amazed at how well the educational elements of a limited democracy as outlined by Benn and Peters in *The principles of political thought* ([1959] 1965) reflect and affirm English educational practice—practice, one might add, that was commonly acknowledged to be aristocratic and elitist at least as early as Tawney's caustic little essay in "The problem of the public schools" ([1918] 1964b). The case they made is clearly Victorian and anti-egalitarian:

"Equality of opportunity" would be consistent with a single educational stream which everyone entered on their same footing, following it as far as his capacity allowed. This is not the theory (whatever the practice) of our present system. We, aim, instead, at a number of streams, to provide educational opportunities appropriate to different types of ability, as well as different degrees. The system is not like a slope that people climb until strength gives out, but more like a transport system in which people are conveyed to different, and appropriate, destinations ...

We carry out an assessment of children's capacities at the age of eleven, and send them accordingly to different schools. We accord them *the same* opportunities only in the sense that all are entitled to be treated alike until relevant grounds are established for treating them differently. Thus they all take the same examination—but its purpose is precisely to establish the different opportunities to be provided thereafter. This is a special application, in the fields of education and recruitment to the professions, of the procedure we have called "equal consideration." If we do not say that opportunities thereafter are unequal, it is because we see the point of the discrimination. Differences in opportunities are compatible with "equality" if we see the point of them—they are "inequalities" when we do not. ([1959] 1965, 137-138)

It was the same sense of equity and democracy that the Norwood Report of 1943 used to deflect the drive for equal education for all between the First and Second World Wars (cf. Lawson and Silver, 1973, 419). The logic of the Norwood Report, like the logic of Benn and Peters, was for the maintenance of the public schools. However intentional or unintentional, in the last analysis it was a stance that worked in the defense of privilege and militated against equal opportunity for all.

## RADIO ADDRESSES

Peters published "four broadcast talks on education" that brought him a certain "public" recognition within the teaching profession just as it helped present education as a public issue (Hirst, 1989). These British Broadcasting Corporation lectures were published as a collection of essays entitled *Authority, responsibility, and education* ([1959] 1966). In the essays we find the same person Peters conceptualized in *The concept of motivation* (1958)—"man the rule following animal" ([1959] 1966, 5). But in *Authority* we find an individual who is not only rule following but also who has lost the source of authority necessary to conduct a life and is desperately seeking a rationally justified life (([1959] 1966, 39). This individual is looking for a shelter from the potential nihilism and the collateral threat of fascism evident in the international politics of the postwar period ([1959] 1966, 40). In this world, Peters's world, the characters "Shane, The Lone Ranger, Philip Marlowe in Chandler's stories, the heroes of *On the waterfront, Manhunt,* and *A man is ten feet tall*— these represent the struggle for decency against naked power" ([1959] 1966, 42-43). *Ethics and education,* of course, was part of this quest for authority in the "struggle for decency against naked power."

In his broadcast talks on education Peters indicated that he had little time for the alienation of the New Left. He wrote that neither Freud nor Marx supported the dark rationality of those who would "merely look back in anger" ([1959] 1966, 79)—a transparent allusion to John Osborne's very successful play *Look back in anger.* Osborne followed *Look back in anger* with *The entertainer.* Both of these plays reflect the collapse of Edwardian and Victorian stability and an emergent strand of social criticism (Lloyd, [1979] 1989, 361). The text of and the critical academic research of the sixties (see Peters, ([1959] 1966). If the old Victorian and Edwardian social and moral authority was lost, Peters was out to generate a modern equivalent.

In Peters's world education *qua* education was not a simple matter of means and ends ([1959] 1966, 79). Education had to do with the attitudes that it generated ([1959] 1966, 92-93), it has to do with the manner of its transmission ([1959] 1966, 118), and the manner in which it provided access to certain values and cultural characteristics through the medium of language ([1959] 1966, 98). This world was not inhabited by Peters alone, it was inhabited by the establishment as well. The reinterpretation of liberal education evident in the last few segments of Peters's radio broadcasts was a rationale and justification for the British public school and the elitism that it supported (cf. Silver, 1983, 162). It was a stance that would provide a warm welcome for Peters within the university establishment.

At Hull University during an influential conference early in 1964 Peters took the initiative and announced that the cure to educational ills was a thorough study of the *disciplines* that contributed most to the study of eduction. As Simon noted Peters was out to sieve the "undifferentiated mush" of educational research (1983).[16] Philosophy would leaven psychology, sociology, and history, and they in turn would transform the educational enterprise (Simon, 1983, 8). The entire area of teacher education became a highly academic enterprise. (Simon 1992, 376).

The main attack, or critique, on existing practice was launched by Richard Peters, a proponent of the 'revolution in philosophy' (involving 'the disciplined demarcation of concepts and the patient explication of the grounds of knowledge and conduct') . . . What was necessary was to identify the various disciplines which underlay, or contributed to, the study of education—nor referred to as the 'the three foundation disciplines' (history was here ignored). (Simon 1991, 376)

The advantage of this approach as far as the establishment was concerned was that educational reforms were largely internal and apolitical. Unlike Reid who had preceded him, Peters brought the outline of a hopeful intellectual gambit with him. Analysis had roused philosophy from its intellectual doldrums and promised to do the same for education. The initiative had already been successfully tried by Israel Scheffler (1960) in the United States with promising results.[17] All that remained was to develop a sophisticated model of analysis that was appropriate to the English scene.[18]

Following this lead, which exploded with considerable vigour, colleges of education (and universities) rapidly appointed specialist philosophers, sociologists, historians, to expanding education departments—many the products of new diploma and higher degree courses mounted at universities. Courses provided by these departments for their students reflected the 'disciplines' approach. Each became established, later setting up societies, publishing journals, organising conferences. the study of education was coming into its own. (Simon 1991, 376)

Peters dominated educational philosophy's intellectual initiatives just as he dominated its institutional initiatives. For example, the manner in which Peters dominated the journal of the discipline was not unimportant for its future. Peters in conjunction with his colleagues at the Institute, and Paul Hirst first at the Institute, then at Kings College, and later at Cambridge monopolized the discipline's literary technology. Peters's initiative created *Proceedings of the Philosophy of Education Society of Great Britain*. In a very important sense he directed the society's voice, and therefore he also controlled the obvious source of intellectual dissent. In addition to the society's journal he also was general editor for Routledge and Kegan Paul's International Library of the Philosophy of Education series. Since Routledge and Kegan Paul was one of the most prolific publishers of book-length manuscripts in philosophy of education, Peters's position was doubly important. As the senior editor on an editorial board comprised of himself, Taylor, Morris, Simon, and Tibble (the chairman)—a board that Paul Hirst later joined—Peters, for all intents and purposes, was the major editor of educational philosophy in Great Britain.

Peters established the Philosophy of Education Society of Great Britain in the 1963-1964 academic year. Peters continued to guide the society for the next ten years. His personal effort established the society and his reputation was linked to it. His involvement as chairman of the society ensured his influence upon British philosophy of education for the period of his chairmanship and beyond. What was unique in all of this was the complete control that Peters and members of the London Institute achieved within the discipline. It was a level of influence that even Dewey's department at Columbia did not achieve in the 1920s (the work of William Heard Kilpatrick, Harold Rugg, George S. Counts, and John L. Childs added immensely to the department's influence and had its own impact and following). Teachers College Columbia had competitors: Harvard, Ohio State, Stanford, the University of California (Berkeley), Chicago, Iowa, Michigan, Minnesota, and Yale all had influential schools of education. But in England there was only the London Institute of Education and only one R. S. Peters—at least in the beginning.

In addition the students of R. S. Peters were appointed to, and soon dominated, England's most prestigious departments of educational philosophy. Peters was instrumental in decisions regarding who would be appointed to Chairs and lectureships. Over the next ten years, the majority of those who would be "important" philosophers of education in Britain either worked at or were trained within the London Institute. To note the most obvious examples: Paul Hirst held the Chair of Educational Philosophy at King's College London and later the chair at Cambridge; Leslie Perry held the chair at Warwick and King's College London; Ray Elliot and Robert Dearden held chairs at the University of Birmingham; Hugh Sockett held a chair at the New University of Ulster and later at East Anglia; and Richard Pring held a chair first at Exeter and then at Oxford.

## R. S. PETERS: INDUSTRY, BUSINESS, COMMERCE, AND A LIBERAL EDUCATION

A host of controversies—about vocational and nonvocational education, technical and nontechnical training, liberal versus professional education, narrowness versus breadth, and all of the other issues common to the discussion of secondary and further or tertiary education since the period between the wars—present themselves in *Ethics and education* (1966). The stance was foreshadowed by the Hadow Committee's (1926) warning against too isolated and narrow school curriculums which was overly responsive to the specific needs of later life; and in the Newbolt Committee's (1921) assertion that technical training might become technical education if not informed by the humanities (Silver, 1983, 164). Peters's comments reflect the inability of earlier educational debates to determine the boundaries between technical and liberal education and to reinterpret concepts of liberal and vocational education without reference to the "narrow frameworks and status structures of the nineteenth and twentieth–century British educational system" (Silver, 1983, 169). For example, Peters wrote in *Ethics and education* (1966): "We do not call a person 'educated' who has simply mastered a skill (30); and "A man might be a very highly trained scientist; yet we might refuse to call him an educated man" (31); and "A man with a 'trained mind' is one who can tackle particular problems that are put to him in a rigorous and competent manner. An 'educated mind' suggests much more awareness of the different facets and dimensions of such problems" (32); and "An educated man is one who has achieved a state of mind which is characterized by a mastery of and care for the worth–while things that have been transmitted, which are viewed in some kind of cognitive perspective" (46-47). His comments reflect a very Victorian view of knowledge and the caustic relationship that existed between science, technology, and classics in the English educational system. They also reflect the inability of the humanities and the sciences to write the terms of some reasonable armistice. An uneasy cease-fire seems likely to continue to exist between them.[19] Peters's argument is more at home with Victorian versions of the *quadrivium* and *trivium* than modern versions of university education.

The stance of the London Line seemed a modern echo of their philosophical predecessors.[20] Peters's intellectual stance is more than vaguely reminiscent of John Stuart Mills' Inaugural address at St. Andrews University" ([1867] 1985), in which Mill argued:

The proper function of a University in national education is tolerably well understood. At least there is a tolerably general agreement about what a university is not. It is not a place of professional education. Universities are not intended to teach the knowledge required to fit men for some special mode of gaining their livelihood. Their object is not to make skilful lawyers, or physicians, or engineers, but capable and cultivated human beings . . .

Whether those whose speciality they are, will learn them as a branch of intelligence or as a mere trade, and whether, having learnt them, they will make a wise and conscientious use of them or the reverse, depends less on the manner in which they are taught their profession, than upon what sort of minds they bring to it—what kind of intelligence, and of conscience, the general system of education has developed in them. Men are men before they are lawyers, or physicians, or merchants, or manufacturers; and if you make them capable and sensible men, they will make themselves capable and sensible lawyers or physicians. What professional men should carry away with them from a University, is not professional knowledge, but that which should direct the use of their professional knowledge, and bring the light of general culture to illuminate the technicalities of a special pursuit. ([1867] 1985, 380-381)

Both Mill and Peters shared the belief that clarity was the key to success in any intellectual pursuit. Mill wrote:

When I consider how very simple the theory of reasoning is, and how short a time is sufficient for acquiring a thorough knowledge of its principles and rules, and even considerable expertness in applying them, I can find no excuse for omission to study it on the part of anyone who aspires to succeed in any intellectual pursuit. Logic is the great disperser of hazy and confused thinking: it clears up the fogs which hide from us our own ignorance, and make us believe that we understand a subject when we do not. (Mill, [1867] 1985, 401)

It was a sentiment with which Peters could only concur.

Similar to the general task that Mill perceived for logic, Peters hoped to rid education of the "fog" that confounded investigations of the discipline and its theoretical and conceptual structures. Substantively, Mill and the London Line were not that far apart.

Clarity was a secondary issue. Formal versions of analysis were about epistemology, British educational philosophy was not. Its analytic function was to disabuse educators of concepts which they only half understood; its substantive function was to "solve the world."

Again, if Peters's discipline had a task, it was to provide a thorough intellectual interrogation of education, just as nineteenth-century social and moral philosophy provided a thorough investigation of "human nature, social forces, progress, marriage and family relationships, economic process, maintenance of government, international relations, elementary jurisprudence, primitive customs, history of institutions, religion, ethics, aesthetics" (Bryson, 1932b, 304). Peters, along with the Victorians, believed that an education must be a *liberal* education. It must serve a utopian purpose and impart some unique moral benefit (see Rothblatt, 1976, 146-147). Although verbally committed in principle to more egalitarian versions of schooling, Peters and the London Line were silent or almost silent in practice on the questions of poverty and deprivation. The London Line co-opted, perhaps unwittingly, the impossible task of defending liberal education as an elite version of schooling from the democratic effects of the comprehensive and the secondary modern. It also sought to protect liberal education from excessive science (see Hirst, 1974) and mundane technology (Peters, 1966)—tasks that England's conservative educational establishment could only applaud.

The postwar reconstruction of the sixties brought a new addition to the university study of education: educational philosophy. Along with its invention and establishment came great expectations. The task Peters defined for it was to build a fundamental educational language within which what educators and academics could say and discursively think about schooling would be contained. It was a grand project that was never realized. The specification of fundamental categories and principles proved to be an elusive task that defied an elegant solution (Hirst, 1982, 8) and the political ultraelitism it presupposed was impossibly anachronistic in the ultrademocratic politics of the counterculture.

## NOTES

1. The aristocracy, civil service, and philosophy have always been tightly related. The relationship remains alive and well in England, as evidenced by the important educational work of philosophers such as Baroness Mary Warnock on government commissions. It is also shown by the important governmental work with which curriculum developers cum philosophers such as Richard Pring, Chair and Professor of Education at Oxford University, are constantly involved.

2. Nevertheless, both the vice-chancellors and the principals of teacher training colleges also believed that if there were anything to know about education, then a first step in raising the status and prestige of teacher education might be found in raising its academic standards. In time this task was inherited by educational philosophy in general.

3. On the other hand, educational philosophy's prosperity in the late 1960s was certainly a result of the success of R. S. Peters's work.

4. Both T. Percy Nunn and Fred Clark were transitional figures. Interesting and important in their time, their work quickly lost importance in the professionalized atmosphere of the sixties.

5. Malet Street was the early address of the London Institute's Department of Philosophy of Education. Later it moved to a terrace house close to the main building of the institute in Woburn Square, and now it is situated in the main building.

6. These men's concerns were with political reform, social welfare, or academic philosophy. It would take another generation to find scholars who would give their lives and careers to philosophy of education.

7. The New Education Fellowship was formed in 1921 in Calais. It was a clearinghouse for disseminating the ideas of progressive education. It presented the ideas of both European and American proponents of "new education". Its journal *The New Era* presented the ideas of Dr. Montessori (Italy); Decroly (Belgium); Claparede (Switzerland); Dr. Reddie (England); and Colonel Parker (U. S. A.). (see Armytage 1967, 74)

8. To be more precise, L. A. Reid was invited by the then director Dr. G. B. Jeffery to be the first occupant of the new chair.

9. The appointment of both Reid and Peters is a demonstration of the English faith in philosophy as well as an admission of the disrepute and "hard times" that many teacher training colleges had fallen upon.

10. The similarity may be coincidental, but there is some parallel between Reid's Easter seminars and with the Easter reading parties that G. E. Moore organized from 1898 to 1914 that were so influential in the development of English philosophy.

11. Reid's books are: *Knowledge and truth* (1923), *A study in aesthetics* (1931), *Creative morality* (1937), *A preface to faith* (1939), *The rediscovery of belief* (1945), *Ways of knowledge and experience* (1960), *Philosophy and education* (1962), *Meaning in the arts* (1970), and *Ways of understanding and education* (1986).

12. Laing along with another individual called Jones were tutors that Reid employed to "improve on my entrance qualification" such that he might attend the University of Edinburgh. Laing was his English tutor and Jones was his tutor for science and mathematics.

13. Peters's attempt to demonstrate the conceptual confusions and low level of argumentation that diminished the theoretical power of psychology is presented in *The concept of motivation* (1958). For example, Peters wrote: "My thesis is that

the concept of 'motivation' has developed from that of 'motive' by attempting a causal interpretation of the logical force of the term. This is made possible by the failure to distinguish different levels of questions" (28). The quote is indicative of both the stance and the purpose of the book and Peters's intellectual stance in general. The extension of the task he had set for himself in psychology was extended to education not long after his appointment and was presented in *Ethics and education* (1966).

14. The exclusive stance of the British society was very different from the egalitarian stance of the John Dewey Society that welcomed all comers. But when it was established in 1940 the Philosophy of Education Society in the United States adopted membership standards that excluded non-professionals.

15. The parallel allusion here, of course, is to Marx's challenge to Feuerbach (vide, Marx, *Thesis on Feuerbach*: Thesis, 11).

16. It should be noted that he was not out to solve the institution of education, but rather to solve the research paradigms of disciplines that studied the institution of education. If philosophy could not be the queen of sciences it would at least be science's tutor. This position did not sell at Birkbeck and it did not sell for long at the London Institute—at least in the social sciences.

17. Israel Scheffler *The language of education* (1960).

18. It would be wrong to conclude that Peters did nothing more than to develop what Scheffler had already tested. The questions that constitute Peters's work are different from Scheffler's. What they really shared was a concern for analysis.

19. See C. P. Snow's *Two cultures* ([1959] 1961).

20. The London Line was the pattern of intellectual reaction to and defense of Peters's version of analytic philosophy that became a pervasive style of professional conduct in England and the Commonwealth.

# 8

# The Counterculture and
# Modern Times

Philosophy's public image in the immediate postwar period was saved by existentialism. Existentialism in its various formulations represented philosophy's resurgent humanism (see Schrader, 1967) in a world that had seen enough manifestations of German philosophy in Hitler's Fascism and Stalin's Gulags. Philosophy's academic image was saved by Wittgenstein's version of metaphysics, epistemology, and analysis. Obsessed with analysis, departments of philosophy in England ignored the continental tradition in favor of a closer identification with analysis and therein the ethos of science. The time marked the genesis of a new philosophical age—an age of analysis (Rorty, 1982, 214–230). The age was as varied as the numerous versions of analyses it generated. Versions varied from those that depended on Russell's theory of descriptions to those that revolved around constructive reformulations of concepts (Tice and Slavens, 1983, 164-165). The similarity with educational philosophy was a methodological similarity. The reservoirs of questions that defined each of the disciplines were different and their natural audiences were radically divergent. Nevertheless, analytic philosophy began as a way of divesting philosophy of its speculative image and endowing it with the virtues of science by the means of "logical analysis" (Rorty, 1982, 227).

Prior to World War I what counted most as academic philosophy was developed domestically by Bertrand Russell, Alfred North Whitehead, and G. E. Moore. The students of Russell, Moore, and their colleagues were appointed to, and soon dominated, England's most prestigious departments of philosophy. Together they dictated what would and would not count as philosophy (McGuinness, 1988). The work of Russell's most famous student assumed pride of place in the philosophical establishment as the epistemology of the *Tractatus* completed in 1918 became the order of the day. But the epistemology of the *Tractatus* was not unproblematic, and variant versions of analysis continued to evolve. J. L. Austin and Gilbert Ryle at Oxford and A. J. Ayer first at Oxford (1929-1945) then at the University of London (1946-1958) and finally back at Oxford (1959-1978) would be principal players in the development of the English versions of analysis. Ryle's *Concept of mind* ([1949] 1964), Ayer's *Language, truth, and logic* ([1936] 1946), and Austin's various philosophical papers were key English contributions. *Language, truth and logic* ([1936] 1946) exemplified analysis to the English philosophers and members of the academic fraternity (Tice and Slavens, 1983, 153). These scholars in concert with Susan Stebbing and John Wisdom at Cambridge consolidated the position of analysis, and these works became common points of reference in analytic versions of educational philosophy.

Peters's natural reference point was academic philosophy, and he assiduously sought to construct educational philosophy within the parameters of that reference. In response to Peters's encouragement, a volume appeared in 1975 entitled *Philosophers discuss education* edited by S. C. Brown. In the volume members of philosophy's establishment addressed the topic of education with almost embarrassingly frequent reference to Peters's work. It would appear that the establishment's effort to discuss education was at best a response to Peters's energy and academic position rather than any honest interest in the topic itself, at least initially. But more was to follow. David Hamlyn, R. S. Downie, Mary Warnock, David Cooper, and Antony Flew all made contributions to educational philosophy. Although modest, their participation and involvement in educational philosophy was more extended and generous than that of their American cousins. Peters's ability to solicit the participation of notable philosophers in the education debate, constructed solid points of contact between philosophy and philosophy of education.

From 1965 to 1975 analytic philosophy was philosophy of education and philosophy of education was the London Line. But while Peters's work established philosophy of education in Britain, the towering stature of his thought obstructed its development; that is, Peters's influence was so pervasive and powerful that neither the staff who taught at the institute nor its graduates seem to have been able to escape the ambit of Peters's thought. It is not merely that they shared a conviction that analytic philosophy was a useful style for the conduct of philosophy of education; it is that those individuals were transfixed by Peters's use of analysis for the investigation of education. Even into the 1990s the London Line has not escaped the range of questions generated by Peters's *Ethics and education* (1966). Despite Paul Hirst's important epistemological contribution to Peters's basic position, the dozen or so titles from the London Line that appear in the International Library of the Philosophy of Education series, and the sea of articles appearing in various journals, those authors touched by the London Line rarely escaped the philosophically enervating affect of Peters's thought. But even more important, the London Line has not managed to generate any philosophically interesting alternatives to its analytic meanderings.

In the 1960s and early 1970s the educational system's Victorian proclivities began to reemerge. The British economy was under great pressure. The press wrote articles about child neglect, abandonment of the aged by governments and families, substandard education, and antiquated hospitals. The fulfillment of the promise of the Beveridge Report and the realization of the 1944 Education Act was in doubt. Questions of social policy were being greeted by a cacophony of opposing voices. In this context the debate over the form of education had been a comparatively academic and distant one; but the New Left would change all that. It, along with collateral social and political issues of the 1950s and 1960s—largely revolving around the promise of the Beveridge Report—would be tinder for the counterculture. Political and social protest was based on concerns about social agendas, poverty, child neglect, medical care, the implications of an open immigration policy, as well as the Vietnam War (Lawson and Silver, 1973, 477).

In the sixties many of England's most influential educators and academics investigated the questions of poverty and deprivation, the unequal distribution of educational resources, the effects of class on educational performance, antiquated and dilapidated schools, the economic exploitation of immigrant groups and the neglect of their children's education, and so forth. England's educational philosophers, however, did not engage in this discourse. They did not participate in the sixties' all-consuming topics. Educational philosophy in Britain was driven by an attempt to find transcendental constants and, perhaps, moral absolution in a boisterous, rowdy, and politically volatile social climate.

The issue of liberal education raised by liberals and conservatives found a place in modern texts like R. S. Peters's *Ethics and education* (1966) and Paul Hirst's *Liberal education and the nature of knowledge* ([1965] 1974). Peters found liberal education as commendable as Arnold did and would share difficulties quite similar to those of the headmaster in commending technical education. It was a faith that Paul Hirst echoed in *Liberal education*, just as the same work signed an uneasy armistice with science. From this point in time and history, Hirst's faith in liberal education seems quite at home with the more articulate versions of Georgian and Victorian culture. Hirst's work was a seminal contribution to educational philosophy. Be that as it may, it is now obvious that what he did, of course, was not to derive a definition of "liberal education" from the nature of knowlege itself, but to derive a definition of knowledge from an English version of a "liberal education."

Hirst was opposed to intellectual anarchy and committed to an altruistic version of social morality that required a subordination of private inclinations and personal advantage to the public welfare. His work found a restraining force in a commonly accepted Victorian canon of taste, summed up in Arnold's refrain "the best that has been thought and said." The transmission of this canon is at the center of Hirst's arguments in *Liberal education and the nature of knowledge* ([1965] 1974). It is at one with the intellectual stance of elitist liberals such as Russell. The London Line's intellectual stance was in good intellectual company but it was difficult to maintain in the 1960s and 1970s.

In the atmosphere of the sixties it was not easy to cling to the social and intellectual elitism of Shaw, Wells, and Russell, while conversely—thanks largely to the activities of the New Left—it was easier to look at the collectivism of the  Webbs straight on. Thus, while the social emotions of educational philosophy were confused at the London Institute its intellectual stance was not. It was for social and educational reform as long as it left the "public schools" alone. Like Russell it was feared that the demands for universal education would reduce schooling to the lowest common denominator.


THE LONDON LINE

In a sense, then, the London Line conducted their investigations within a nineteenth-century context. It was an indiscretion that was common to philosophy and educational philosophy. As Bryson (1932a, 1932b, 1932c) points out, moral philosophy, the traditional ambit of educational questions, had always offered detailed discussions of human relations and institutions. Education was a traditional part of these discussions. But these investigations were isolated from their empirical counterpart and largely scholastic in their content.[1] Empirical questions were left for sociology. As a result the reference of educational philosophy's reflections seemed to be more a part of the natural history of philosophy than the empirical questions of education. In retrospect the work of the London Line seems strangely isolated from the time and history of its writing. And perhaps even more unfortunate, it touted the results of their investigations as philosophically correct and educationally veridical. They ignored the political interests of both the Right and the Left—perhaps as a matter of principle. In a sense they acted as if philosophy was its own excuse.

The London Line's intellectual work seemed to have more to do with aspiring to philosophy than it did with solving the idea of education or its worldly difficulties. In fact, the work generated little interest from academic philosophy. From a modern perspective the work seems profoundly conservative. What educational philosophers of the London Line assumed to be transcendental, objective, and eternal was English, ethnocentric, and reactionary. The work of the London Line was socially and intellectually removed from a world that was trying to respond to the egalitarian ideology of the Beveridge Report, the social criticism of the old and New Left, and the irony, sarcasm, and self-indulgence of the counterculture. They endeavored to convince themselves and professional educators (rather successfully) and their professional colleagues and the public (rather unsuccessfully) that there was something essentially important for the conduct of education yet to be found in the realm of metaphysics (cf. White, 1987, 155-157).

The metaphysical stance retains some currency in academic philosophy.[2] It was a fairly common custom in departments of philosophy—at least those with some commitment to the analytic philosophy—to assume that intellectual success in educational philosophy had more to do with philosophy than schools. Peters aspired to this task with Stakhanovite vigor. And to a degree his stance was a realistic understanding of the needs of the emerging discipline. Unfortunately it was a stance that confused conforming to the demands of English academic culture with solving questions about education and schooling.

There was tremendous pressure on Peters to induct the study of education into the university establishment. His task was to instantiate university academic standards in a discipline that was deemed by English academics in general and many university vice-chancellors to have little or no academic content or standards. The expectation was clear; Peters was to bring the rigorous academic standards of philosophy to education as some sort of academic tonic. In this atmosphere it was impossible to conceptualize a version of educational philosophy that did not aspire to the philosophical and academic fashions of the day. Nevertheless, whatever success Peters had in meeting these demands did little to meet the more compelling demands for the resolution of England's urgent educational questions.

SIXTY-EIGHT

Peters's and therein the London Line's philosophical stance was more comfortable with the Victorians than with the "hip" people of Carnaby Street and Petticoat Lane or the successful and aggressively egalitarian Labor party of the Sixties. Carnaby Street and Petticoat Lane were lexical icons of the sixties that vaguely alluded to the appalling poverty of London's Victorian East End. The hip people displayed a solidarity with labor and England's political Left— fashionable at the time. When even the Beatles were singing about revolution and the Stones were discovering that there was big money in being bad (Gitlin, 1987, 199).[3] Peters's "worth-while" seemed out of touch. It seemed more in touch with Gilbert and Sullivan's *Pirates of Penzance* than Bob Dylan's bittersweet allegory "Blowin' in the wind."[4] "The Stones completed a trinity: The Beatles were the ultimate romantics, Dylan was cerebral, and the Stones stood for sex" (Kaiser, 1988, 210). The Beatles were the counterculture's utopian romantics, Dylan its connection with the politics of the old and New Left, and the Stones transcended England's vestiges of Victorian morality. All of them were for the "here and now".

What made sixty-eight different from all of the years that went before it was that it was the moment when practices set free by the collapse of Victorianism were socially and ethically sanctioned. Victorian morality had remained a persistent version of social conduct until the late 1950s. The Festival of Britain in 1951 had firm connections with the late-Victorian era. In many respects, both social and political, England had remained Victorian (Seaman, 1985, 5). The Festival of Britain did not seem all that far from the Crystal Palace. But all that was about to change. The counterculture pulled in one direction and the old and New Left in the other, and Victorianism came tumbling down. What emerged was a liberated Britain. It would be a Britain that was free from the social constraints that had endured for more than a century.

Morality, social graces, polite entertainment (theater), and conversation (middle-class discourse) had remained Victorian since the turn of the twentieth century. "Matters which the Victorian had buried under shame and evasion were now entering fully into the public domain" (Marwick, [1982] 1988, 152). Nudity, homosexuality, sexual intercourse, profanity, poverty, deprivation, child abuse, neglect of the aged, exploitation of the underclass, socialism, and communism were topics that entered the public arena with a new legitimacy. Sexually explicit language became a part of ordinary discourse, at least for the literati and those who aspired to cultural sophistication. A Britain in which hip girls wore transparent blouses, topless swimming costumes, and condemned bras and corsets to the British Museum was at odds with its Victorian history and establishment present.

Theatrical censorship remained in place until 1968. Frank social commentary, nudity, and sex—near enough to the real thing—would find expression in London's experimental theater. Pushed by plays like Peter Brook's *Marat/Sade*, in 1964 Victorian censorship collapsed—just in time for *Hair* to open in the West End. Not only did *Hair* silence the counterculture's Victorian critics, it provided a powerful two-fisted legitimation of hip cultures' new social code (Caute, 1988, 248). *Hair* consolidated the zeitgeist of the sixties. After *Hair* the new code could not be dismissed as "willful exhibitionism and self-indulgence."

And if live theater was out of hand, the movies had checked out altogether. In the period just after the war happy and hopeful American musicals like *Oklahoma* and *Annie get your gun* dominated stage and screen. By the sixties the celebration of the social imperium ended. *Alfie* (1966) took a new look at the working class and questions of abortion, a situation that government took up in the 1967 Abortion Act sponsored by David Steel. The film *The ruling class* starring Peter O'Toole demonstrated that—as was proclaimed in the *Pirates of Penzance*—"Peers will be Peers!" But the system of aristocracy was looking out of place in the twentieth century to both the working and middle classes. *If,* a surrealistic film opening in the final month of 1968 with dreamlike or, perhaps, nightmarelike qualities, outlined a stinging critique of authoritarian and sadomasochistic conduct of the "public schools" and—similar to *The ruling class*—named the aristocracy for complicity in something more than a social misdemeanor (Caute, 1988, 251). If an unlimited supply of child labor had been essential for Victorian industry it was disastrous for members of the working class and postindustrial society. No longer a source of wealth or required by modern industry accidental and unlimited families were on the way out. The Pill and family planning were "in." Topics unthinkable to Victorian England had become "clinical" questions.

Soft pornography appeared on page 3 of "respectable" newspapers. In personal conduct English society began to abandon the "double standard" of the Victorian moral code. Kingsley Amis became a literary institution. Between *Take a girl like you* ([1960] 1961) and *I want it now* ([1968] 1969) Amis was able to chronicle in fictional guise the complete revision of the Victorian sexual code (Marwick, [1982] 1988, 139; see Salwak, 1992). Not only was the code being informally revised and chronicled, but also it was being persuasively critiqued by feminists. Feminists were drafting both a sexual revolution and a politics for themselves. The liberation of the third world and the ghetto's underclass was fine but, frankly, they were more concerned with their own oppression (Gitlin, 1987, 371; Caute, 1988, 237). They were demanding a new social accord in which they might participate in rewriting the articles of the gender contract. The terms of endearment rapidly evolved.

Society was being tested by assertive young women and men who were hip to the politics of the Right and the Left. January 1969 was the time of the Tet offensive. Tet redrew the image of the war and redrew the practice of domestic politics. By "sixty-eight" the young men were hip, Vietnam was a monument to America's political ambitions. To many the only thing that was at stake in Southeast Asia was the American political imperium. *Hair* attested to the fact that war was no longer a matter of politics by another means. The war was too serious to be left either to the generals or the to politicians. Although no English soldiers went to Vietnam, Britain's moral support for the war was more than enough to consolidate the protest of the old and New Left. It was a protest that would extend to domestic arrangements of empire as well.

A New Left was in the streets, and the counterculture had taken possession of the country's imagination. Only nominally connected to labor, the New Left was largely comprised of the sons and daughters of the new class. Alienated and disappointed in their elders' generation, they were out to realize new values or, perhaps, just to live up to the values their parents espoused. "The most fundamental characteristic of the New Left was its libertarian distrust of state power, parties, competition, leadership, bureaucracies and, finally, of representative government" (Caute, 1988, 20). The distinguishing characteristic of this group was its belief that anything was possible. The counterculture was the mirror image of the New Left. Libertine to the core, it elevated license over the more traditional virtues of liberty, and self-indulgence over the Calvinist ethic of hard work. The counterculture lacked the New Left's bad conscience (Gitlin, 1987, 35). The New Left was more in tune with the *Discreet charm of the bourgeoisie*. Intellectual and sophisticated, the New Left knew that the West's bourgeoisie had abandoned the workers to pursue a home in the suburbs. The disciplines of politics and the protocol of the New Left was often overwhelmed by the counterculture's lack of reverence for almost everything. It was difficult for the New Left to accept a clown for a partner in revolution. Reciprocally, it was just as difficult for the children of the counterculture to tolerate the terminal seriousness of the New Left. The New Left was full of plans, manifestos, and opposition politics. The counterculture just "let it all hang out"—one government or vanguard was as untrustworthy as another. The counterculture was for the Beatles and Sgt. Pepper.

The counterculture brought the idea of social revolution to the English public school. Schools for the privileged were looking out of place even if Prime Minister Wilson (a grammar school boy himself) and his government couldn't quite bring themselves to abolish them. Still, the comprehensive was in the ascendant and government was talking about schools in terms of "equality of educational opportunity". It was a striking change from the period just before the close of World War II when the Norwood Committee (1943) recommended, without the slightest blush or hesitation, a curriculum that reaffirmed class prejudices dating from the Victorian period (Lawson and Silver, 1973, 422).

England differed from the United States. Americans were influenced or, perhaps, just more in tune with Camus's existential humanism and operated from the perspective of a relatively secure world in which the "bomb" was safely remote in the citizenry's collective unconscious. American radicals were more interested in social justice than in undoing the "system"—except for a small group of the Weather Left. But in Europe, as in Britain, the left was driven by a powerful intellectual base that was more accommodating and more accustomed to direct action. Sartre's socialist ideology was more familiar to the old Left of Britain and Europe than to the transcendental socialists of the American New Left. The New Left of Britain and Europe was driven by a sense of betrayal (Caute, 1988, 26-27) and style (Marwick, [1982] 1988, 135). They felt betrayed by the Old Left that seemed more interested in settling old scores than in "changing the world." Socialism had produced the "welfare state"—a holding tank for the underclass. Poverty and deprivation were not going away; they were just being moved off the street and out of sight. It seemed that someone or perhaps everyone had betrayed the social covenant that had closed World War II. If their parents would not honor the contract, they would. On the other hand they were driven by a sense of style and relative wealth (Caute, 1988, 27). They were social revolutionaries of a special brand. They knew the shops of Mary Quant and Alexander Plunkett-Green, Carnaby Street. The knew the songs of the Beatles and the Stones. They read Mao, Kurt Vonnegut, Jr., Hermann Hesse, and Tom Wolfe. They were the relatively privileged agitating on behalf of "the wretched of the earth" as well as on behalf of themselves. Their movement *was* radical-chic.

Still, the English New Left, unlike the American New Left, was deeply connected to Europe's intensely intellectual establishment. The English New Left believed it was the new vanguard and that it would inherit the establishment. They had no time for the hip chemically stoned revolt of the counterculture and its unbridled libido. They wanted real power with no distractions.

The student revolt was driven by its own history. Like their compatriots on the continent, British students knew their elders were running scared. Faced with what looked like the final collapse of Victorian England and its values, the establishment was in disarray and, finally, unsure of itself and its place in the scheme of things. The establishment's failure of nerve found spontaneous opposition by its historical nemesis, the intellectual Left. Like the Fabians before them, the instant Left was abstract, articulate, and disconnected—outside of a few temporary alliances—from any significant working-class power base (Caute, 1988, 76; cf. Pugh, 1984). But unlike the Fabians they managed at least for a short period of time to parlay the question of formal representation for students in British universities into a broader political alliance. This alliance revolved around the issues of racial discrimination, the subordination of women, nuclear armaments, the Vietnam War, and more complex questions regarding the social, political, and economic exploitation of the third world.

In addition, the political scene had become menacing. Stories about the bomb were more compelling in Europe and Britain than in the United States. Hungary had been occupied and subdued by Soviet troops. Faced with indigenous opposition to the Soviet brand of democratic centralism, Russian troops invaded Czechoslovakia on 20-21 August 1968. They removed Dubcek and crushed that country's version of socialism with a human face. As far as the Soviets were concerned, satellites were satellites and that was that. In March 1968 Italian university students exploded in protest and closed the university system. Mexican students clashed with riot police in September, shortly before the opening of the Olympic Games. In March of 1968 Franco closed Madrid University ostensibly to rid the nation of Bolshevik agitators. Franco's age and a native demand for democracy were the real causes. In April 1968 Martin Luther King, Jr. was assassinated on his hotel balcony. American blacks rioted and torched the ghettos in which many of them lived. Dany Cohn-Bendit and the Nanterre Eight faced the university disciplinary committee on 6 May 1968, and French students were at the barricades.

But unlike the Italian system the English system was finally opening up to those that structure had excluded from university education. Colleges of art and design moved up on the prestige scale, teacher training colleges were closely associated with universities, certain colleges became universities, and totally new universities such as Sussex, York, Kent, Warwick, Lancaster, East Anglia, Essex, and Stirling were created (Marwick, [1982] 1988, 154-155). Although never deeply involved in social protest the new student populations supported the more radical student politics found at the London School of Economics (LSE) and in the crusades of the Radical Student Alliance (RSA). The RSA membership was probably never in excess of a thousand (Caute, 1988, 303), but with the widespread support of the socially egalitarian aspiring burghers of the new universities and widely covered by the media, their political and social impact far exceeded their numbers.

It is interesting to note that the students of the London Institute of Education—the home of educational philosophy in Britain—never seriously participated in the protests of the sixties. Although Lionel Elvin, the Institute's director, had prepared a contingency plan for the day when the politics of LSE would boil over to the institute, that day never arrived. The politics of the institute were establishment, and the politics of its students were those of the Department of Education. According to the reminiscences of the director, the institute's students were too busy preparing for their professional careers to participate in student politics (Elvin, 1989). Years later Lionel Elvin would write *The place of commonsense in educational thought* (1977). It was a turgid defense of liberal education and indicative of the director's politics. The institute was a conservative place.

The cry for "participatory democracy" in England's colleges and universities attracted liberal students in the way the "instant Left's" anti-imperialistic rhetoric never could. In the end the liberal students would be the movement's political base. But chauvinist to the end, the instant Left would alienate the feminists, labor, minorities, and other incipient sources of political support. It was by no means a unified alliance. Friction and enmity characterized the politics of the New Left, and by the end of the decade it would dissolve in "fratricidal knife-play" (Caute, 1988, 27).

But all of the former changed professionalized versions of educational philosophy very little. By 1975 the development of Peters's version of analytic philosophy of education had become so inwardly turned that even Peters would state that the London Line had entered a rather scholastic period, repeatedly rehearsing and refining the arguments of a previous time (Peters, 1983, 35). It was a form of discourse that educational philosophy in Great Britain rehearsed throughout the 1980s.

And perhaps most surprizing of all—perhaps tired of waiting for intellectual initiatives—the civil service reasserted its dominion over fundamental (philosophical) educational questions in 1988. The 1988 Education Act declared a new fund of conservative (fundamental philosophical) questions and answers for the institution of education (cf. Simon 1991). It left educational philosophy as it did many elements of the university study of education gasping for breath and attempting to reassert its place in the game.

## NOTES

1. By scholastic I mean an insistence upon and traditional educational doctrines and dogmas.

2. As recently as 1985 D. W. Hamlyn has claimed that educational philosophy must show academic philosophy that it is pursuing substantive philosophical issues. ("Need philosophy of education be so dreary?" *Journal of Philosophy of Education* (19): 159-165). Hamlyn's was not an isolated stance. It has its philosophical proponents in Britain, the United States, and Australasia.

3. The Beatles, (1968), *White* album.

4. This is not an ad hominem attack on Peters, it is a comment; that is, both the *Pirates of Penzance* and "Blowin' in the Wind" were about the brutality and disappointments generated by what appeared to be pointless wars. The difference is that the *Pirates of Penzance* was generated by the Boer War, and "Blowin' in the Wind" was generated by the Vietnam War.

# 9

# Conclusion: Great Britain

Britain was "ripe" for the establishment of educational philosophy as early as the closing years of the Victorian period.[1] The questions of educational philosophy were ready for immediate investigation. The radical utilitarians had prepared the intellectual groundwork necessary for the establishment of the discipline, and Herbert Spencer had translated philosophical questions about education into a contradictory but modern format. The literary guild had made education a public issue. And the National Association for the Promotion of Social Science had imported questions of social reform into the compass of educational studies. It had also appropriated educational questions out of the realm of moral philosophy and firmly established them within the ambit of social science. But without an intellectual champion, without a university environment that was, for all intents and purposes, supportive of social science (education among them), the opportunity to establish education and therein educational philosophy was lost.

But the reservoir of questions remained. Education's philosophical questions were appropriated by social science and public administration, gathered comments from the occasional intellectual tourist, and were advanced by Britain's great intellectual families prior to and during the period between the World wars. The failure of educational philosophy to establish itself in the period prior to World War II was not the result of inadequate intellectual resources. Individuals of great intellectual ability were deeply concerned with the philosophical problems of education. The failure of educational philosophy to establish itself early was generated by an absence of institutional support.

The establishment of the discipline awaited the development of the London Institute and a general infrastructure that made the establishment of a "professional forum" possible. The institute launched the Philosophy of Education Society of Great Britain under the management of R. S. Peters, and the society marked the establishment of educational philosophy in Britain. Although the opportunity was ripe at the turn of the century the environment was not "susceptible" to its establishment.[2] A suitable professional forum for the discussion of the conceptual elements of the discipline was not established. Without it neither the discipline nor its constitutive ideas were capable of development.

On an academic level professionalization meant gaining a place in the academic establishment of the university in its own right. It also meant gaining intellectual control of the nation's colleges of teacher education and displacing the preeminence of informal versions of teacher education. On a professional level educational philosophy sought to extend its position in the academic community and pursue its own special interests in the theory and practice of education that is, the discipline sought to extend its own technical interests—by exposing the theoretical muddles of its professional competitors, psychology, and sociology—with the sponsorship and assistance of its professional ally, philosophy. In this role educational philosophy sought a more influential position among professional educators and in society at large.[3]

In *The future of intellectuals and the rise of the new class* (1979) Alvin Gouldner points out that the new class is a group—often academic—that has found and appropriated an identity for itself based upon their monopoly possession of arcane knowledge. This group pursues its own interests and aggrandizement. And as Gouldner points out, more often than not, it ignores, when possible, the culture of critical discourse to attend to its "narcotizing technical obsessions" (Gouldner, 1979, 66). If one extends Gouldner's argument to include both critical and conservative political persuasions as members of the new class, it is easy to see that English educational philosophy, of course, was no exception to the class's tendency to indulge its technical obsessions. In seeking to extend its own technical interests it lost sight of its professional audience. Its technical obsessions became their own excuse.

Although as author of *Ethics and education* (1966) R. S. Peters was committed to some version of "secondary education for all" in principle, he was silent in practice on the questions of poverty and deprivation: the irrational distribution of educational resources, the effects of class on educational performance, antiquated and dilapidated educational plants, the economic exploitation of immigrant groups, and the neglect or plain inappropriateness of parts of immigrant children's education. In the last analysis *Ethics and education* (1966) was a quest for authority in a world that seemed to have lost respect for all authority.

## PROFOUND CONSERVATIVISM

One standard Australian critique of Peters's version of analytic philosophy argues that it was socially unconscious. It was not unconscious, it was profoundly conservative. This critique of the London Line accuses it of a surfeit of grammatical analysis and a paucity of social concern. In an eminently practical profession like educating it is undoubtedly correct to point out that it is a matter of no small amount of bad faith to pose social questions as matters of linguistic nuance. Turning one's ear to linguistic nuance is not enough in a world that is asking social, not linguistic, questions. Nevertheless, Peters and the London Line in general were anything but socially unconscious. The London Line reflected the Victorian stance of the classical aristocratic educational tradition out of which it had sprung. Peters was committed to a version of education familiar in spirit to the liberal education that was so valued by Arnold of Rugby and John Ruskin.

The London Line argued for the "education" and the "worth-while" as if they were, respectively, an eternal truth and a moral transcendental aesthetic. In historical perspective, it was all too clear that the arguments were, in modern dress, a rather traditional defense of the virtues of a peculiarly British definition of "education"—which generated a Victorian, classical, socially segregated, and morally focused version of schooling. But at the time the stance seemed a solid defense of a version of education that produced the "best and the brightest," a defense against educational Luddites who had constructed in the name of egalitarianism schools without academic or, more important, intellectual merit.

## NOTES

1. See Stephen Toulmin, (1972), *Human Understanding* (vol. 1), (Princeton, N. J.: Princeton University Press), 211-213. This volume contains an excellent statement about "ripeness" in science. By easy extension it can be made available for discussions of the social sciences.

2. An account of the discipline's prologue is important because it describes the "susceptibility" of the wider social and intellectual environments to support a "new" academic project such as educational philosophy. Without a susceptible environment, no matter how large or dramatic the discipline's intellectual potential, it usually never reaches the takeoff point. The case of philosophy of education in Britain is an excellent example of a discipline that did not reach that point until well after World War II. An interesting discussion of susceptibility can be found in Stephen Toulmin, (1969), "Innovation and the problem of utilization," In *Factors in the transfer of technology*, eds. William H. Gruber and Donald G. Marquis (Cambridge: MIT Press).

3. Initially educational philosophy was only concerned with extending its dominion over education's theoretical structures. Nevertheless, its tactical interest extended to acquiring a place of special interest first in the London Institute of Education. In this it was successful. Its strategic interest extended to obtaining a place of special influence in government, which it failed to acquire, and in the university establishment, which it did achieve.

# Part III

# Philosophy of Education in Australasia

# 10

# The Early Days in Australia

A primary factor in the history of Australian education and therein Australian educational philosophy is the nation's ominous origins. Australia began as a penal colony. Robert Hughes, in *The fatal shore* (1987), a graphic and horrific account of the nation's history, demonstrates that its convict past is an irreducible element of Australia's social history. Prior to the gold rush in the 1850s, which brought thousands of immigrants to Australia, the majority of the continent's European inhabitants were convicts who had been transported to Australia from England's prisons. This fact was a significant element of the Australian ethos at the turn of the twentieth century, just as it remains a significant element of Australia's domestic worldview today.[1]

Convictry produced a social organization of work within which the initial development of British (European) settlement and social distinction was dependent upon convict labor. In response to the nation's convict history and its position in the British Empire an economically and socially segregated educational system evolved. Advanced learning through the use of tutors or private schools was largely the monopoly of social, economic, and intellectual privilege, while elementary education in charity schools of the Society for the Propagation of the Gospel or the Clergy and Schools Corporation of the Church of England was, for the most part, a proprietary monopoly of religious organizations held in trust for those who had little or no claim on privilege (see Barcan, 1988; Burnswoods and Fletcher, 1980, 12-15).

For the dispossessed convictry meant a very moral version of education:

The educational work of this early penal period evolved as a governmental and church response to social and moral needs to train up the "rising generation" to be better behaved than their convict parents. Most schools established were for the "lower orders", the children of parents who could not afford an education for their children or who were indifferent to their children's needs. Schools such as the Female and Male Orphan Schools and the Native Institutions were specifically designed to separate pupils from the "vicious example" of their environment and to perform a moral and religious reformation in the children, usually by combining a programme of basic literacy and religious instruction with training in an industrial occupation suited to social expectations. (Burnswoods and Fletcher, 1980, 13)

On the other hand, for social elites, education meant something fundamentally different.

For the children of more well-to-do parents the services of tutors were normally engaged until the child was old enough to be sent "back home" to an English boarding school. However, in the early 1800s several small academies were begun in Sydney and Parramatta, some teaching advanced subjects for boys, and at the same time select academies sprang up, offering the "polite accomplishments" for girls. These trends continued well into the first half of the nineteenth century. (Burnswoods and Fletcher, 1980, 13)

"In the later nineteenth century the main activity of the urban upper class in education was its support for the major private schools" (Barcan, 1988, 335). Nothing demonstrated elite social standing and economic privilege better than the casual but undeniable statement made by the school tie of an elite GPS (Greater [Public] Protestant School) school. Janet McCalman (1989) points out that 97 percent of Australia's social elite attended Victoria's Greater Protestant Schools or one of the slightly less prestigious independent Protestant schools. Australians were and are ruled, judged, cured, financed, sermonized, and taught by the graduates of Victoria's GPS schools (McCalman, 1989).

The monopoly of advanced learning was supported not only by the nation's social ethos but also by an educational system in which a small number of places in the secondary system and an even more restricted number of university places assured the monopoly of educational privilege that the nation's ethos suggested. The last major educational initiative of urban elites in the middle to late nineteenth century was "the establishment of Sydney University as an aristocratic, Anglophile institution" (Barcan, 1988, 335). Donald Horne (1967, 199) has noted that  universities were shrouded in conservatism and dedicated to servicing the establishment professions. "The University remained a conservative, English, classical enclave in colonial society. Its classical version of a liberal education served to isolate it from the practical, pioneering community" (Barcan, 1988, 103). Australia's primary and secondary schools reflected that isolation.

## MATESHIP

Society was characterized by a dialectical social solidarity. It was a solidarity of those who had come to Australia of their own volition or the requirements of duty, against those who had been sent as transportees. The solidarity of free men (the Protestant ascendency) was accomplished at the price of opposition to convicts, Aboriginals, freed men, and women. The last were in opposition to all men—convicts and free men. Contempt and animosity affected gender relations. Homosexuality in the colonial tradition was the most horrible crime of all. "Their sexual preference was doubly damned: first, because it was a crime under law, and second, because it was mainly committed by those who were convicts already" (Hughes, 1987, 272). Convicts, Aboriginals, and women were part of a perpetual underclass that was the object of the hostility and aristocratic and nonaristocratic fantasies of masculine privilege. In this oppositional solidarity Aboriginals were the least equal of all. But they were closely followed by women. Women were the primary objects of male oppression:

The upper ranks were hardly free of cruelty, on ships any more than in society at large. Still, I'd stick to my general proposition in both these domains: the lower the status of men in the nineteenth century, the more brutalized they were and the more brutal their attitude towards women. Their capacity to "thingize" women matched that of their social betters . . . (Dixon, 1976, 96)

Women were defined by men in terms of their usefulness as a source of food and labor, their fitness for sexual release, as well as—according to the church—their seminal role as a moral inspiration. Anne Summers ([1975] 1976) remarked that they were deemed to be "damned whores and God's police" in a book by the same title. Insofar as they were educated, daughters of the "well-to-do and land-owning classes" were given a refined and domestic education consistent with their future roles as mothers and homemakers. Daughters of lower-class families received what education circumstances would allow. Even the "bush school" was not an egalitarian place (Kyle, 1988).

Australia's oppositional solidarity is part and parcel of both the country's egalitarian bonhomie and a defensive two-class resentment that marks its social relations. Being far removed from the icy control of Victorian England, the colony dissolved some of the more deplorable elements of the English class system (Hughes, 1987, 595-596). Australia never developed a system of aristocratic social relations or politics. Nevertheless, the egalitarian "mateship" of Australian society existed at the cost of "defensive, static, levelling, two-class hatred that came out of convictry" (Hughes 1987, 596). In the nineteenth century many factors limited the growth of education, but none was as significant as the absence of an educationally ambitious middle class. Barcan (1988, 103) notes, "An industrial middle class hardly existed, the commercial middle class was unambitious educationally and was weakened by religious divisions." This absence sustained the distinction that commended elementary education for all, while reserving secondary education and particularly private secondary education for the privileged few.

The construction of the Australian ethos was accomplished by the obsessive cultural enterprise of forgetting and sublimating the convict realities of Australian colonial history, along with the social and personal consequences that history engendered. As Robert Hughes writes,

A "Centennial Song" published in the Melbourne *Argus* struck the right note of defensive optimism, coupling it with an appeal to censor early Australian history—or, preferably, not to write it at all.

> Is it manly, fair or honest with our early sins to stain
> What we aimed at, worked for, conquered—aye—an honest, noble name?
> And those scribes whose gutter pleasure is to air the hideous past,
> Let us leave them to the loathesome mould in which their mind is cast.
> Look ahead and not behind us! Look to what is sunny, bright—
> Look into our glorious future, not into our shadowed night.

At the heart of each proclamation of renewal was a longing for amnesia. (Hughes, 1987, 597)

The country's convict history was denied by the well-to-do and influential members of Australian society (Hughes, 1987, 595). Real culture, literature, and history were British. Only the largely inarticulate recollections of the dangerous elements of the working class in general and the working class Irish retained an interest in their convict past (Hughes 1987, 595). This element also opposed and even celebrated their opposition to individuals of vested social and economic privilege. But to polite Australian society, the penal colony origins of their society were something grossly obscene and best forgotten. The content of official education was little different than the content of official culture.

OFFICIAL CULTURE

Official culture omitted or maginalized bushranger folkheroes and their almost inevitable fate upon the gallows. Australian women and Aboriginals were invisible elements of the country's history. Authorized versions of Australian history began with the gold rush and the 1850s (cf. Horne, 1972, 210). Authorized history was largely British history. Shirley Hazzard provides an illustration of this history in her seminal novel *The transit of Venus* (1980):

Australian History, given once a week only, was easily contained in a small book, dun-coloured as the scenes described. Presided over at its briefly pristine birth by Captain Cook (gold-laced, white-wigged, and back to back in illustrations with Sir Joseph Banks), Australia's history soon terminated in unsuccess. It was engulfed in a dark stench of nameless prisoners whose only apparent activity was to have built, for their own incarceration, the stone gaols, now empty monuments that little girls might tour for Sunday outings . . .
Australian History dwindled into the expeditions of doomed explorers, journeys without revelation or encounter endured by fleshless men whose portraits already gloomed, beforehand, with a wasted, unlucky look—the eyes fiercely shining from sockets that were already bone.
That was the shrivelled chronicle—meagre, shameful, uninspired; swiftly passed over by teachers impatient to return to the service at the Abbey. (Hazzard, 1980, 32)

Colonial Australia was a creature of the British Empire and its Victorian culture. The colony's history and ideology was a mixture of Victorian culture, morality, and apologetics. Australian children were

made to read the novels of Walter Scott and the deeds of Sir Francis Drake, to recite like parrots the names of English kings, the dates of unexplained events like the Rump Parliament and the Gunpowder Plot, the lengths of European rivers they would never see . . . It [was] impossible to find, in any history book used in Australian schools up to the mid-1960s, a satisfactory or even coherent account of penal Australia. (Hughes, 1987, 599)

The period between Australia's 1888 centenary celebration and its horrific casualties in World War I was a time of unchallenged allegiance to England and the Empire:

Australian politicians conceived and ran the Centenary as a lavish feast of jingoism, a tribute to the benevolent, all-embracing British Empire. Without Britain's market, Australian business could not survive; without her institutions, especially the Monarchy, Australian morality would decay; without her dreadnoughts, Australian blood would be yellowed by hordes of invading junks. Bunting, flags, parades, speeches and more bunting were rammed down the popular throat, and only republicans gagged on them. (Hughes, 1987, 598)

Australia's alienation from Empire began as the colony entered her "great widowhood" during World War I. As the losses in France and

Gallipoli grew to nightmare proportions, unthinking allegiance to Empire and European politics became a matter of public concern. The colony's relationship with the Empire became politically problematic, and Australia began slowly and painfully to disentangle its own history from the luck and history of John Bull and the British establishment. Australia's estrangement from the British Empire was complete by the end of World War II. The country's devastating losses in World War I allowed the Australian Prime Minister to withdraw Australian troops from the African campaign during World War II to protect Australian shores when the British abandoned the defense of Australia and left the nation huddled behind the Brisbane line after the collapse of Singapore. Putting Australian national self-interest before the concerns of Empire would have been unthinkable just twenty or thirty years before. The Australians finally understood that they were on their own.

## AUSTRALIA'S NEW HISTORY

An informed, realistic version of Australia's history prior to the gold rush did not appear until after the Festival of Britain in 1951, which celebrated the end of World War II, the return to a peacetime economy, and unobtrusively foreshadowed the final collapse of Victorian: culture and morality. As in all elements of the Commonwealth the collapse allowed Australia to bring the continent's own history to light. What was unspeakable in the 1930s and 1940s became a matter of intense interest in a period when history, whatever its origin, became acceptable, if not fashionable. In an era filled with antiheroes, a convict history was not all that impossible to accept. The New Left and the counterculture created the cynical attitudes necessary to penetrate the "lavish feast of jingoism" and false consciousness that had formed the Australian ethos and its history. The change in public consciousness allowed the academic and intellectual establishment to construct a version of its own history that was proud of its present and able to look directly at its origins.

Australia discovered its own history in the sixties. Australians rewrote their history and their present in terms consistent with the optimistic ethos generated by World War II. The euphoria of the postwar period produced books like Donald Horne's *Lucky country* ([1964] 1965). This widely read text was a part of the feast of nationalism that swept the country after the war. It presented a version of the country's history that was happy to accept its own present and to share in the Commonwealth's glory. But according to

Horne the country was not ready to acknowledge all of its past. At a later point in time authors like Humphrey McQueen brought a new set of verities to the story of the nation's past and present. McQueen's *A new Britannia* (1970) paved the way for Australia's modern history. In a sense, *A new Britannia* was heir to Russell Ward's *Australian legend* (1958). Ward's account of the Australian ethos referenced its heritage to its own domestic situation, rather than to the British experience. He constructed a "people's account" of the Australian ethos in a manner reminiscent of Frederick Turner's thesis on the significance of the frontier for the American experience. Later Ward's account of the Australian ethos found a sympathetic ear in Australia's counterculture.

Social psychology, sociology, and history all conspired to form a new Australian identity suitable for modern times. It was an ethos that drew Australia's indigenous worldview more into line with the intensely intellectual and liberal ethos of Europe. It formed a link between the social critiques of European and Australian society. It questioned liberal interpretations of Australian society and turned from rationales of British imperial politics to explore new topics. The motifs of labor, class, gender, race, mateship, and convictry all became grist for the new academic radicals just as they became subject to counterattack by the academic establishment and conservative journals like *Quadrant*.

Robert Conway's *Great Australian stupor* (1971) was one of the first successful attempts to mount an assault upon the Australian ethos in general and the elements of "mateship" in particular. R. W. Connell's *Ruling class ruling culture* (1977) was an academic critique of privilege in Australia. It is an interesting text not only for what it argues but for what it indicates as well, that is, some new and contemporary cracks in the Australian academic establishment's relationship with social and economic privilege. Anne Summers in *Damned whores and God's police* ([1975] 1976) and Miriam Dixon in *The real Matilda* (1976) discovered the history of Australian women. Under the careful and artful work of Summers and Dixon women emerged from the margins of the Australian ethos.

The establishment of educational philosophy was part of the construction of a new Australian ethos, of the attempt to disentangle Australia and the idea of Australia's institutions from their British parentage. The conservative intellectual agendas of Australian educational philosophy had reference to the work of R. S. Peters, Paul Hirst, and the London Line in order to maintain an ideological continuity with British educational traditions and ideas. The alienation of Australian educational philosophy's new radicals and liberals from that inspiration was part of the discovery of Australia's own identity and history. It was generated by all those social, economic, political, and historical forces that found their focus in World War II and the consequences that flowed from the Allied victory.

## NOTE

1. An interesting presentation of Australia's contemporary ethos can be found in (1985) *Daedalus* (114) 1. It is the first number of the journal to be dedicated to a single country.

# 11

# John Anderson and C. D. Hardie

Professor John Anderson was responsible for the only important domestic school of philosophy in Australia in the period between the world wars. Anderson, born in Scotland, was the son of a politically radical headmaster. He received his education at the University of Glasgow and "lectured at Cardiff (1918-1919), Glasgow (1919-1920), and Edinburgh (1920-1927) before accepting an appointment in 1927 as professor of philosophy at the University of Sydney, Australia" (Passmore, 1967a, 119). Although Anderson remained forever faithful to the spirit of the Scottish Enlightenment, he brought the radical social politics that he had acquired at his father's knee with him to Australia. Some of the first important fractures in the academy's relationship to the English ethos can be traced to the appointment of John Anderson to the Chair of Philosophy at Sydney University.

Anderson was responsible for some of Australian educational philosophy's most important philosophical antecedents. He generated a distinctive Australian philosophical voice. Donald Horne noted:

Around the artist Norman Lindsay in the 1920s gathered a number of people who proclaimed a renaissance of world culture in Sydney with artists who had "gay hearts and the courage of their desires"; and around the philosophy professor John Anderson in the 1930's was a group that saw Sydney University as the only significant centre of philosophy in the contemporary world. (1972, 212)

Anderson's work provided an inspiration to educators that the work of the first professor of educational philosophy, C. D. Hardie, never did. For example, Margaret Mackie at Armidale Teachers College was inspired by Anderson's work. Anderson's example, presented largely through the philosophy department at Sydney University inspired Australia's younger educational philosophers to speak with their own voices and to be suitably suspicious of all things English—as were all good Scots, Anderson included!

Anderson's philosophical stance had reference to Kant, Hegel, and, most interesting of all, to Samuel Alexander (Passmore, 1967a, 120; Baker, 1979, 6). It was the thought of the expatriate Australian, Samuel Alexander [1859-1938], who along with William James, provided the intellectual means that allowed Anderson to reject Idealism. Alexander's 1915 Gifford lectures at Glasgow University, the university which Anderson attended in 1916-1917, were an immensely influential part of Anderson's intellectual development.[1] Alexander and James convinced Anderson to adopt a modified empiricism. This conversion allowed him to construct a cultural politics that found, at least for a time, a middle way between radical Scottish and Marxist thought—an Australian way.

Soon after his arrival in Sydney his liberal and, for the times, radical politics brought him into opposition with Christianity, social welfare work, jingoistic patriotism, censorship, and the "new education" (Passmore, 1967a, 119). He quickly became "doyen of Sydney's radical intellectuals" (Gilbert, 1988, 44). In 1931, four of Anderson's essays on education were published under the title *Education and politics* (1931). Anderson's comments on education were written when Victorian Australia, torn from its unquestioning and jingoistic patriotic relationship with Empire by the realities of war and the questions of its own domestic relations generated by the Depression, began to reconstruct its own history and domestic realities. Although Anderson was firmly committed to Scottish versions of a "liberal education," his sympathies for Marxist thought provided a critical counterpoint for jingoistic Victorianism. Anderson returned to the topic of education on many occasions just as he returned on numerous occasions to his troubled allegiance with Marxist politics and social theory. By the 1950s his Marxism would fade, while his allegiance to Victorian values would remain (Baker, 1979).

Anderson's seminal *Education and politics* (1931) was an important contribution to Australian educational thought. Its four essays displayed an allegiance to Victorian versions of a liberal education, but at the same time it recognized an obligation to a more egalitarian Australia. Nevertheless, like many Victorians, Anderson's egalitarianism did not extend to utilitarian versions of education. He deemed such departures from traditional schooling to be a prostitution of his version of nonscholastic classicism—to his mind the only preparation for the real questions of life (Baker, 1979, 75).

Anderson wrote:

Culture is not a leisurely affair, but is something that a man must put into his work, and that liberality of thought is opposed to every sort of exclusiveness and thus to the very notion of the "gentleman," or of social rank in general. But I also maintain that all education must be liberal, and that training of a "utilitarian" character, by being illiberal, is at the same time, uneducative . . .

The view I shall maintain is that a liberal education is one which enables us to live freely. It is a training, not for a particular job or service, but for a whole life . . .

If education is to be for a whole life, it must be *political* . . .

Education properly understood, then, is liberal; it implies the most thorough-going democracy, the rejection alike of privileged ideas and of privileged persons. (Anderson, 1931, 53-54, 55, 56, 63)

In part Anderson's stance on liberal education is little different than J. S. Mill's "Inaugural address at St. Andrews University" ([1867] 1985). The stance is this: Classical wisdom should inform practice. What is different in Anderson's stance is its pervasive egalitarianism. Anderson's concern for a "thorough-going democracy" was part of his intellectual legacy to the philosophy department of Sydney University. The department would pass on that gift to the "Sydney School" of educational philosophy through the people it trained.

John Anderson's philosophy department at Sydney University and, similarly, R. M. Crawford's history department at Melbourne University were profoundly influential elements in the structure of the two institutions that supplied the graduates to the most important positions in their respective states (Head, 1988, 30). Together with the cultural cliques and journals that they intellectually sponsored, supported, and to which they responded, Anderson's philosophy department and Crawford's history department controlled the character of political, cultural, and educational discussions in the nation's two major cities.

A most notable feature of the Australian university system in the period before World War II was its diminutive size:

The university sector began slowly, with capital city universities opening for undergraduate teaching in Sydney (1852), Melbourne (1855), Adelaide (1876), Hobart (1893), Brisbane (1911), and Perth (1913). Student numbers remained small in the decades before the Second World War. There was a complete lack of resources for postgraduate studies, reinforcing the lack of research on local topics and the overseas drift of talents. (Head, 1988, 18)

Unlike departments in the United States, Anderson's and Crawford's departments faced no significant intellectual challenge to their ideas from social science. Conservative attitudes committed to the English idea of a "liberal education" assured the humanities pride of place in the Australian university system (Bourke, 1988, 47-56):

In 1901 . . . the small society of around 3.5 million people had only six universities in capitals and no national journals, organizations or conferences. The very term "social sciences" was a rare one and the only large association, the Australasian Association for the Advancement of Science, had a few sections for the social sciences and the humanities. (Alomes, 1988, 70)

Social science, like science, would have to wait until well after the close of World War II to establish and consolidate a position in the university system.

Australians interested in social science had little choice but to pursue advanced training somewhere else in the Empire or cross the Pacific and seek graduate training in America. Of course the absence of postgraduate work within the country had its impact on the path of academic careers in Australia. Small staffs and large work loads left little time for research (Alomes, 1988, 74). Postgraduate numbers and research resources were either nonexistent or so small that Australia's best social scientists left the country to pursue their careers overseas.[2]

In the inter-war period a number of distinguished social scientists left Australia to make their careers elsewhere. Among them were Clarence Hunter Northcott, Meredith Atkinson, H. Duncan Hall, A. Radcliffe Brown, Persia Campbell, George Elton Mayo, Stanley Porteous, Herbert Heaton and Thomas Griffith Taylor . . . Some, like Atkinson, Radcliffe Brown and Heaton, were not native Australians but they did invest substantial years of their lives here; the significant point is that they did not stay. (Bourke, 1988, 60)

The tendency for Australian social scientists both to study and to realize their careers overseas contributed to the attitude that "real" academics like "real" ideas came from America or Britain. It was an attitude that delayed the establishment of the university study of social sciences, education among them, until after World War II.

"Before the 1960s Australian intellectuals had been seen as too insignificant to greatly influence the course of national life, or as too timid to try" (Head, 1988, 28). This level of nominal participation in the course of national life changed in the sixties when Australian academics and intellectuals acquired a heretofore unheard of importance in the cultural life of the nation. In the mid-sixties Sydney Andersonians championed a place for liberal politics in a conservative establishment while the old and New Left sensed new political opportunities in the romantic ethos of the counterculture and the Labor party. The election of the Whitlam government in 1972 marked the time when Australian academics in general and social scientists in particular entered a new place in the university establishment and the social and cultural politics of Australia. The liberal economic approach of the Priorities Review Staff and the general direction of national policy for enhanced educational opportunities, consumer protection, and other liberal or "egalitarian" policies gained the general support of Australia's intellectual elite (see Kemp, 1988). The political mandate to extend educational opportunities consolidated a place for the university study of the social sciences. This extension supported, of course, the establishment of the university study of education in general and thereby educational philosophy. Anderson's work certainly foreshadowed the early sympathy for the discipline in the Faculty of Education at the University of Sydney.

## C. D. HARDIE

Another academic career that was as important as Anderson's to the discipline's establishment was that of C. D. Hardie.[3] In 1942 C. D. Hardie's *Truth and fallacy in educational theory* ([1942] 1962) was published in Britain, after which Hardie was given the Chair of Education at the University of Tasmania. In the years that followed Hardie was a central figure in the discipline's prehistory. In a sense, he was the discipline's antihero.

Despite his long tenure at that southern institution, and despite the fact that Hardie's work preceded the pioneering work of O'Connor (1957), Scheffler (1958), and Peters (1966) by at least a decade, Hardie did little to establish the place of analytic philosophy in Australasia. Interestingly enough *Truth and fallacy in educational theory* ([1942] 1962) was a work that probably would have remained largely unacknowledged by the academic community except for the work of James E. McClellan and B. Paul Komisar, who brought it to the attention of American philosophers of education through their sponsorship of the publication of an American edition by Columbia University in 1962. American scholars had been introduced to analytic philosophy of education through the work of Israel Scheffler in 1958 and were receptive to Hardie's work, which became more widely known in North America than it was in Australasia—at least in the early 1960s. It is probably the case that it was the analytic work of Hardie and D. J. O'Connor's *An introduction to the philosophy of education* (1957) that first attracted Australia and New Zealand's nascent college to analysis (cf. Marshall, 1982, 19; Beck, 1991, 312). It was Hardie and O'Connor who aroused Australasia's invisible college from "its dogmatic slumbers," the work of these two dissolved interest in more traditional versions of a systematic study of educational ideas gleaned from the "Great Educators." Later, when analytic philosophy attracted wide interest in Australasia and New Zealand, it was R. S.

Peters's version of analytic philosophy that enchanted Australasian philosophers of education, not O'Connor's or Hardie's.

Nevertheless, Hardie's *Truth and fallacy in educational theory* ([1942] 1962) is an important artifact in the history of Australasian philosophy of education (cf. Snook, 1969, 17). It is significant not only because it was a foundational contribution to the establishment of analytic philosophy in the study of educating but because it offered a version of analytic philosophy that was far closer to the spirit of Wittgenstein's work, as we know it today, than was the thought of those analytic philosophers of education whose major work would follow in a decade's time. Unlike his academic contemporaries, Hardie was not concerned with the invention, production, or application of any technical view of philosophy to educational thought or practice. Instead, just as Wittgenstein attempted to free philosophy from the doctrinal and technical constraints and confusions of metaphysics (cf. Janik and Toulmin, 1973, 256-257), Hardie foreshadowed an educational project designed to liberate educational discourse from the artificial constraints of any technical or metaphysical view of philosophy (Hardie, 1974). His work, at its best, was an attempt to guard against foundational versions of philosophy that purported to direct education from some ethical or epistemological high ground (Hardie 1974, 94). He argued that metaphysics and various technical versions of philosophy generated needless impediments to powerful discourse about the practice of educating (Hardie, 1974).

Hardie was interested in the struggle to free mind from the intellectual obstacles generated by philosophy, rather than in the application of philosophy either "pure" or "educational" to the problems of schooling. As far as Hardie was concerned, genuine problems of educating were sometimes empirical, and therefore to be addressed by either science or one of the social sciences; or they were analytic, and therefore to be addressed through logic or mathematics. In his opinion education had suffered unduly from its historical links with philosophy. He wrote, "It was unfortunately true that the study of education in universities had been initiated largely as an off-shoot from the study of philosophy, so that with the disappearance of philosophy as a serious subject, the subject of education inevitably became suspect in the eyes of many" (Hardie, 1974, 94). Hardie disassociated himself from the "technical'" and "professional" versions of philosophy and philosophy of education that had become the hallmark of the analytic tradition, and from the prescriptive tasks that marked traditional versions of philosophy of education.

The establishment of societies for the study of philosophy of education in the United States and Great Britain was, as far as he was concerned, merely symptomatic of the attempt of philosophy, an academic discipline that had become intellectually bankrupt thirty or forty years previous, to reestablish itself in the unguarded euphoria of the post-World War II educational boom.

Philosophy of education in Australasia is a once and future thing. It might have begun in the late 1940s after the publication of C. D. Hardie's *Truth and fallacy in educational theory* ([1942] 1962) and his appointment to the Chair of Education at the University of Tasmania. His book and his tenure in Tasmania could have become a plausible predicate for a society dedicated to the professional conduct of educational philosophy. In other words, Australasia could have established a modern analytic form of the discipline while in the United States the profession was still struggling to free itself from Dewey's transfixing stare and the plethora of "isms" that shadowing philosophy had generated (cf. Dykhuizen, 1973)—and while the British approach remained either a Cook's tour of comments upon education by individuals important in the construction of the intellectual or educational history of the West or a series of intellectual adventures conducted by individuals whose main concerns were something other than educating.

Unfortunately, the early Australasian opportunity was lost. It was lost partially because of Hardie's intellectual consistency and his attitude toward philosophy; it was lost partially because philosophy of education had yet to become a significant part of the Australian university establishment; and finally, the opportunity was lost partially because of a Victorian conceit that "real" intellectuals and academics resided in Great Britain. And perhaps it was also lost because Hardie was a man with a difficult personality not well suited to the academic politics necessary for building an academic discipline.

Hardie believed in education and believed that education could not help but suffer from a connection with a pseudodiscipline like philosophy, and might suffer even more from a close affiliation with a pseudo-pseudodiscipline like philosophy of education (Hardie, 1974, 94). He was a member of the editorial board of *Educational Philosophy and Theory* for about six years and contributed two articles to early volumes but he did little to further the development of philosophy of education as a discipline.[4] His membership on the editorial board was largely a formality—or a courtesy may be a better description. His authorship of two articles in the journal indicates that he was more willing to follow his own ideas than he was to promote the discipline. His support for philosophy of education in Australasia was largely passive. It is impossible to argue that he took an active or important role in the establishment of educational philosophy—as a discipline—

in the region. He did not promote the establishment of either Chairs or lectureships in the "philosophy of education" (Hardie, 1985); nor did he involve himself in the establishment of *Educational Philosophy and Theory* in the late 1960s or the Philosophy of Education Society of Australasia when it was established in the early 1970s. His lack of support for philosophy of education as a disciplinary undertaking was not a matter of disaffection, it was a matter of remaining consistent with his belief that philosophy had nothing to offer to the practice of schooling—schooling was an empirical question or, in the odd instance, a logical one.

On a purely pragmatic note, it must be remembered that philosophy of education was not taught in Australian universities until the mid-to-late 1960s. Thus, even if Hardie or any of his colleagues who shared his concern for philosophy and education—residing, at that time, mostly in teachers colleges—had decided to press for the establishment of a society for the study of philosophy and education, there was precious little in the way of infrastructure for them to call upon. Partially the opportunity was lost because the Australian university system was not ready to support it.

On the other hand, if Hardie's work had achieved critical acclaim in Britain, all might not have been lost for Australian philosophy of education. Early critical acclaim in Britain might have manufactured enough academic interest in Australasian universities and teachers colleges to have generated a few lectureships as well as a pertinent professional society. But England was busy with World War II and deeply involved in postwar economic recovery immediately thereafter. Except for some initial recognition by academics such as D. J. O'Connor (see 1957, v), Hardie's book languished in obscurity and quietly went out of print.

## NOTES

1. Samuel Alexander's 1915 Gifford lectures on "Space, Time and Deity," later written up in a book by the same title ([1933] 1966), seem to be a common point of reference among educational philosophy's intellectual antecedents. And insofar as educational philosophy and philosophy share a concern for a common corpus of literature, Alexander's Gifford lectures may be an important but neglected antecedent. As one reads the prehistory of educational philosophy, reference to Alexander's lectures appear, often obliquely, again and again. Their place among educational philosophy's antecedents deserves further research.

2. It might be profitably recalled at this point that some of Australia's best educational philosophers followed a similar career path.

3. Hardie's work is a chronological though not a conceptual or logical link with the work of John Anderson.

4. C. D. Hardie, (1969), "Does education stand on its foundations?" *Educational Philosophy and Theory* (1) 1; C. D. Hardie, (1971), "The philosophy of educational research," *Educational Philosophy and Theory* (3) 1.

# 12

# The Right Climate, Australia
# and New Zealand

The development of the pool of talent that eventually would populate philosophy of education in Australia and reform the country's educational system in general can be explained by reference to the postwar baby boom, the rise of industrialism with its white-collar class, and the consequential expansion of primary, secondary, and tertiary education. Changes in the Australian education system were demographically driven. Educational reforms that took place during and immediately after the war were not driven by political philosophy or systematic intellectual reappraisals of the educational system.

Nevertheless, the war years in Australia witnessed the emergence of a viable and virulent reform movement in education, after nearly two decades of stagnation or aridness. Yet despite the strength of this reform movement there are no national or even state education landmarks to testify to its success. Australia is bereft of reforms comparable in significance to the 1944 Education Act in England and Wales, or to the "GI's Bill of Rights" legislation in USA, or the "Langevin Plan" for secondary school reorganization in France. (Spaull, 1982, 162)

The entire system of Australian education was entering upon a period of qualitative transformation parallel to that of Australian society as a whole. The demand for tertiary education first evidenced itself in Australia's teachers colleges: "Developments in teachers' colleges in the 1950s responded closely to the changes in primary and secondary education. As enrollments in primary schools rose after 1946, teachers' colleges increased in size and number. In 1946 there were only seven State teachers' colleges in Australia. By 1962 there were twenty-eight" (Barcan, 1980, 338). But despite the massive development of teachers colleges, recruitment drives, and lower standards of admission to the profession of teaching, short courses were still needed to fill the demand for primary teachers (Barcan, 1980, 338; Burnswoods and Fletcher, 1980, 213). When the demand for primary teachers finally abated in the late 1950s, the crisis was quickly replaced by a desperate shortage of secondary teachers. Accordingly, the percentage of university graduates teaching in secondary schools markedly declined after 1944.[1] By the mid-sixties the demand for teachers, and therefore for tertiary education, seemed to be in a period of unrestrained growth. In the early 1960s a higher birth rate, increased levels of immigration, and higher levels of student retention coupled with a seemingly ever-increasing resignation rate, elevated the demand for teacher training to a previously unheard of level. (Barcan, 1980, 338; Burnswoods and Fletcher, 1980, 212-215)

The university system was also expanding, but at a pace not quite as rapid as that of the colleges. Industrialization, the professionalization of work, and an increasing level of prosperity generated an unquenchable demand for tertiary education in general, and university education in particular. The expansion of the university sector of tertiary education in Australia was evident in the proliferation of universities in the 1950s and thereafter. The Australian university establishment extended beyond its usual boundaries of government cum civil service, clergy, and the law; added were medicine, dentistry, engineering, architecture, and a cohort of collateral professions. The institutions themselves proliferated. In 1954 the University of New England gained its autonomy from Sydney University, partially in response to the elevated demand for university education and partially as a result of its willingness to establish correspondence courses in teacher education (Barcan, 1980, 331). In 1958 the University of Technology became the University of New South Wales. Monash University in Melbourne, also founded in 1958, first enrolled students in 1961. Macquarie University was established in 1963. The Wollongong division of the University of New South Wales became Wollongong University College in 1962, and Newcastle became an independent university in 1965 (Barcan, 1980, 334). The climate of expansion continued into the early 1970s with University College at Townsville becoming the James Cook University of North Queensland in 1970. In Brisbane, Griffith University was established in 1971 and like Murdoch University in Perth, it was opened in 1975 (Barcan, 1980, 376). "Between 1967 and 1973 the number of [university] students increased by 39.6 per cent—from 95,380 to 133,126" (Barcan, 1980, 376).

The expansion of the Australian tertiary system began in the early 1950s and was ended in the mid-to-late 1970s by economic recession. The expansion vastly extended the number of student places available to the country's populace. Nevertheless it continued to be true that most students who went to university were there because their parents could afford to buy them a career (Horne, 1967, 199). The vast majority of Australians could not afford such a luxury. The expansion of the college and university system marked only a semicollapse of the monopolies of learning that the Australian "carriage trade" had held to itself since the 1850s.

But "by 1971 Australia had fifteen universities and over thirty well-known journals in the humanities, social sciences and pubic affairs, and a proliferation of associations and their conferences" (Alomes, 1988, 70). The creation of the Philosophy of Education Society of Australasia and *Educational Philosophy and Theory* was part of the general growth of journals, associations, and their collateral conference structure during this period. As argued later in this section, these two academic institutions had their own history and a separate paternity, but they were also part of the general fruition of the social sciences and the tertiary (postsecondary) establishment in the 1970s.


## NEW ZEALAND

The factors leading to the development of the pool of talent that would populate philosophy of education in New Zealand were not greatly different from those at play in Australia. In New Zealand, the explosive and prolonged expansion of the demand for primary, secondary, and tertiary education in the period immediately after World War II was the key feature in the establishment of philosophy of education in universities and teachers colleges. That same demographically driven expansion of the educational establishment was accelerated by the prewar promises of social reconstruction of the then newly elected Labour government. In 1939, Peter Fraser, minister of education in New Zealand's first Labour government, declared that it was his administration's objective to ensure "that every person, whatever his level of academic ability, whether he be rich or poor, whether he live in town or country, has a right, as a citizen, to a free education of the kind for which he is best fitted and to the fullest extent of his powers" (Appendices to the Journals of the House of Representatives, 1939, E-I, 2-3, in McLaren, 1974, 3).

As in the case of many wartime promises, living up to the letter of those commitments, or in this case even the spirit of those promises, proved most difficult. Reaching some practical compromise between wartime promises and postwar realities would have to wait until well into the 1960s (Cumming and Cumming, 1978, 315-318). Nevertheless, the support of every Minister of Education after the war for the egalitarian sentiments enunciated by New Zealand's first Labour Government was an important political force fueling the expansion of the educational establishment.

The most serious obstacle to the fulfillment of Labour's egalitarian intentions was a desperate shortage of teachers of any description—let alone well-trained and well-educated teachers (Cumming and Cumming, 1978, 318). Part of the shortage was Labour's own doing. By raising the school leaving age to fifteen in 1945 as part of the attempt to fulfill prewar promises, Labour exaggerated the already assured shortage of qualified teachers. Educational planners were able to anticipate the immediate increase in school populations that the higher school leaving age and typical factors of postwar demography would generate. But no one foresaw the protracted demand for school use (McLaren, 1974, 97-99; cf. Parry, Andrew, and Harman, 1960; Cumming and Cumming, 1978, 317).

The repatriation, retention, and recruitment of teachers was a major problem for ministers of education in the postwar world (Cumming and Cumming, 1978, 318). The rate of enlistment among male teachers and teachers college students was high, and, tragically, that enlistment rate was more than matched by the percentage of those killed in action (McLaren, 1974, 101). In addition, repatriated teachers were reluctant to return to the classroom (McLaren, 1974, 101). The retention and recruitment of teachers was made more difficult because of several factors: low wages (compared to the salaries available in the private sector), very heavy teaching loads, overly large and unresponsive classes, and diminishing public esteem (McLaren, 1974, 120-125).[2]

In response to the demand for teachers and also in response to the demand for a "progressive improvement of social and professional services" (Parry et al., 1960, 7-13; Beeby, 1983), there was a tremendous expansion of the range, sophistication, and diversity of courses offered in technical institutes, teachers colleges, and universities (McLaren, 1974, 134). The expansion of tertiary education began in 1945, but its most significant development occurred after 1960. The Education Vote by the end of the 1960s had become one of the largest elements of government expenditure, and by 1971-1972 it had claimed 16.4 percent of total government disbursements (McLaren, 1974, 29).

As part of the general postwar expansion and revision of tertiary education, New Zealand's teacher education program in the 1960s was profoundly influenced by British versions of teacher training. The recommendation for a distinctive professional degree for teachers—generated by the Robbins Committee on Higher Education in Great Britain in 1963—was carefully considered in New Zealand (Cumming and Cumming, 1978, 314). But only the universities of Waikato and later Massey were willing to introduce a Bachelor of Education degree. The other four universities of Auckland, Wellington, Canterbury, and Otago refused to establish a first degree in education. Nevertheless, they did agree to offer courses catering to the needs of teachers in response to the initiatives generated by this report in New Zealand (McLaren, 1974, 151). The profound influence of the Robbins Report and the fact that New Zealand universities recruited their teaching staff from their own graduates and from the universities of the United Kingdom assured the influence of English versions of teacher education (Parry et al., 1960, 51).

Under the influence of English versions of teacher education, professors and principal lecturers generated a new demand for philosophy of education. And philosophy of education in the English context meant the work of R. S. Peters (Clark, 1982, 104). Although the Illinois School and the Sydney School have had a significant impact upon the conduct of the discipline, initially the London Line dominated philosophy of education in New Zealand (cf. Clark, 1982, 104).[3]

## SOCIAL FACTORS

In Australia the political and intellectual reassessment of the educational system (government, private, and religious) would have to wait until the late 1960s and early 1970s—after postwar governments were able to satisfy the egalitarian demand for schools and teachers for all (Burnswoods and Fletcher, 1980, 212-215). Nevertheless, a time for the political and intellectual reappraisal of the Australian educational system would come in the sixties as the social issues generated by the "hip" revolution and the Vietnam war forced a reassessment of many establishment values and reinforced the "new" pluralistic values of postwar immigrants and the values of a newly emerging white-collar class (Barcan, 1980). The intellectual reassessment of Australian education followed the general thrust of issues raised by radicals and conservatives in England and the United States ten years previously; nevertheless, it also developed out of its own social and political context. The thrust of this reassessment was also influenced by the evolution of ideas about what constituted political issues.

Like many Australian institutions during this period, education lost its political innocence. It was all too apparent that schooling played a major role in the production and reproduction of social advantage and disadvantage (cf. Encel, 1970; Fitzgerald, 1976). The proper role of schooling was widely debated. Ultimately what was at stake was nothing less than the kind of society Australians wished to live in and the part to be played by education in achieving it. The debate was couched in terms of egalitarian attacks upon elitist versions of schooling and conservative defenses of academic standards. Schools were perceived by conservatives, liberals, and radicals to be an important resource for the maintenance or achievement of a good society. Conservatives held that the contribution of schooling to the support of Australia's Westminster system of government's culture and social-welfare capitalist economic system was the only serious alternative to totalitarianism, despotism, and poverty. Radicals maintained that Australia's schools—knowingly or unknowingly—betrayed the egalitarian and democratic ideals they espoused and were dominated by socioeconomic groups that exploited the schools for the purpose of maintaining their position of social and economic privilege.

Conservatives argued that postwar redirection of social and educational policy would generate a reorganization and redistribution of social and economic privilege. It was widely believed that the massive expansion of the educational franchise would lead to the reconstruction of Australian society in terms of a more egalitarian model. But as time passed it became clear that the expected gains in equity were not developing. The most invidious aspects of discrimination on the basis of race, class, and sex remained; and, despite the disclaimers to the contrary, many influential Australians lost their faith in the potential of education to undo well-entrenched social inequities.

In the 1970s and later, social reformers as well as liberal and radical educators argued that education alone could not reconstruct Australian society. These groups turned their attention away from questions of educational achievement and the "culture of poverty" that putatively defeated the efforts of disadvantaged groups to liberate themselves from social disadvantage, to questions about social structures that were fair in form but discriminatory in practice. In sociology Peter Gilmour and Russell Lansbury's *Ticket to nowhere: Training and work in Australia* (1978) and Keith Windschuttle's *Unemployment: A social and political analysis of the economic crisis in Australia* (1979) are excellent examples of this genre of literature. Educational philosophers of the New Left joined in this critique with a certain vigor. Kevin Harris's *Education and knowledge* (1979) and Michael Matthews's *Marxist theory of schooling* (1980) explored the "fair in form but discriminatory in practice" thesis, among others. Robert Mackie's *Literacy & revolution* (1981) explores a similar thesis in a series of articles.

Within the analytic and explanatory terms of the new politics of schooling—counterculturalist or Marxist—it seemed that the production and reproduction of social advantage and disadvantage was immune to any form of remedial social action; and within the terms of the new hermeneutical cum qualitative sociology it seemed equally unlikely that individuals could liberate themselves from the "culture of poverty." The fatalistic pronouncements of counterculturalists and the almost gleeful vanguardism of some Marxist sociologists and economists (see R. W. Connell, 1977) that proclaimed the bankruptcy of all social reform and individual "self-help" were politically and intellectually unacceptable outside of a small group of the radical New Left.

Liberal and conservative academics, professional educators, and parents rejected fatalistic conclusions. They were unwilling to abandon the Enlightenment project directed toward a rationally controlled self and a rationally directed society. They asserted a less fatalistic analysis of society and its social systems—educational and otherwise. Liberal sociologists took the lead in these alternative investigations. The best that can be said for the most significant elements of this liberal venture is that they produced a more "socially conscious" database from which, it was to be hoped, more successful egalitarian programs of social reform and individual self-help could be launched.

Nevertheless, the inability of both the Whitlam and the Fraser governments to change the profile of social and educational disadvantage substantially in Australian society was highlighted by a conservative critique that was presented by the press in the pages of the *Australian,* the national newspaper, and influential publications such as the *Institute of Public Affairs Review* and *Quadrant.* The apparent failure of the new liberal analysis was the linchpin of educational debate in the 1980s and early 1990s. It launched a conservative resurgence that blamed the "failure of government schools" (the decline in academic standards in secondary schools in particular) upon liberal and radical curriculums hostile to traditional social and academic values. Conservatives maintained that the liberal/radical hostility to tradition was being expressed in curriculums fostering moral relativism and devaluing academic standards. On a more positive note, conservatives argued that contemporary social tension and the "obvious" academic decline in the nation's schools could be halted by a return to curriculums that supported traditional values and moral standards with a focus upon the fundamental aspects of numeracy and literacy.

This conservative critique was part of the "back–to–basics" movement in curriculum development and classroom practice. In the pages of the *IPA Review* and *Quadrant*, Geoffrey Partington (1982), Lauchlan Chipman (1984), and Peter McGregor (1985), among others, attacked reconstructionist views of political philosophy, sexual politics, social morality, and education. They argued that the reconstructionist views that encourage and exalt regional, linguistic, ethnic, and Aboriginal cultural differences destroy social continuity and national unity. They also argued that revisionist moralities were little more than self-indulgence and an unsatisfactory basis upon which to build any society.

Kemp in summing up the differences between liberals and conservatives writes,

Liberals from Mill through to Hayek had acknowledged the particular dilemmas arising from the role of values in education. Hayek had concluded that since education could not avoid the teaching of values, public compulsory education had to teach some basic uniform values in a liberal society, including the value of liberal institutions and liberal principles of tolerance and intellectual rationality. Conservative and liberal thought in this respect converged in opposition to the deliberate promotion of cultural diversity by the liberal state. Despite the tendency of liberal principles of social organization to promote diversity, liberals held that they would also promote of their own accord an underlying cultural unity in support of freedom and tolerance. (1988, 343)

During the late 1960s, Jürgen Habermas (1971) and the new hermeneutic sociology had become very popular with the New Left. That popularity was shadowed by the investigations of Australian educational philosophers into the secondary effects of schooling in the production and reproduction of social inequality. These studies highlighted the importance of the school's curriculum in the social construction of reality. They argued that the curriculums reflected—in the production and reproduction of social advantage and disadvantage evident in race, class, and gender relations—the vested interest of dominant social groups. The discussion of education was within the parameters of the new definition of politics and was, in fact, central to the Sydney School of educational philosophy.

Unfortunately a liberal school of educational philosophy never evolved into any solid form. The closest thing to a liberal philosophical scheme revolved around Peter Karmel's *Schools in Australia* (1973). A government report, *Schools in Australia* seriously addressed the issue of equality of educational opportunity that was close to the core of liberal philosophical concerns. Struggling with the revelations of the New Left, liberals were incapacitated by "bad conscience." They were unable to "make up" their minds or present their own analysis. As a result liberals continued to fraternize with both the New Left and the conservatives while they unsuccessfully tried to define a stance that was significantly independent of the New Left and conservative ideologies. In the end they emerged as the discipline's "go-betweens"—occasionally opposing the New Left and conservatives—while they attempted to find some compromise that would satisfy everyone. In the end, liberals even managed to find solidarity with the conservatives.[4]

In this contemporary debate liberals and Marxists found a distinctive if not unified Australian voice. Liberals and Marxists agree that Australia's education system has been struggling to emerge from its elitist past, an educational past based not so much on distinctions of natural ability as on the distinctions of class privilege, gender, and race (R. W. Connell, 1977; Harris, 1979; Matthews, 1980; Sharp, 1980; cf. Smith, 1977, 11). But they also hold that Australia's educational system has not been completely successful in abandoning its elitist past and that it is quite likely that it might return to that past without a determined effort to continue developing a more egalitarian educational system.

Both libertarians and Marxists are likely to argue . . . that while you attempt to deal with the problems in terms of the existing frame of reference, the difficulties are likely to continue. They are problems to do with the system, not with particular people. Marxists are likely to add that the problems are not ones which can be solved within the school, either. They have to be solved in society as a whole first. Libertarians are less sure of this. (Rubenstein, 1979, 7-17)

Nevertheless, even at its best their voice was less than monolithic.

## NOTES

1. The percentage of teachers working in State secondary schools who were university graduates fell from 84.6 percent in 1944 to only 41.5 percent in 1966 (Barcan, 1980, 302).

2. New Zealand teachers taught on average 30 or 31 periods during a 35 period week.

3. At this point in the text there should be a separate history of specific social factors attached to the establishment of philosophy of education in New Zealand. There are significant differences in the national ethos of philosophy of education in New Zealand, but I do not have the research resources to provide that history here. All I can do is apologize to my colleagues in New Zealand. As it stands, this history overemphasizes Australia in a history that clearly should be focused upon Australasia—Australia and New Zealand.

One further aside, the original charter of the Philosophy of Education Society of Australasia included members from Australia, New Zealand, and New Guinea. But the element of the society that was based in Port Moresby never evolved into a significant segment of the society.

4. The liberal agenda never found enduring support even among liberals themselves. Only a few years later Karmel, in *Quality of education in Australia* (1985), revised his opinion on the primacy of equality of educational opportunity in favor of a new and more conservative focus upon "equal outcomes."

# 13

# Philosophy of Education Society of Australasia

The disciplined study of philosophy of education began in the United States in 1935 and in Great Britain in 1964. Philosophy of education did not begin in Australasia until 1970, when the discourse of Australasia's nascent "invisible college" of educational philosophers was routinized by the founding of a professional organization dedicated to applying the genius and literary style of philosophy to questions generated by the practice and theory of educating and to specifying, accepting, and commending specific research programs consistent with the intellectual ambitions of said "invisible college."

As previously mentioned several contributions from philosophy stand as seminal antecedents to the field in Australasia. John Anderson's *Education and politics* (1931) is probably among the earliest and most important publications in what would be the discipline's area of scholarship. The work of C. D. Hardie ([1942] 1962) and D. J. O'Connor (1957) also was antecedent and a seminal part of the discipline's establishment just as the chapters on analytic philosophy and education that John Passmore contributed to the 1965 volume of *Melbourne Studies in Education* are part of philosophy's legacy.

Just as important to this history of the discipline is the work produced by a small nucleus of academics at Armidale Teachers College and the University of New England in New South Wales. At Armidale Margaret Mackie followed her own mind and the inspiration of John Anderson to write at length about education in a philosophical tone. In the early days she wrote: *Education in the inquiring society: An introduction to the philosophy of education* (1966); *Educative teaching* (1968); *What is right?* (1970); and *Philosophy and school administration* (1977). Furthermore in the early 1960s Clive Beck joined Nirmal Bhattacharya and Gordon Eastwood at the University of New

England, where Bhattacharya and Eastwood had labored for some time in the seemingly pointless effort, or so at least Beck argues, of attempting to instruct diploma of education students in the analytic approach to educational philosophy (Beck, 1991, 313). Following the general career pattern of many of Australia's best social scientists—the tendency for Australian academics both to study and to realize their careers overseas (cf. Bourke, 1988, 60)—the core of this nucleus left the University of New England to make important and significant contributions to the discipline in North America.

The work of individuals at Sydney Teachers College and Sydney University also was part of the discipline's heritage. Anna Hogg and Bill Andersen made important contributions through the development of some of the first Australian courses in philosophy of education.

Others at other instiutions and various places around Australia were busy preparing an indigenous literature for the discipline. In the mid-to-late 1960s Les Brown published *General philosophy in education* (1966); Jim Gribble published *Introduction to philosophy of education* (1969); and D. C. (Denis) Phillips wrote *Theories, values and education* (1970).[1]

In New Zealand arguably the most important early contributions to the discipline were the books of Ivan Snook. He authored *Indoctrination and education* (1972b) and edited *Concepts of indoctrination* (1972a); both published by Routledge and Kegan Paul. Nevertheless, it should be pointed out that Snook was writing on similar topics long before his books appeared. In the 1960s Snook published these articles: "Education and the philosopher: A reply to J. P. Powell," *Australian Journal of Education* (1966a); "Philosophy, education and a myth," *Australian Journal of Higher Education* (1966b); and "Philosophy of education: Today and tomorrow", *New Zealand Journal of Educational Studies* (1969). In New Zealand the body of work Snook inspired was misleadingly named the "Illinois School."[2]

Snook earned his doctorate at the University of Illinois. His doctoral study was influenced by R. S. Peters's powerful work (Snook, 1986). Later in New Zealand, Snook and Peters became good friends and in the passing years Peters became a regular visitor in the Snooks' home—at least as regular as a visitor from halfway around the world could be—and spent several extended periods with the Snooks (Snook, 1986). Thus, although the almost mischievous reference to the "Illinois School" might lead the unwary reader to assume a more Americanized intellectual stance—Broudy, Scheffler, Dewey, and so forth—the stance of the "Illinois School" is doubtlessly British.

But a discipline is not reducible to its texts. As was argued at the beginning of this book, the form of any professional undertaking can seldom be explained without reference to the professional organization that rationalized and gave shape to the pool of participants and the collection of questions and answers that constitute that field of endeavor. Surprisingly, or perhaps not so surprisingly, the professional organization that is largely responsible for initially giving form to the practice of philosophy of education in Australasia is a British one. The adoption of analytic philosophy as the dominant mode of practice of the Australasian society can be explained almost without reference to the domestic pool of academics who would populate the society upon its establishment, but it cannot be explained without reference to R. S. Peters and the Philosophy of Education Society of Great Britain.

The Philosophy of Education Society of Great Britain was launched by Peters in 1963-1964 academic year. It was dominated by Peters's department at the London Institute of Education, if not by Peters, himself as chairman of the British society from 1965 to 1975 (Dearden, [1979] 1984; Peters, 1983). The "London Line" attached itself to the defense of liberal education (see Peters, 1966; Hirst, [1965] 1974) when English definitions of a "worth-while" and liberal education were being besieged on all sides by socially egalitarian versions of comprehensive schooling. In some ultimate sense, philosophy of education was about what counted as a "worth-while education"—in English and Victorian terms. Only obliquely did it join the educational debate of the period, which addressed the concepts of poverty, social justice, social class, social change, fairness, equality of access, opportunity, streaming, testing, selecting, school use, and success. The literature of the time that examined educational disadvantage and deprivation was intensely political (see Silver 1983, 265, 267). Educational philosophy's discussions of the same phenomena, however indirect, were always cool, detached, and intellectual.

The defense of liberal education in due course became the research agenda of the first generation of the Australasian society. It should not be surprising to find that the research agenda of the Philosophy of Education Society of Great Britain dominated the formative years of the Australasian society when it is remembered that Peters, the London Institute of Education, and the Philosophy of Education Society of Great Britain had an important supporting role in the events that surrounded the formation of the Australasian society.

## LOCAL AND IMPORTED INFLUENCES

The intellectual relationship between Australian culture and overseas cultures to which it has primary reference and affinity are "the single most important issue in understanding the characteristics of Australia's intellectual life" (Head, 1988, 9). In 1974 the intellectual influence of R. S. Peters and the London Line was enormous. Peters's influence was important in its own right, but in the 1970s it was redoubled by the mere fact that it shadowed the dependent character of academic life that was characteristic of Australian intellectual life in the period between the wars.

In this era Australia was very much an intellectual province of Britain and to a lesser extent of the USA. Good students were sent to Britain (and in economics and education increasingly to North America) for postgraduate training. Visiting experts were welcomed and fêted, if not worshipped, and the latest books and articles from overseas were devoured with interest and with due deference. (Alomes, 1988, 82)

When Peters came to Australia to work at Australian National University he was "welcomed and fêted, if not worshipped."

By way of contrast the philosophical work of North Americans like James and Dewey was more important for Australasian educational practice than educational theory. Australian educational history refers to progressive education and one of the few Progressive schools established by the New South Wales Department of Education: Brighton-le-Sands (see Barcan, 1988, 210-211). But it is hard to find reference in Australian material to American philosophers writing about education. There are references to Kilpatrick's *Project method* (1918), and associations like the New Education Fellowship did find it useful to borrow from the ideas presented by Americans such as Dewey, Counts, Kilpatrick, and Rugg. When speaking with philosophers of education who were important actors in the events that surrounded the society's early days, they willingly acknowledge Dewey's place in the scheme of educational philosophy; nevertheless, upon closer inspection it is obvious that John Anderson, Professor of Philosophy at Sydney University, was at least as profound an influence upon philosophy and education in Australasia as were the North American giants, William James and John Dewey.

It is important to remember when discussing the English influence upon philosophy of education in Australasia that there was a significant North American influence. Among liberals and individuals who received their training in North America, it must be admitted that American thought was influential. "John Dewey was recognized as a giant in the field, and *Democracy and education* in particular was widely read" (Beck, 1991, 312). Dewey had a powerful disciple in Professor W. F. (Bill) Connell at Sydney University. Connell's support for Dewey's thought was fervent, and he pressed education graduate students to read and study his work (Walker 1985). American universities were also influential in the discipline's intellectual concerns. The University of Illinois awarded doctorates to seven individuals who would practice philosophy of education in Australasia: Brian Hill, Felicity Haynes, Bruce Haynes, Brian Crittenden, Gabrielle Lakomski, Ivan Snook, and Donald Vandenberg all received their doctoral degrees from the University of Illinois. Not all of these individuals were native Australians, but all of them spent a major portion of their careers in Australasia, and all of them have played a significant part in the Philosophy of Education Society of Australasia.

In addition, the domestic intellectual establishment was not without its influences upon Australasian educational philosophy. Clive Beck has stated that he "did a a degree in philosophy of education at U. W. A. [University of Western Australia] from 1956 to 1960 under the tutelage of Bert Priest, who was a fan of Hardie's and Scheffler's work and already a committed analyst" (Beck, 1991, 313). Beck further noted that several individuals were already applying the analytic work of Hardie, O'Connor, and Scheffler to the conceptual muddles of education just as others were responding to the inspiration of John Anderson. But Beck's description of the discipline's establishment implies a depth of enterprise and study that just did not exist. The Australian university system in the period before World War II was diminutive in size and had no place for philosophy of education. In the 1950s there were no journals and or professional associations to support structurally the study of philosophy and education. Postgraduate numbers and research resources for education were either lacking altogether or were so small that many of Australia's best scholars left the country to pursue their graduate training, and in some cases their careers, overseas. Nevertheless, Beck is correct in identifying an incipient cohort of "progressive, liberal, middle-class academics" concerned with both philosophy and education who were more or less at home with the study of philosophy and education. But it would not be until the late-1960s that this group achieved the critical mass necessary to transform a modest personal project dedicated to the study of philosophy and education into a professional and disciplined undertaking established in the nation's universities.

This group was fueled by the graduates of Australasia's rapidly expanding academic establishment who were examining the ideals of the New Left. Those who had some sympathy or allegiance with the New Left had more than some little difficulty with the English atmosphere. In 1975 it seemed that the most significant intellectual work in progress was the use of various left intellectual social critiques to loosen the grip of Peters's philosophy. The group constructed its

intellectual concerns on critical reason and social democratic, if not
Marxist, versions of democratic participation in the region's social and
political institutions (cf. Head, 1988, 29). The Sydney School focused
upon the critical rationality and rhetoric of Althusser, Lacan,
Bourdieu, Gramsci, Poulantzas, and others; important as well were Wal
Suchtin, John Burnheim, and David Armstrong at Sydney University's
Department of Philosophy.

Nevertheless, with all of this said, the centrality of the English
influence cannot be denied. As Harris (1988, 55) acknowledges, "Bill
Andersen studied with Peters in London and subsequently introduced
Peters' work into education courses at Sydney University in 1969." And
as Andersen has noted, "There was a London Line at Sydney University,
I introduced it" (Andersen, 1985). Jim Gribble attested to his debt to
Peters in the preface to *Introduction to philosophy of education* (1969),
and Ivan Snook wrote his doctoral thesis in response to Peters's work.
Andersen, Gribble, and Snook were central figures in the discipline's
early days. But perhaps even more important, Kevin Harris, a key
player in the Sydney School of educational philosophy, has admitted
the importance of both Peters and Hirst in his own work. As Harris
states in the first words of his preface to *Education and knowledge*
(1979):

If this work could carry a second sub-title, that sub-title would in all probability
be: "A New Introduction to Philosophy of Education"; for whereas this work is
concerned mainly with its own thesis, the need to write it grew partly out of a
general dissatisfaction with what philosophy of education has become, and with
what philosophers have brought to the study of education over the past decade
and a half. This secondary concern will account for what might otherwise appear
as disproportionate attention given in the text both to philosophy of education,
and to some of its exponents, especially R. S. Peters and P. H. Hirst. (1979, vii)

Philosophy of education in Australasia is a creature of its own
history and with its own theses; nevertheless, its predicate or "the
need to write" a domestic text for the discipline was conditioned by
what came on license from the London Institute. Forgetting the English
predicate has become a practiced and, perhaps, necessary part of the
evolution of what has become philosophy of education in Australasia
(see Marshall, 1982; 1987; and Harris, 1988). The repression of the
dependent character of academic life (part of a vital cultural
nationalism) was necessary to convince the nation's own universities
that Australian philosophy of education—some of the world's best—
was worthy of undergraduate and graduate study and that its domestic
practitioners (again, some of the world's best) were sufficiently
accomplished to hold chairs of educational philosophy in their own
country (cf. Phillips, 1988, 136). Forgetting the English predicate was

also part of transcending a time when Australia was "little more than 'a congeries of colonies' . . . an intellectual province of Britain" (Alomes, 1988, 82) and responding to the vital domestic intellectual culture that has become part of the Australian scene since the end of World War II. Nevertheless, the predicate remains. The early game revolved around Peters and, to some extent, Hirst, and what philosophy of education had become in the Commonwealth.

## EDUCATIONAL PHILOSOPHY AND THEORY

In May 1969 the first number of *Educational Philosophy and Theory* appeared. Initially, the journal was produced, published, and financed entirely independent of the society. In 1967 and 1968 Les Brown, associate professor at the University of New South Wales, canvased for subscriptions and did the groundwork—securing initial finance and institutional subscriptions, contracting publishers, soliciting manuscripts, and so forth—necessary for the publication of the journal. During the journal's first years Brown's editorial policy was directed toward consolidating an administrative and financial base and establishing an international circulation.

Initially, there was at least the appearance of an informal affiliation between the journal and the society. The interlocking directorate of the society and the journal—Brown was foundation president of the society and founding editor of the journal—gave the impression of a unity of institutional base, purpose, and editorial policy. But the journal belonged to Brown, and the society belonged to itself. The unity implied by the interlocking directorate did not, in fact, exist.

Many members within the society assumed that the relationship between the society and the journal was or would evolve into a relationship not unlike that of the *Proceedings of the Philosophy of Education Society of Great Britain* and the Philosophy of Education Society of Great Britain.[3] In the British instance, one was the creature of the other. It was easy to assume in this historical context that the relationship of *Educational Philosophy and Theory* and the Australasian society would be similar to the British precedent. R. S. Peters was editor of the *Proceedings of the Philosophy of Education Society of Great Britain*, Les Brown was editor of *Educational Philosophy and Theory*; R. S. Peters was chairman of the British society, Les Brown was president of the Australasian society—the analogy was close enough to encourage even the most cautious individuals to make the unfounded but logical jump.

The society published the proceedings of its second (Flinders) conference by means of the publication system Brown had established for *Educational Philosophy and Theory*. The second volume of the *Proceedings* (Philosophy of Education Society of Australasia, 1972b) was being prepared for publication under the assumption that one or more articles of R. S. Peters, who was participating in the Christchurch conference in 1972, would be made available for publication in the *Proceedings*. When it became apparent that Peters's work was to be published in other places and would not be available for publication in the *Proceedings*, the editorial committee decided not to publish the *Proceedings* that year. According to the minutes of the Ordinary General Meeting the society decided to terminate the publication of the *Proceedings* because of their "uneven quality" (Philosophy of Education Society of Australasia, 1972a).

In fact, the *Proceedings* never reappeared because of Brown's opposition to their production. Brown believed that the pool of manuscripts that was available to the society for production in the *Proceedings* would not support an annual publication, and he resisted its resurrection. It was a fateful decision. The *Proceedings* never reappeared on a commercial basis or in a professional format. Although the society attempted to revive the production of the *Proceedings*, without Brown's assistance the task proved formidable.[4] The suspension of the publication of the *Proceedings* foreshadowed a profound political disagreement over the editorial control of *Educational Philosophy and Theory* that eventually led to the formal disassociation of the society from the journal. On the domestic level the alienation of the journal from the society created a politics of discontent in which the journal was a major icon.

In 1973 when *Educational Philosophy and Theory* ran into financial difficulty the Australasian society proposed to support its further publication (Minutes of the Ordinary General Meeting, Hobart, 1973) and did so in 1974 and 1975. Collateral with the society's financial commitment to the journal, and in anticipation of fuller participation in the operation of the journal, with Brown's agreement the society selected Brian Crittenden, then president of PESA, I. Snook, J. Walker, and J. Gribble to represent the society on the editorial board of the journal (Minutes of the Ordinary General Meeting, Canberra, 1974). Then in a singularly prepossessing gesture, the society elected Brown to the editorship of the journal that he had established, published, and edited (Minutes of the Ordinary General Meeting, Canberra, 1974). It would seem that influential members of the society had discussed and tentatively agreed among themselves that the society should select, if not control, the editorship and editorial control of *Educational*

*Philosophy and Theory*—the journal with which they had psychologically, not to mention financially, identified themselves. The discussion and tentative approval of elected editorships (probably prior to the Canberra conference) also assumed the transportation of the journal from institution to institution as the editorship changed.

Fortunately, or unfortunately—only history can judge—Brown did not share the society's enthusiasm for a movable feast or for a rotating editorship. He believed that the society's mooted policy took no account of his central role in the establishment and maintenance of the journal, or of the economic realities of publishing, or of the importance of a stable venue for the administration and production of a journal (Brown, 1985). By 1976 the journal was again financially viable and no longer in need of the support of the society. Brown repaid the society and returned the journal to his personal control.

For its part, the society responded by severing its connection with the journal. Although the society did not formally disestablish itself from the journal until 1981 (Minutes of the Ordinary General Meeting, La Trobe conference, 1981), for all intents and purposes the break was complete in 1976.

Brown's decision to sequester the journal had important consequences for *Educational Philosophy and Theory*, consequences that were outside of the manifest purpose of preserving the journal's editorial continuity and administrative base. The most important consequence was the generation of competitive journals. Partially in response to the alienation of some members of the society from *Educational Philosophy and Theory* and partially in response to apparent intrinsic intellectual promise of New Left critiques for the transformation of Australian society, *Radical Education Dossier (RED)* appeared in October of 1976. *RED* was, partially, a spin-off of the June 1976 conference led by Herbert Gintis and Samuel Bowles, the radical American economists who had published the immensely successful *Schooling in capitalist America* (1976). The first issue of *RED* was compiled by a committee, many of whom were active and visible members of the Philosophy of Education Society of Australasia. For that matter, *RED* was cofounded by Jim Walker, then lecturer of educational philosophy at Sydney University. Walker has been a significant contributor to educational philosophy since the formative years in the 1970s.

*RED* helped produce a clearer distinction between liberal, Andersonian, and neo-Marxist versions of educational theory. It also brought into sharp focus the tentative generation alliance between Australasian liberals, progressives, and neo-Marxists. Reading *RED* was a mark of alliance between those who placed their intellectual loyalties with the New Left or the counterculture. This alliance eventually dissolved along ideological lines and the necessities of careerism. Nevertheless, it was a factor in the intellectual politics of the discipline. The new journal quickly became a competitor of *Educational Philosophy and Theory*, but the competition was relatively short-lived. *RED* fell into disfavor among members of the society involved in its production as political activists muscled them out of positions of influence and off the editorial board (Walker, 1985).

The origins of *Educational Philosophy and Theory's* more enduring competitors were as much a function of the times as they were of the political intrigues that separated the journal from the society. Nevertheless, the alienation of the society from the journal opened a pool of manuscripts and institutional support that otherwise would not have been quite so available to other academic journals. A journal called *Discourse* was first published in 1980 by Ted D'Urso with the help of Michael Macklin (D'Urso, 1986). Both men were educational philosophers at the University of Queensland. And in New Zealand Jim Marshall and Colin Lankshear at the University of Auckland launched a newsletter-type publication called *Access*. The format of *Access* prevented it from becoming a serious competitor. *Discourse*, on the other hand, has proved to be an important competitor for manuscripts. Although Ted D'Urso, the editor of *Access*, did not see it as a competitor, a quick review of his journal's contents reveals numerous articles that might have appeared in *Educational Philosophy and Theory*—if things had been different.

Radical elements of the society were isolated from control of the journal by the continuing editorship of Brown and Gribble. They were never able to control the journal's ideological superstructure. The persistent and important antihegemonic education critique that the New Left championed found only erratic support in *Educational Philosophy and Theory*. The journal remained a bastion of Australian liberalism. The journal's editorial policy remained definitely liberal and middle-of-the-road. They were never able to dominate the intellectual means of production (the journal).

The decision to terminate its relationship with *Educational Philosophy and Theory* deprived the society of the most obvious means of presenting itself and the work of the society to an international audience. The society retained a presence and was recognized by similar academic societies in Britain and the United States. But its international profile, the editorial style and content of the journal, was determined by Les Brown and Jim Gribble. The journal did not shadow the changing concerns and dynamics of the society. In that sense the editorial policy of *Educational Philosophy and Theory* remained intellectually fixed for a period of almost twenty years in a way that journals which have had a more diverse set of editors do not.

Journals, societies, and "invisible colleges" provide a forum within which disciplines evolve and mature. Journals and societies interact to present ideas that are "deserving" of consideration to authoritative reference groups who determine the ideas' standing within the academic community. In this fashion the profession and its "publics" are protected from novices, charlatans, and quacks as well as from intellectual innovations that are "utterly without merit." In other words, the interaction of the institutional elements of a discipline identifies the pool of intellectual "possibilities" that constitutue of the discipline (cf. Ziman, 1968, 102-142). The split between the society and the journal marginalized this interaction in Australasia.

Within the politics of the Australasian society philosophers of education devoted to R. S. Peters's version of analytic philosophy, and to existentialism, liberal humanism, and conservative versions of social contract theory secured places and influence within the aegis of the journal and controlled a majority of principal elected positions within the society. At the same time Marxists, romantics, and those "second generation" members and conference participants trained outside of the influence of R. S. Peters and the London Institute (often in a domestic context) secured positions of intellectual influence and places to publish their work in the commercial academic press.

These two groups became the major intellectual counterpoints within the society and were major contenders for authority within the politics of Australasian philosophy of education. Both groups have sought to shape the intellectual ambitions of the discipline in terms of their intellectual (explanatory), political, and social ideals. The competition between these groups in the society and the journal has been a major factor in construction and deconstruction of philosophy of education in Australasia. As Toulmin notes, "The creation of authoritative reference-groups and journals has a particularly significant part to play in the maturation of a would-be discipline" (1972, 390).

Members of the society have produced important contributions to the philosophy of education, and there has been determined effort upon the part of the editors of *Educational Philosophy and Theory* to foster the international standing of the journal. Yet, both the society and the journal have been hampered in achieving academic status equivalent to the Philosophy of Education Society (of the United States) and the Philosophy of Educational Society of Great Britain. Part of that failure can be attributed to demographics and the physical isolation of Australasia. As well, the separation of the society from the journal has militated against the pragmatic and qualitative goals of both the society and the journal.

On the international level the fragmentation of philosophy of education has disrupted the ordinary process through which individuals become established and recognized "authorities" within the worldwide "invisible college." On a domestic level, excessive rivalry has been generated between intellectual factions and professional generations. And on an individual level the importance of publication in the *Educational Philosophy and Theory* and membership and active participation in the society has been depreciated. This devaluation has meant that both the society and the journal have lacked the usual degree of influence on the ordinary academic progress that leads through the usual career sequence of membership, fellowship, editorships, and promotion that in turn lead to university chairs, academic kudos and other vestiges of intellectual "authority."

Whether *Educational Philosophy and Theory* will emerge in the 1990s as an authentic, lucid, and representative voice of the society and its membership is yet to be seen. In 1986 Les Brown and Jim Gribble transferred the journal's management to the society, under the editorship of James S. Kaminsky, then Senior Lecturer at the University of New England. When Kaminsky accepted the position of Associate Professor, Auburn University, in the United States the editorship devolved to a committee and then to David Aspin of Monash University. Early indications were that the journal's direction would both reflect the society's goals and promote the Australasian cohort's place in the international arena.


## THE SIXTIES

By the late 1960s many Australasian academics were directing the literary style and culture of educating and philosophy at the idea of education—particularly as it had appeared in the intellectual history of the West. The pattern of the discipline's establishment followed a meter similar to that of the English experience. As in England, the absence of any great sympathy for social science in general or the university study of education in particular meant that there was no place for the discipline until social science became an integral part of the university in the period following World War II. Simon (1983) notes—a matter of common knowledge—in the English academic establishment there is an important distinction between the public study of social science, education included, and the university study of social science. The former has always been tagged with the opprobrium of amateurism; the latter, of course, carries the approbation of the establishment and its collateral aura of legitimacy and rigor. Prior to the solid establishment of the social sciences in the early 1970s the university study of the social sciences in general and educational philosophy in particular—as was previously noted—was a diffident enterprise conducted by a few academics in departments of philosophy, social science, and education. In an important sense the study of education and educational philosophy arrived along with the social sciences in the Australian university establishment.

In the late Sixties Australia and New Zealand were hard pressed to find enough educational philosophers to fill the demand generated by the implementation of British and American models of "university teacher education." Postgraduate programs in educational philosophy were created. And, in a reciprocal fashion, postgraduate programs stimulated the demand for yet more philosophers of education. A relative "ocean" of positions appeared, and many of the individuals who were asked to teach courses in educational philosophy had not yet competed their graduate training. As a result, educational philosophy quickly generated the reputation of attracting enthusiasts or apologists whose philosophical investigations were "too utopian, too dated, or perhaps just too endlessly boring" (cf. Keifer, 1980, 81).[5]

In the two decades following World War II academic studies of education and philosophy attempted to define a "Socratic" role for themselves. During this "honeymoon" period academics encouraged educators to adopt a philosophy of education to articulate "their own" philosophy of education. Educators were invited to articulate their philosophy of education after studying the ideas of the "Great Educators" for guidance. Thus, in Socratic fashion they set out to assist educational practitioners to develop their own philosophy of education—that is, to develop a set of informed convictions about the practice of educating.

To complicate matters, the relationship of education to the Department of Philosophy at Sydney University was highly problematic. In the 1940s, 1950s, and 1960s philosophy was busy defending its intellectual legitimacy and its place within the academic establishment. It used as its defense a demonstration of the low level of logical rigor and theoretical argument of its scientific competitors. The philosophy department at Sydney University saw itself as the bulwark of the defense against the decline of education and academic standards produced by the antitheoretical and utilitarian forces created by the general extension of tertiary education to the general populace. In Anderson's words:

We have to take a pluralist view of the University as well as of society in general and to see that, within any so-called academic institution, there are non-academic and anti-academic activities—that what is academic (for it is a question of movements and traditions, and not of "individuals") has to fight for survival against pseudo-academic Philistinism as well as against the incult social mass, that the struggle of culture against "bourgeois society" exists also on the campus.

This has always been the case; but the academic had more of a fighting chance when any member of staff might be assumed to have had a liberal education in which he acquired some knowledge of the classics of literature and philosophy. The absence of that condition today explains the absence of any distinctive and recognized academic view of public affairs; its place is taken by the naive and unlettered views which emanate not merely from scientists but from psychologists and educationists. (1960, 5)

The university study of education was just another indicator of the decline of academic standards and the marginalization of departments of philosophy and classics to Anderson's mind and to the minds of most professors of philosophy and classics. In other words, educational philosophy attracted a certain disrepute by association. The general disdain with which the English academy held the study of education in particular and the new utilitarian idea of the university in general was extended to academic studies of philosophy and education.[6]

Despite the opposition of departments of philosophy and conservative elements of the university, the idea of establishing a professional society for the study of philosophy of education was "in the air." Les Brown, founding editor of *Educational Philosophy and Theory* and associate professor of education at the University of New South Wales, had canvased the idea of establishing a professional society at least as early as 1968 (Brown, 1986a; 1986b). But he abandoned further efforts at that time because professorial support (particularly that of C. D. Hardie) could not be obtained. Nevertheless, Brown's initial investigation was part of the ambient environment that augured well for the establishment of the discipline.

By 1969 things had changed enough for tentative steps toward the establishment of a professional society to be taken. Bill Andersen, then a senior lecturer at Sydney University, was responsible for providing the initial impetus (Andersen, 1985). While it is probably impossible to isolate one individual as "the" author of the Philosophy of Education Society of Australasia, Bill Andersen's seminal role in establishing courses in philosophy of education at Sydney University, directing the energy of Warren Fenley's passion for educational philosophy, and his work behind the scenes at the Peters's seminar seems an irreducible part of the society's establishment.

While he was a doctoral student under the supervision of R. S. Peters at the London Institute in 1967 and 1968, Andersen had recognized the need and virtue of establishing an Australasian society similar to the ones in Great Britain and the United States. Upon returning to Sydney University, Andersen arranged a seminar on the "Concept of 'Education'" to be given by R. S. Peters, who was working at the Australian National University while on leave from the London Institute. Andersen convened the seminar, firstly to take advantage of Peters's presence in Australia, and secondly to bring together a nucleus of potential members for a philosophy of education society. Thus, early in third term of 1969 at the "Peters Seminar," Warren Fenley presented Andersen's proposal for the formation of a society (Andersen, 1985). It was a preliminary proposal, but there was sufficient interest for the seminar to proceed with further plans.

Andersen's preliminary initiative resulted in the formation of a provisional committee comprised of: Les Brown, associate professor of education at the University of New South Wales; Anna Hogg, principal lecturer at Sydney Teachers College; R. Precians, Macquarie University; and Bill Andersen, senior lecturer at Sydney University. This organizational committee drafted a preliminary constitution for the society, issued the initial call for members, and made plans for an inaugural conference to be held in May of 1970 at the University of New South Wales with Brown acting as convener and host. It should be added that Brown's contribution to the establishment of the society as founder of *Educational Philosophy and Theory* and host and convener of this conference is, in all probability, just as irreducible a part of the society's establishment as was the impetus that Andersen provided.

The conference was opened by P. H. Partridge, vice-chancellor of the Australian National University. At the conference the constitution was accepted by those present. A council was elected and an executive committee was appointed, comprised of Les M. Brown, president; Anna Hogg, vice-president; W. E. Andersen, secretary; and R. Precians, treasurer. Hogg is, undoubtedly, one of the most important and yet largely invisible players in the establishment of philosophy of education in Australasia. While her name appears here and there in the documents these records do not reflect her profound role in recruiting and socializing members of the profession who would play important roles in what would come to be known as the Sydney School of educational philosophy and in actively—not passively—supporting the establishment of the discipline.

In a sense, then, philosophy of education in Australasia began at Bassar College, University of New South Wales, on 20 May 1970 (Brown, 1985; cf. Clark, 1982). But unlike similar societies in the United States and Great Britain, whose initial membership and research program evolved in terms of their own ecologies, the

Australasia society adopted as its own, and unproblematically held, at least initially, the analytic method and research agenda of the Philosophy of Education Society of Great Britain: the defense of "liberal education." The defense of "liberal education" inspired, defined, and declared the pool of questions and answers that would constitute the research program of educational philosophy in Australasia (see Philosophy of Education Society of Australasia, 1972b).

Further, many of the senior members of the Australasian society evolved outside of their own ecology and in terms of a peculiarly distinctive (intellectually elitist) English environment; that is, they had traveled to England, trained at the London Institute, and defined themselves in terms of the reserve of questions and answers that were constitutive of, and pertinent to, the English scene and Peters's version of philosophy of education. But by the mid-1970s many of the society's newer and younger members, trained in Australia and/or the United States, found the research agenda and methodology of the London Line problematic. In a sense the reaction of this latter group to the London Line was consistent with the pattern of reaction and dissent typical of English philosophy of education—e.g., philosophy of education at the London Institute of Education. Many of the society's younger members were unwilling to accept the pattern of reaction and dissent to Peters and the London Line as definitive of their research agenda. The philosophical agendas of this group argued for a return to partisan philosophy of education in a society whose early days had been dominated by a concern for the analytic defense of liberal education.

## COUNTERCULTURE AND THE NEW LEFT

To return to the point made very early in this section, convictry produced a social system in which suppressed resentment affected most social transactions between those who had come to Australia of their own volition or the requirements of duty and those who had been sent as transportees. In the nineteenth century many factors limited the growth of education but none was as significant as the remnants of two-class animosity and the absence of an educationally ambitious middle class (cf. Barcan, 1988, 103). But by the early 1960s

a democratic form of corporate State capitalism was emerging. In the new society the largest class was the white collar or salaried middle class, a class of "employees" with a strong basis in the administrative bureaucracy of the State and large corporations. Family influence and religious influence had weakened. The new values and the new ideology were sometimes described as "permissive". Drugs and sex became more important, religions less. The puritan ethic was giving way to the social ethic. (Barcan, 1980, 345)

Under the pressure of the new middle class the Australian system of "mateship" started to collapse. Conway's *Great Australian stupor* (1971) articulated what middle-class Australians were feeling about mateship and the Australian version of Victorianism that it supported. White collar workers and the salaried middle class Australians questioned support for American imperialism in Vietnam. They were willing to consider extending political rights to Aboriginals. Australian women—who were reading Kate Millet's *Sexual politics* (1970)—redefined themselves as something more than "damned whores and God's police" (see Altman, 1988, 312). And the *Summer of the seventeenth doll* (1957), a drama depicting mateship, the sad relationship of two Australian couples, and an Australian society in the twilight of a very Victorian social order, convinced audiences all over Australia that it was time for other things. Censorship collapsed. Plays like *Hair* and *Oh Calcutta!* (1969) invited Australians to consider social and moral alternatives that previously were considered outrageous. *Lady Chatterly's lover* (Lawrence, [1928] 1932), *Tropic of Cancer* (Miller, [1934] 1961), *God's little acre* (Caldwell, 1933), and other "pornographic" books that previously had been prohibited by a Victorian morality and the Australian Customs Office became commonly available.

Traditional Australian political economy was encapsulated in W. K. Hancock's often-quoted aphorism of the 1930s: "To the Australian the State means collective power at the service of individualistic "rights'" ([1930] 1966, 55-6). It was a politics of self-interest. The collapse of English Victorianism and its politics of self-interest is dated to the Festival of Britain in 1951; the breakdown of Victorian mores arrived in Australia a decade later. The social effect of that collapse was Australia's version of the counterculture that came into existence in the mid-to-late 1960s. Its political image was the Australian New Left. The final failure of Victorianism produced a vigorous analysis of politics directed against establishment values and social privilege. It produced a socially conscious politics.

In the New Left's scheme of things politics was no longer in the service of vested self-interest. Politics was in the service of the "good society"—a society that unfortunately was beyond the power of the New Left to define or create. Nevertheless, the New Left directed its political efforts at a socially conscious politics. The antiwar movement, ecology, and various "Green" questions, antinuclear protest, Aboriginal rights, feminist and gay movements, consumer protectionism, and social democratic medicine were all elements of its political agenda. The

New Left failed to give coherent definition to its personal, participatory, and interested politics that made special reference to socially maginalized groups.[7]

The New Left formulated its ideology in terms of "participatory democracy." Always small in numbers, the New Left depended upon its political alliance with liberals—as it did in America and Britain—to remain a viable political force. Participatory democracy was the glue of a common cause with the counterculture. Thus, when Peters's version of educational philosophy presented itself in the late Sixties and early 1970s, when it was still new and exciting, it found itself embedded in an Australasian intellectual matrix that was similar to but in certain ways quite different from the cultural matrix out of which Peters's analytic work had evolved.

Australasian educational philosophy's second generation tended to see themselves as members of or at least in sympathy with the New Left or the counterculture. The New Left and "free liberals" were inspired by their own intellectual ecology and the counterculture heroes of the 1960s and 1970s. They responded to the work of Goodman, Reimer, Holt, Kozol, Postman, Weingartner, Marcuse, Bowles and Gintis, Freire, Fanon, and Illich, just as they responded to the more intensely intellectual concerns of Althusser, Adorno, Marcuse, and later Foucault, to name only a few.

Australasia's educational philosophers also responded to their own ecology. An Australian version of the counterculture was spawned by the new postwar university educated professional, intellectual and academic establishment (cf. Docker, 1988, 299). This counterculture ethos drew inspiration from America and Europe with equanimity. The combination of radical humanists like Goodman with Frankfurt School types like Marcuse and Adorno reflected a new style of social and intellectual political activism that revolved around opposition to the Vietnam War and support for personal liberation (Altman, 1988, 309). It was a political and intellectual activism that was generated by the radical, libidinal, and egoistic humanism of the counterculture as much as it was a part of the serious politics of the New Left. Personal liberation was a realization of the possibilities of the collapse of Australian versions of Victorian morality. The New Left's immediate contribution to Australia's rapidly evolving national ethos was a critique of traditional politics in which socially marginal groups had been excluded. In this New Left politics gays, Aboriginals, women, and immigrants found a place. The counterculture contributed an erotic and not too serious version of personal liberation that encouraged a daring liberalism. The repressed asceticism of the New Left politics generated its own intellectual and sober ethos.

The New Left cum counterculture stance generated a new gambit in educational philosophy. In this version of the discipline analyses of ethnicity, gender, sexuality, ideology, politics, and economics created a new education discourse. It supported liberation movements of all types. This support extended to Aboriginals in the same way that it extended to Algeria and its desperate politics that Frantz Fanon described in *Wretched of the earth* ([1963] 1965)—a touchstone among educational philosophers during the period.[8] Educational philosophers explored all of the topics of the new education discourse. Of course it should be remembered that these topics were generated not only by the unique history and personnel of Australian educational philosophy, but also by the new Australian ethos that was rapidly evolving in the "hothouse" environment of the counterculture.

The society's younger members were marked by a technical competence coupled with the romanticism and politics typical of the New Left, on the one hand, and "free liberals" on the other. Many were suitably hip Marxists and were openly aligned with members of the counterculture. And, of course, they deemed their group to be far more competent than their older colleagues. What bound the New Left and "free liberals" together was a shared willingness to debate the appropriate social, political, cultural, and moral basis for Australian society and the role of education in creating that society. Free liberals brought the North American personal politics of Goodman, Reimer, Holt, Kozol, Postman, and Weingartner to the debate just as the New Left imported the ideas of Marcuse, Adorno, and other members of the European Left.

But the New Left and the counterculture produced the seeds of their own intellectual transformation. The counterculture became tainted by a lack of seriousness, drugs, and eroticism; it lost itself in a vortex of self-indulgence, just as it had in America. Similarly the New Left lost itself in self-righteousness, seriousness, and epistemic privilege:

In terms of radical activity, the New Left has also been both liberating and innovative, and limiting and enclosing. It animated radical activities in terms of protest against American imperialism in Vietnam and against racism in general; it spawned the liberation movements; it led to activity on behalf of oppressed minorities and "marginals". Yet the very energies released by the new movements, as gays worked for gay liberation and women for women's and blacks for black liberation, led to a fissuring and fragmentation of radical activity—to separate movements that scarcely related to each other—that makes it difficult to see how any united actions could ever again be mounted and sustained. (Docker, 1988, 304)[9]

## TRANSFORMATION IN THE 1980S AND 1990S

The intellectual element that is unique to philosophy of education in Australasia in the 1980s and early 1990s is the qualitative transformation of the discipline's intellectual dependency. In the decade of the nineties educational philosophy established a discipline with its own Australasian identity. It is no longer reliant upon Europe or North America for intellectual leadership or postgraduate training. Individuals trained in Australasia have become the discipline's "authoritative individuals," holding chairs of education and many of the most significant offices in the Philosophy of Education Society of Australasia.

The 1980s and 1990s found a new generation of academics in possession of the discipline. Educational philosophers who began their careers at about the same time as the establishment of the Philosophy of Education Society of Australasia—many of whom held chairs or professorships of Education (at the time of writing)—became the discipline's authoritative individuals. The discipline's second generation consolidated a position of influence in various Australian universities. Relative to its small size, the discipline was amazingly successful.

## NOTES

1. For a more complete record of Australian publications in educational philosophy, see Brian S. Crittenden. 1988. "Philosophy of education in Australia." In *Australian education: Review of recent research*. Further, see James S. Kaminsky's 1988a. "Comprehensive author index of articles in *Educational Philosophy and Theory* 1969-1988."

2. For a more complete record of publications in educational philosophy in New Zealand should see John Clark. 1982. "Philosophy of education in New Zealand." *Journal of Educational Studies* (17) 2; and James Marshal's 1987. *Positivism or pragmatism: Philosophy of education in New Zealand*, vol. 2.

3. The first eleven volumes were published under the title *Proceedings of the Philosophy of Education Society of Great Britain*; the title of the periodical was then changed to the *Journal of Philosophy of Education*.

4. At a later point in time the society attempted to produce the *Proceedings* on an informal basis but the effort was unsuccessful.

5. Of course the pattern of professional development was little different than that of its counterpart in England, where Peters drafted his best students into lectureships and worked them mercilessly teaching the institute's courses while at the same time demanding that they finish their degrees and publish in the academic press.

6. The disdain of departments of philosophy and classics for studies of philosophy and education, putative or real, has remained part of the folklore of the profession. In a convoluted way, the same explanation appealed to professors of educational philosophy, but only as a convenient device for the control of excessive intergenerational competition. The perverse appeal of this assessment to professors of educational philosophy will continue to exist, in all probability, for as long as academic generations compete for professional honors—tenure, fellowships, editorships, chairs of education, and the presidency of national and international organizations. Nevertheless, this criteria of excellence (the opinion of departments of philosophy) has lost much of its prominence as the profession has matured, and educational philosophy has achieved a certain grudging respect from the more conservative elements of the university.

7. Kevin Harris's "Philosophers of education: Detached spectators or political practitioners?" (1980) is, perhaps, the best short example of an attempt to formulate a personal, participatory, and interested politics to appear directly in *Educational Philosophy and Theory*.

8. Australasian educational philosophy's search for new topics was evident in its concern for politically and economically marginalized elements of the third world. This willingness to embrace new topics is evident in an excellent little book edited by Robert Mackie, *Literacy & revolution* (1981). An extension of this concern is also evident in the discipline's concern for the work of Illich. In recent years another piece—that addresses similar topics—*Literacy, schooling and revolution* (1989) was written by New Zealander Colin Lankshear.

9. In a rather scathing review of Kenneth A. Strike's *Liberal justice and the Marxist critique of education* (1989), Kevin Harris (1991) shows that the Antipodean (or perhaps, the general) Marxist critique has not completely lapsed. But the list of correct and incorrect Marxist authors that Harris cites to demonstrate the contemporary vitality of the Left critique is too old and too small to be convincing evidence of a vital intellectual stance.

# 14

# Conclusion: Australasia

Australasian educational philosophy in the early 1990s continues to struggle with its identity within the university establishment. The discipline had gathered to itself an interesting and important place in the university study of education, but it still labors to some degree within the cultural attitude that declares that "real" academics like "real" ideas come from the United States or Britain (cf. Bourke, 1988). As a result the discipline's academic identity has remained fluid, even if it is marked by a strong sense of place (cf. Alomes, 1988).

The contemporary concerns of educational philosophy in Australasia can be traced to the social ethos of the discipline's inception in the 1970s. Many of that new generation of educational philosophers who assumed authoritative positions in the discipline during the mid-to-late 1980s began their careers as part of or at least had sympathy for the New Left and/or the counterculture. And in many instances, they followed the concerns of the Department of Philosophy at Sydney University.

That generation previously had been committed to a large number of social and political issues. But their commitment to Aboriginals and oppressed minorities, gay groups, the handicapped, feminist issues, and women's liberation—as well as the traditional issues of philosophy of education and philosophy—generated the same kind of fragmentation within the discipline that the counterculture and the New Left experienced. After the collapse of the New Left and the counterculture no lingering allegiance to the working class or the counterculture arrested their intellectual ambitions or careers. The solidarity of the new generation with their social and political alliances originally forged in the sixties and seventies remained only insofar as they were

consistent with their technical, material, intellectual, and career
ambitions (cf. Gouldner, 1979, 12). Having gained control of the
important and influential offices of the society and having acquired
control of the technical means of intellectual production (the journal),
the new generation was free to pursue their own political, technical,
and intellectual fetishes (cf. Gouldner, 1979, 60).

The younger members of the discipline's second generation were part
of Australia's university-trained, professional middle class, and they
shared many of the virtues and faults of that class:

The professional middle class in modern history has always seen itself as the
ethically superior class, the one group in society that does not, like traditional
employing and working classes, pursue its own sectional interests, but which
speaks to society and history's universal values, which indeed tries to create
those values and live them out in its own life-styles and sensibility for the rest of
society to follow. (Docker, 1988, 299)

Their technical interests still retain reference to their own history,
life-styles, and sensibilities as a statement and example "for the rest of
society to follow." They assumed, as all of the professional middle
class tends to assume, that "All should be as they are" (Docker, 1988,
300).

As a result, in the early 1990s they continued to argue that Australian
people and the education system they support should not be "sexist,
anti-homosexual, racist, anti-sensuous, anti-sexual experiment, 'anti-
genderbendering' . . . People in Australia should live in communal
households either in the country, close to the rhythms and mystic
secrets of the natural world, or in the inner city. Relationships, of . . .
adults and children, should be fluid, unproprietorial, un-nuclear,
open . . . People should drink at inner-city Bohemian pubs where the
bar is open to women" (Docker, 1988, 300).

In commenting upon Helen Garner's *Monkey grip* ([1977] 1981), an
Australian novel of the late 1970s about bohemian life in Melbourne,
Nicholas Jose notes that

Even at its most urbanized, Australian life offers an ancient picture of shore
dwellers . . . She exposes the laws by which the loose [bohemian Melbourne] sub-
community lives, and understands that its values are an attempt to socialize a
deeper moral quest for personal integrity, freedom with responsibility, and
selfhood within community. For Garner's venturing men and women, none of those
things is chimerical. (1985, 329)

Jose's comments can be extended to the practice of educational
philosophy in Australia. Australia's practice is different from that of
the United States or Great Britain. The last two present an undertaking
that is disinterested, professional, and driven by impersonal historical

forces. Philosophy of education in Australasia is personal, intense, and driven by an attempt to find selfhood within a responsible community.

Philosophy of education remains what it always has been—a merchant of nonstandard ideas to a centralized and conservative educational establishment. As in the United States and Great Britain, the future of the discipline depends in part upon the willingness of governments to continue their support of the humanities and social science in a world where the idea of the university is coming to be defined by its role in economic competition. But while the future of educational philosophy in the United States and Great Britain will largely be determined by their ability to pursue the discipline's technical agendas, in Australasia the challenge will be to transcend biography and focus the discipline's fluid intellectual identity within the Australasian university establishment.

# Bibliography

Abrams, Philip. 1968. *The origins of British sociology: 1834-1914*. Chicago: University of Chicago Press.

Adams, Douglas. 1980. *The restaurant at the end of the universe*. London: Pan Books.

Adams, John. 1928. *The evolution of educational theory*. London: Macmillan.

Addams, Jane. [1935] 1974. *My friend, Julia Lathrop*. New York: Arno Press.

Albinski, Henry. 1985. "Australia and the U.S." *Daedalus* (114) 1.

Allan, John S. 1968. *Teacher education*. Wellington: A.H. & A.W. Reed.

Alexander Samuel. [1933] 1966. *Space, time, and Deity*. 2 vol. New York: Dover Publications.

Alomes, Stephen. 1988. "Intellectuals as publicists 1920s to 1940s." In *Intellectual movements and Australian society*. Eds. Brian Head and James Walter. Melbourne: Oxford University Press.

Altman, Dennis. 1988. "The personal is the political: Social movements and cultural change." In *Intellectual movements and Australian society*. Eds. Brian Head and James Walter. Melbourne: Oxford University Press.

American Social Science Association (ASSA). 1866. *Constitution, adresses, and list of members*. Boston: Wright and Potter.

————1869. "Introductory note." *Journal of Social Science* (1) 1.

————1873. "Eulogy for John Stuart Mill." *Journal of Social Science* (5) 136.

Amis, Kingsley. [1960] 1961. *Take a girl like you*. New York: Harcourt, Brace & World.

————[1968] 1969. *I want it now*. New York: Harcourt, Brace & World.

Andersen, W. E. 1985. [Notes, interview with the author.]

Anderson, Archibald, W. 1951. "The task of *Educational Theory*." *Educational Theory* (1) 1.

————1959. "Fostering study in the theory of education." *Educational Theory* (9) 1.

Anderson, John. 1931. *Education and politics*. Sydney: Angus & Robertson.

————1954. "Democratic illusions." *Hermes*. N.p.

————1960, 16 June. "The place of the academic in modern society." *Honi Soit*.

Apple, M. 1979. *Ideology and the curriculum*. London: Routledge & Kegan Paul.

Armytage, W. G. 1967. *The American influence on English education*. London: Routledge & Kegan Paul.

Arnstine, Barbara. 1981. "To whom may it concern." *Educational Theory* (31) 1.

Atkin, Myron, J. 1973. "Practice oriented inquiry." *Educational Theory* (2) 7.

Axtelle, George E. 1965. [Taped interview]. Philosophy of Education Society, Archives.

Axtelle, George E., and Burnett, Joe R. 1970. "Dewey on education and schooling." In *Guide to the works of John Dewey*. Ed. Jo Ann Boydston. Edwardsville: Southern Illinois University Press.

Axtelle, George E., and Wattenberg, William W. Eds. 1940. *Teachers for democracy*. Fourth yearbook of the John Dewey Society. New York: D. Appleton-Century.

Ayer, A. J. [1936] 1946. *Language, truth, and logic*. London: V. Gollancz.

Bain, Alexander. 1889. *Education as a science*. New York: D. Appleton.

Baker, A. J. 1979. *Anderson's social philosophy*. Sydney: Angus & Robertson.

———1986. *Australian realism: The systematic philosophy of John Anderson*. Cambridge: Cambridge University Press.

Baker, Ray Stannard. [1920] 1971. *The new industrial unrest*. New York: Arno Press.

Barcan, Alan. 1980. *A history of Australian education*. Melbourne: Oxford University Press.

———1988. *Two centuries of education in New South Wales*. Kensington, NSW: New South Wales University Press.

Barrow, Robin. 1983. "Does the question 'What is education' make sense?" *Educational Theory* (33) 3 & 4.

Beard, Charles A. 1913. *An economic interpretation of the Constitution of the United States*. New York: Macmillan.

———1932. *A charter for the social sciences*. New York: Charles Scribner's Sons.

———1934. "Property and democracy." *The Social Frontier* (1).

Beck, Clive. 1991. "North American, British and Australian philosophy of education from 1941 to 1991: Links, trends, prospects." *Educational Theory* (41) 3.

Beck, Robert. 1965. [Taped interview]. Philosophy of Education Society, Archives.

Beeby, C. E. 1983. "Is the university a part of the education system?" In *The university and the community*. Ed. Ian Carter. Auckland: N.p.

Beineke, John. 1989. "A Progressive at the pinnacle: William Heard Kilpatrick's final years at Teachers College Columbia University." *Educational Theory* (39) 2.

Bellamy, Edward. [1887] 1926. *Looking backward: 2000-1887*. Boston: Houghton Mifflin.

Benjamin, Harold. Ed. 1950. *Democracy and the administration of higher education*. Tenth yearbook of the John Dewey Society. New York: Harper and Brothers.

Benn, S. I., and Peters, R. S. [1959] 1965. *The principles of political thought* (also published as *Social principles and the democratic state*). New York: The Free Press.

Benne, Kenneth D. 1966. [Taped interview]. Philosophy of Education Society, Archives.

———1974. "The education professoriate." *Society of Professors of Education*. (Occasional Paper No. 4). Minneapolis: University of Minnesota.

———1988. [taped telephone interview with the author].

Berger, Peter L., and Luckmann, Thomas. 1967. *The social construction of reality*. New York: Doubleday and Co.

Bernstein, Richard J. 1966. *John Dewey*. NEW YORK: Washington Square.

———1983. *Beyond objectivism and relativism*. Oxford: Basil Blackwell.

Best, John Hardin. 1988. "The revolution of markets and management." *History of Education Quarterly* (28) 2.

Bestor, A. [1953] 1985. *Educational wastelands*. Urbana: University of Illinois Press.

Black, C. E. and Helmreich, E. C. 1964. *Twentieth-century Europe*. New York: Alfred A. Knopf.

Blanshard, Brand, and Ducasse, Curt J. 1945. "The basic courses in philosophy: Metaphysics." In *Philosophy in American education*. Ed. Brand Blanshard. New York: Harper and Brothers.

Blanshard, Brand, Ducasse, Curt J., Hendel, Charles W., Murphy, Arthur E., and Otto, Max C., Eds. 1945. *Philosophy in American education.* New York: Harper and Brothers Publishers.

Bloom, Allan. 1987. *The closing of the American mind.* New York: Simon and Schuster.

Bode, Boyd. 1935. "Education and social reconstruction." *The Social Frontier* (1) 4.

Bourke, Helen. 1988. "Social scientists as intellectuals: From the First World War to the Depression." In *Intellectual movements and Australian society.* Eds. Brian Head and James Walter. Melbourne: Oxford University Press.

Bourne, Randolph S. 1913. *Youth and life.* Boston: Houghton Mifflin.

Bowers, C. A. 1964. "*The Social Frontier* journal: A historical sketch." *History of Education Quarterly* (4) 3.

————1969a. *The Progressive educator and the depression.* New York: Random House.

————1969b. "Social reconstructionism: Views from the Left and the Right, 1932-1942." *History of Education Quarterly* (10) 1.

Bowles, S., and Gintis, H. 1976. *Schooling in capitalist America.* London: Routledge & Kegan Paul.

Boydston, Jo Ann. 1969. "John Dewey and the journals." *History of Education Quarterly* (10) 1.

————Ed. 1970. *Guide to the works of John Dewey.* Edwardsville: Southern Illinois University Press.

Bradley, F. H. [1876] 1927. *Ethical studies.* Oxford: Clarendon Press.

Brameld, Theodore. 1933. *A philosophical approach to communism.* Chicago: University of Chicago Press.

————1935. "Karl Marx and the American teacher." *The Social Frontier* (2).

————Ed. 1941. *Workers' education in the United States.* Fifth yearbook of the John Dewey Society. New York: Harper and Brothers.

————1956. *Toward a reconstructed philosophy of education.* New York: Dryden Press.

Brickman, William W. 1970. "Dewey's social and political commentary." In *Guide to the works of John Dewey.* Ed. Jo Ann Boydston. Edwardsville: Southern Illinois University Press.

Broudy, Harry S. 1987. [Taped interview with the author].

————[1979] 1981. "Philosophy of education between yearbooks." In *Philosophy of education since mid-century.* Ed. Jonas F. Soltis. New York: Teachers College Press.

Broudy, Harry S., Ennis, Robert H., and Krimerman, Leonard I. Eds. 1973. *Philosophy of educational research.* New York: John Wiley & Sons.

Browder, Earl. 1935. "Education—an ally in the workers' struggle." The Social Frontier (1) 4.

Brown, L. M. 1966. *General philosophy in education.* New York: McGraw-Hill.

————1985. [Personal letter to the author].

————1986a. [Personal letter to the author].

————1986b. [Personal interview with the author].

Brown, S. C. Ed. 1975. *Philosophers discuss education.* London: Macmillan.

Brubacher, John S. 1942. *Philosophies of education.* The forty-first yearbook of the National Society for the Study of Education. Ed. Nelson B. Henry. Bloomington, IL: Public School Publishing.

Brubacher, John S. Ed. 1944. *The public schools and spiritual values.* Seventh yearbook of the John Dewey Society. New York: Harper and Brothers Publishers.

————1955a. "The challenge to philosophize about education." In *Modern philosophies and education.* The fifty-fourth yearbook of the National Society for the Study of Education. Ed. Nelson B. Henry. Chicago: University of Chicago Press.

———Ed. 1955b. *Modern philosophies and education*. The fifty-fourth yearbook of the National Society for the Study of Education. Ed. Nelson B. Henry. Chicago: University of Chicago Press.

Bryson, Gladys. 1932a. "The comparable interests of the old moral philosophy and the modern social sciences." *Social Forces* (11).

———1932b. "The emergence of the social sciences from moral philosophy." *International Journal of Ethics* (42).

———1932c. "Sociology considered as moral philosophy." *Sociological Review* (24).

Burnett, Joe R. [1979] 1981. "Whatever happened to John Dewey." In *Philosophy of education since mid-century*. Ed. Jonas F. Soltis. New York: Teachers College Press.

Burns, J. H. 1959. "J. S. Mill and the term 'social-science'." *Journal of the History of Ideas* (20) 3.

Burnswoods, Jan, and Fletcher, J. 1980. *Sydney and the bush*. Sydney: New South Wales Department of Education.

Burston, W. H. 1969. *James Mill on education*. Cambridge: Cambridge University Press.

Caldwell, Erskine. 1933. *God's little acre*. New York: Modern Library, Random House.

Carneiro, Robert L. Ed. 1967. *The evolution of society*. Chicago: University of Chicago Press.

Caswell, Hollis L. Ed. 1946. *The American high school*. Eighth yearbook of the John Dewey Society. New York: Harper and Brothers.

Caute, David. 1988. *Sixty-eight: The year of the barricades*. London: Hamish Hamilton.

Chalmers, David. 1958. "Ray Stannard Baker's search for reform." *The Journal of the History of Ideas* (19).

Chambers, John H. 1983. *The achievement of education*. New York: Harper & Row.

Chambliss, J. J. 1968. *The origins of American philosophy of education*. The Hague: Martinus Nijhoff.

Champlin, Nathaniel (chairman), Adams, David, Krash, Otto, Mason, Robert, and Villemain, Francis. 1954. "The distinctive nature of the discipline of the philosophy of education." *Educational Theory* (4) 1.

Chandler, Alfred D, Jr. 1977. *The visible hand: The managerial revolution in American business*. Cambridge, MA: The Belknap Press of Harvard University Press.

Chesney, Kellow. 1970. *The Victorian underworld*. Bristol: Western Printing Services.

Childs, David. 1988 [1979]. *Britain since 1945*. London: Routledge.

Childs, John L. 1931. *Education and the philosophy of experimentalism*. New York: The Century Co.

———1936. "Can the teacher stay out of the class struggle?" *The Social Frontier*. April.

Chipman, L. 1984, (January/February). "Failing Australia's children." *Quadrant*.

Church, Robert L. 1976. *Education in the United States*. New York: The Free Press.

Clark, F. 1940. *Education and social change*. London: Sheldon Press.

Clark, John. 1982. "Philosophy of education in New Zealand." *Journal of Educational Studies* (17) 2.

Clifford, Geraldine Jonçich and Gutherie, James W. 1988. *Ed school*. Chicago: University of Chicago Press.

Collins, Philip. 1964. *Dickens and education*. London: Macmillan.

Comte, Auguste. [1830-1842] 1893. *The positive philosophy of Auguste Comte*, (Vols. 1-2) Trans. Harriet Martineau. London: Kegan Paul.

Connell, R. W. 1977. *Ruling class ruling culture*. Cambridge: Cambridge University Press.

Connell, W. F. 1950. *The educational thought and influence of Matthew Arnold*. London: Routledge & Kegan Paul.

————1980. *A history of education in the twentieth century world.* New York: Teachers College Press.
Conway, Robert. 1971. *The great Australian stupor.* Melbourne: Sun Books.
————1976. *The end of the stupor.* Adelaide: Griffin Press.
Coughlan, Neil. 1973. *Young John Dewey.* Chicago: University of Chicago Press.
Counts, George S. 1922. *The selective character of American secondary education.* Chicago: University of Chicago Press.
————1927. *The social composition of boards of education.* Chicago: University of Chicago Press.
————1929. *Secondary education and industrialism.* Cambridge, MA: Harvard University Press.
————1930. *The American road to culture.* New York: John Day.
————1932. *Dare the school build a new social order?* New York: John Day Company.
————1934. "Collectivism and collectivism." *The Social Frontier* (1) 2.
————1935a. "1,105,921." *The Social Frontier* (1) 4.
————1935b. "Teachers and labor." *The Social Frontier* (1).
————1935c. "Teachers and the class struggle." *The Social Frontier* November (2).
Crane, Steven. [1893] 1896. *Maggie: A girl of the streets.* New York: D. Appleton.
Cremin, Lawrence A. 1954. *A history of Teachers College Columbia University.* New York: Columbia University Press.
————1959. "John Dewey and the Progressive-education movement." 1915-1952. *School Review* (67).
————[1961] 1964. *The transformation of the school.* New York: Alfred A. Knopf.
————1988. *American education: The metropolitan experience 1876-1980.* New York: Harper & Row.
Crittenden, Brian S. 1988. "Philosophy of education in Australia." In *Australian education: Review of recent research.* Ed. John Keeves. Sydney: Allen and Unwin.
Cumming, Ian, and Cumming, Alan. 1978. *History of state education in New Zealand.* Wellington, New Zealand: Pitman Publishing.
Dallmayr, Fred R., and Mc Carthy, Thomas A. 1977. *Understanding and social inquiry.* Notre Dame, IL: University of Notre Dame Press.
Dana, James Dwight. [1894] 1896. *Manual of geology.* New York: American Book Company.
Darwin, Charles. [1859] 1860. *Origin of species.* Chicago: Donohue, Henneberry & Co.
Dearden, R. F. 1976. *Problems in primary education.* London: Routledge & Kegan Paul.
————[1979] 1984. "Theory and practice in education." In *Theory and practice in education.* Ed. R.F. Dearden. London: Routledge & Kegan Paul.
————1980a. "Education and politics." *Journal of Philosophy of Education* (14) 2.
————1980b. "Theory and practice in education." *Journal of Philosophy of Education* (14) 1.
————1982. *Philosophy of education 1952-1982.* London: Routledge & Kegan Paul.
DeBenedetti, Charles. 1990. *An American ordeal: The antiwar movement of the Vietnam era.* New York: Syracuse University Press.
Dennis, Lawrence J. 1989. *George S. Counts and Charles A. Beard: Collaborators for change.* Albany, New York: State University of New York Press.
Dennis, Lawrence J., and Eaton, William Edward. 1980. *George S. Counts: Educator for a new age.* Carbondale and Edwardsville: Southern Illinois University Press.
Dennis, Lawrence. 1935. "Education—The tool of the dominant elite." *The Social Frontier* (1) 4.
Department of Superintendence. 1935. *Social change and education.* Thirteenth yearbook of the Department of Superintendence. Washington, DC: The Department of Superintendence of the National Education Association.

———— 1937. *The improvement of education*. Fifteenth yearbook of the Department of Superintendence. Washington D.C.: The Department of Superintendence of the National Education Association.

———— 1947. *Schools for a new world*. Twenty-fifth yearbook of the Department of Superintendence. Washington D.C.: The Department of Superintendence of the National Education Association.

Dewey, Jane M. 1939. "Biography of John Dewey." In *The philosophy of John Dewey*. Ed. Paul Arthur Schilpp. Chicago: Northwestern University Press.

Dewey, John. 1896, July. "The reflex arc concept in psychology." *Psychological Review* (3).

————[1897] 1959. "My pedagogic creed." In *Dewey on education*. Ed. Martin S. Dworkin. New York: Teachers College Press.

————[1899] 1959. "School and society." In *Dewey on education*. Ed. Martin S. Dworkin. New York: Teachers College Press.

————1902a. "Academic freedom." *Education Review* (23) 11.

————1902b. *The child and the curriculum*. Chicago: University of Chicago Press.

————[1916] 1966. *Democracy and education*. New York: The Free Press.

————[1920] 1950. *Reconstruction in philosophy*. New York: The New American Library of World Literature.

————[1922] 1957. *Human nature and conduct*. New York: Random House Inc.

————[1925] 1958. *Experience and nature*. New York: Dover.

————1933. *How we think*. Chicago: Henry Regnery.

————1935. *Liberalism and social action*. New York: G.P. Putnam's Sons.

————1936, May. "Class struggle and the democratic way." *The Social Frontier* (3).

————1937. "Education and social change." *The Social Frontier* (3) 26.

————1938. *Experience and education*. New York: Collier Books.

————[1938] 1982. *Logic: The theory of inquiry*. New York: Irvington.

————1939. *Freedom and culture*. New York: Putnam.

————[1927] 1954. *The public and its problems*. Denver, CO: Alan Swallow.

————[1930] 1962. "From absolutism to experimentalism." In *Contemporary American philosophy*. Eds. George P. Adams and Wm. Pepperell Montague. New York: Russell & Russell.

Dewey, John and Dewey, Evelyn. 1915. *Schools of to-morrow*. New York: E.P. Dutton.

Dickens, Charles. [1837] 1974. *Oliver Twist*. London: Oxford University Press.

————[1839] 1983. *Nicholas Nickleby*. New York: Crown Publishers.

————[1843] 1911. "A Christmas carol." In *Christmas Books*. New York: P. F. Collier & Son.

————[1849-1850] 1981. *David Copperfield*. Oxford: Clarendon Press.

————[1854] 1931. *Hard times*. London: J.M. Dent & Sons.

————[1861] 1931. *Great expectations*. New York: Macmillan.

Dilling, Elizabeth. 1934. *The red network*. New York: Arno Press.

Dixon, Miriam. 1976. *The real Matilda*. Ringwood, VIC: Australia: Penguin Books.

Docker, John. 1988. "'Those halcyon days': The moment of the New Left." In *Intellectual movements and Australian society*. Eds. Brian Head and James Walter. Melbourne: Oxford University Press.

Dorfman, Joseph. 1934. *Thorstein Veblen and his America*. New York: The Viking Press.

Dreiser, Theodore. 1912. *The financier*. New York: Harper and Brothers.

————1914. *The titan*. New York: John Lane.

Durbin, Paul T. Ed. 1980. *A guide to the culture of science, technology, and medicine*. New York: The Free Press.

Durkheim, Emile. 1955. *Pragmatism and sociology*. Trans. J. C. Whitehouse, Ed. John B. Allcock. Cambridge: Cambridge University Press.

D'Urso, T. 1986. Taped telephone interview with the author.

Dykhuizen, George. 1959. "John Dewey: The Vermont years." *Journal of the History of Ideas* (20) 4.

———1973. *The life and mind of John Dewey.* Carbondale: Southern Illinois University Press.

Eaton, William Edward. 1975. *The American Federation of Teachers, 1916-1961.* Carbondale: Southern Illinois University Press.

Edel, Abraham. 1956, Spring. "What should be the aims and content of a philosophy of education?" *Harvard Educational Review* (26).

Elliot, Emoy. 1988. *Columbia literary history of the United States.* New York: Columbia University Press.

Elvin, Lionel. 1977. *The place of commonsense in educational thought.* London: George Allen & Unwin.

———1989. Interview with the author.

Encel, S. 1970. *Equality and authority.* Australia: F.W. Cheshire Publishing Pty. Ltd.

Engels, Friedrich. [1845] 1958. *The conditions of the working class in England* [Orig. title: Conditions of the working class in England in 1844). Trans. and ed. W. O. Henderson and W. H. Chaloner. Oxford: Basil Blackwell.

Fanon, Frantz. [1963] 1965. *The wretched of the earth.* New York: Grove Press.

Fawcett, Edmund, and Thomas, Tony. 1982. *America and the Americans.* (also: *The American condition; America, Americans*) Glasgow, Great Britain: Fontana/Collins.

Feibleman, James K. 1987. *Education and civilization.* Dordrecht: Martinus Nijoff.

Feuer, Lewis S. 1958. "John Dewey's reading at college." *Journal of the History of Ideas* (19).

———1959. "John Dewey and the back to the people movement in American thought." *Journal of the History of Ideas* (20) 4.

———1969. *The conflict of generations.* New York: Basic Books.

Feyerabend, Paul. 1975. *Against method.* London: Redwood Burn Limited, Trowbride & Esher.

Filler, Louis. (1968) 1976. *The muckrakers.* University Park: Pennsylvania State University Press.

Fitzgerald, R. T. 1976. *Poverty and education in Australia.* Canberra: Australian Government Printing Service.

Foner, Philip S. 1947. *Jack London: American rebel.* New York: The Citadel Press.

Frankena, William K. 1965. *Philosophy of education.* New York: Macmillan.

Freedman, Samuel G. 1990. *Small victories.* New York: Harper & Row.

Furner, Mary O. 1975. *Advocacy & objectivity.* Lexington, KY: University of Kentucky Press.

Garforth, F. W. 1979. *John Stuart Mill's theory of education.* New York: Barnes and Noble.

Garland, Hamlin. 1892. *A spoil of office.* Boston: Arena Publishing.

Garner, Helen. [1977] 1981. *Monkey grip.* New York: Seaview Books.

Gay, Peter. 1987. "Introduction." In *On the social contract.* Trans. and ed. Donald A. Cress. Indianapolis/Cambridge: Hackett.

Giarelli, James M., and Chambliss, J. J. 1991. "The foundations of professionalism: Fifty years of the Philosophy of Education Society in retrospect." *Educational Theory* (41) 3.

Gilbert, Alan. 1988. "Anti-suburbanism." In *Australian cultural history.* Eds. S. L. Goldberg and F. B. Smith. Cambridge: Cambridge University Press.

Gilmour, Peter and Lansbury, Russell D. 1978. *Ticket to nowhere.* New York: Harmondsworth.

Gingell, John. 1982. "Philosophy of education and the B. Ed." *Educational Analysis* (4) 1.

Ginsberg, Allen. [1956] 1986. *Howl.* New York: Harper & Row.

Gitlin, Todd. 1987. *The Sixties: Years of hope, days of rage.* New York: Bantam Books.

Glenn, Charles Leslie, Jr. [1987] 1988. *The myth of the common school.* Amherst: University of Massachusetts Press.

Goldberg, S. L. and Smith F. B. Eds. 1988. *Australian cultural history*. Cambridge: Cambridge University Press.

Goodman, Paul. 1960. *Growing up absurd*. New York: Random House.

Gouldner, Alvin W. 1979. *The future of intellectuals and the rise of the new class*. New York: Oxford University Press.

————1985. *Against fragmentation: The origins of Marxism and the sociology of intellectuals*. New York: Oxford University Press.

Graetz, Brian. 1988. "The reproduction of privilege in Australian education." *The British Journal of Sociology* (39).

Graham, Patricia Albjerg. 1967. *Progressive education: From arcady to academe*. New York: Teachers College Press.

Green, Joe. 1981. "The function of speculative thought in the philosophy of education." *Texas Tech Journal of Education* (8) 2.

Green, Thomas. 1971. *The activities of teaching*. New York: McGraw-Hill.

Gribble, James. 1969. *Introduction to philosophy of education*. Boston: Allyn and Bacon.

Guarneri, Carl. 1991. *The utopian alternative: Fourierism in nineteenth-century America*. Ithaca, NY: Cornell University Press.

Gutek, Gerald, L. 1983. *George S. Counts and American civilization*. Macon, GA: Mercer University.

Habermas, Jürgen. 1971. *Knowledge and human interests*. Boston: Beacon Press.

Hadow, W. H. (chair). 1926. *The education of the adolescent*. London: Her Majesty's Stationery Office.

Hamlyn, D. W. 1985. "Need philosophy be so dreary?" *Journal of Philosophy of Education* (19): 159-165.

Hancock. W. K. [1930] 1966. *Australia*. Brisbane: Jacaranda.

Harap, Henry. 1970. "The beginnings of the John Dewey Society." *Educational Theory* (20 ) 2.

Hardie, C. D. [1942] 1962. *Truth and fallacy in educational theory*. New York: Teachers College Press.

————1969. "Does education stand on its foundations?" *Educational Philosophy and Theory* (1) 1.

————1971. "The philosophy of educational research." *Educational Philosophy and Theory* (3) 1.

————1974. "One hundred years of the university study of education." *The Australian University* (12) 2.

————1985. [Personal letter to the author].

Harrington, Michael. 1962. *The other America*. New York: Macmillan.

Harris, Kevin. 1979. *Education and knowledge*. London: Routledge & Kegan Paul.

————1980. "Philosophers of education: Detached spectators or political practitioners?" *Educational Philosophy and Theory* (12) 1.

————1988. "Dismantling a deconstructionist history of philosophy of education." *Educational Philosophy and Theory* (20) 1.

————1991. "An Antipodean philosopher's stone [Review]." *Journal of Philosophy of Education* (25) 1.

Haskell, Thomas L. 1977. *The emergence of professional social science*. Urbana: University of Illinois Press.

Hazzard, Shirley. 1980. *The transit of Venus*. New York: The Viking Press.

Head, Brian. 1988. "Introduction." In *Intellectual movements and Australian society*. Eds. Brian Head and James Walter. Melbourne: Oxford University Press.

Head, Brian and Walter, James. Eds. 1988. *Intellectual movements and Australian society*. Melbourne: Oxford University Press.

Hirsch, E. D. 1987. *Cultural literacy*. Boston: Houghton Mifflin.

Hirst, Paul H. 1963. "Philosophy and educational theory." *British Journal of Educational Studies* (12).

————[1965] 1974. *Liberal education and the nature of knowledge*. London: Routledge & Kegan Paul.

————1973. "The nature and scope of educational theory." In *New essays in the philosophy of education*. Eds. Glenn Langford and D. J. O'Connor. London: Routledge & Kegan Paul.

————1974. *Knowledge and the curriculum*. London: Routledge & Kegan Paul.

————1982. "Philosophy of education: The significance of the sixties." *Educational Analysis* (4) 1.

————1989. [Taped interview with the author].

Hirst, P. H. and Peters, R. S. 1970. *The logic of education*. London: Routledge & Kegan Paul.

Hobbes, Thomas. 1651. *Leviathan*. London: Printed for Andrew Cook.

Hoffman, Abbie. 1968. *Revolution for the hell of it*. New York: Dial Press.

Hofstadter, Richard. [1944] 1945. *Social Darwinism in American thought*. Milford: Oxford University Press.

————1955. *The age of reform*. New York: Alfred A. Knopf.

————1963. *The Progressive movement*. Englewood Cliffs, NJ: Prentice-Hall Inc.

Hoggart, Richard. 1957. *The uses of literacy*. London: Chatto & Windus.

Honderich, Ted. [1976] 1980. *Violence for equality*. London: Richard Clay (The Chaucer Press).

Hook, Sidney. 1939. *John Dewey: An intellectual portrait*. New York: John Day.

————1956, spring. "The scope of philosophy of education." *Harvard Educational Review* (26).

————1987. *Out of step: An unquiet life in the 20th century*. New York: Carroll & Graf Publishers.

Horne, Donald. [1964] 1965. *The lucky country*. Baltimore, MD: Penguin.

————1967. *The education of young Donald*. Sydney: Angus & Robertson.

————1972. *The Australian people*. Sydney: Angus & Robertson.

————1985. "Who rules Australia?" *Daedalus* (114) 1.

Hughes, H. Stuart. 1958. *Consciousness and society*. New York: Alfred A. Knopf.

Hughes, Robert. 1987. *The fatal shore*. London: William Collins and Sons.

Hunter, Evan. 1954. *Blackboard jungle*. New York: Simon and Schuster.

Hunter, Robert. [1904] 1965. *Poverty*. New York: Harper & Row.

Hutchins, Robert M. 1936. *The higher learning in America*. New Haven, CT: Yale University Press

Huxley, Thomas Henry. [1880] 1888. "Science and culture." In *Science and culture and other essays*. Ed. Thomas Henry Huxley. London: Macmillan.

Jacoby, Russell. 1987. *The last intellectuals: American culture in the age of academe*. New York: Basic Books.

Jaffe, Naomi, and Dohrn, Bernardine, 1968, March 18. "The look is you . . . ." *New Left Notes*, Chicago, Ill.

James, William. 1890. *Principles of psychology*. New York: H. Holt.

————[1896] 1904. *The will to believe and other essays in popular philosophy*. New York: Longmans Green and Company.

Janik, Allan, and Toulmin, Stephen. 1973. *Wittgenstein's Vienna*. New York: Simon and Schuster.

Jencks, C. et al., 1972. *Inequality*. New York: Basic Books.

Johnson, Henry C., jr. 1977. "Reflective thought and practical action: The origins of the John Dewey Society." *Educational Theory* (27) 1.

Jose, Nicholas. 1985. "Cultural identity: 'I think I'm something else.'" *Daedalus* (14) 1: 281-291.

Kaiser, Charles. 1988. *1968 in America*. New York: Weidenfeld & Nicolson.

Kaminsky, Jack. 1967. "Spencer, Herbert." *The encyclopedia of philosophy* (vol. 7). Ed. Paul W. Edwards. New York: Macmillan.

Kaminsky, James S. 1986. "The first 600 months of philosophy of education—1935–1985: A deconstructionist account." *Educational Philosophy and Theory* (18) 2.

————1988a. "Comprehensive author index of articles in *Educational Philosophy and Theory* 1969-1988." *Educational Philosophy and Theory* (21) 1.

————1988b. "The first 600 months . . . revisited: A response to Harris." *Educational Philosophy and Theory* (20) 1.

————1988c. "Philosophy of education in Australasia: A definition and a history." *Educational Philosophy and Theory* (21) 1.

————1991. "Some antecedents of educational philosophy in Britain with particular reference to social science." *Educational Studies* (17) 3.

————1992. "A pre-history of educational philosophy in the United States: 1861 to 1914." *Harvard Educational Review* (62) 2.

Karier, Clarence J. [1967] 1986. *The individual, society, and education.* Urbana: University of Illinois Press.

Karmel, Peter, (chair). 1973. *Schools in Australia.* Canberra: Australian Government Printing Service.

Karmel, Peter, (chair). 1985. *Quality of education in Australia.* Canberra: Australian Government Printing Service.

Katz, Michael B. (1971) 1975. *Class, bureaucracy, and schools.* New York: Praeger.

Kaufmann, Walter. [1956] 1968. *Existentialism: From Dostoevsky to Sartre.* New York: The World Publishing Company.

Keifer, Howard. 1980, summer. "Some reflections on the philosophy of education." *Philosophic Exchange* (3).

Kemp, David. 1988. "Liberalism and conservatism in Australia since 1944." In *Intellectual movements and Australian society.* Eds. Brian Head and James Walter. Melbourne: Oxford University Press.

Keniston, Kenneth. 1965. *The uncommitted.* New York: Harcourt, Brace & World.

Kennedy, James G. 1978. *Herbert Spencer.* Boston: Twayne.

Kerouac, Jack. 1957. *On the road.* New York: Viking Press.

Kilpatrick, William H. 1918. "The project method." *Teachers College Record* (19).

————Ed. 1930. *John Dewey: The man and his philosophy.* Cambridge, MA: Harvard University Press.

————1936. "High Marxism defined and rejected." *The Social Frontier.* June.

————Ed. 1937. *The teacher and society.* First yearbook of the John Dewey Society. New York: D. Appleton-Century.

————Ed. 1947. *Intercultural attitudes in the making.* Ninth yearbook of the John Dewey Society. New York: Harper and Brothers.

Klier, Betje Black. unpublished manuscript. *Marie Howland of Topolobampo and Fairhope.* Curriculum and Instruction, Auburn University, Auburn, AL.

Kneller, George F. 1964. *Introduction to the philosophy of education.* New York: John Wiley & Sons.

————1966. *Logic and the language of education.* New York: John Wiley & Sons Inc.

————1984. "The proper study of education." *The UCLA Graduate School of Education, Emeriti Lecture Series* (1).

Koch, Donald F. Ed. 1976. *Lectures on psychology and political ethics: 1898—John Dewey.* New York: Hafner Press.

Koestler, Arthur. 1959. *The sleep walkers.* New York: Macmillan.

Kyle, Noeline. 1988. "Co-education and the egalitarian myth in colonial Australia." *Journal of Educational Administration and History* (20) 2.

Lagemann, Ellen Condliffe. 1989. "The plural worlds of educational research." *History of Education Quarterly* (29) 2.

Langer, Susanne. 1956. "On the relations between philosophy and education." *Harvard Educational Review* (XXVI) spring.

Lankshear, Colin. 1989. *Literacy, schooling and revolution.* London: Falmer Press.

Larson, Margali Sarfatti. 1977. *The rise of professionalism.* Berkeley: University of California Press.

Lasch, Christopher 1965. *The new radicalism in America [1889-1963].* New York: Alfred A. Knopf.

Laslett, Peter, and Cummings, Philip W. 1967. "Political philosophy: History of." *The encyclopedia of philosophy* (vol. 6) Ed. Paul W. Edwards. New York: Macmillan.

Lawler, Ray. 1957. *Summer of the seventeenth doll*. New York: S. French.
Lawrence, D. H. [1928] 1932. *Lady Chatterly's lover*. London: Heinemann.
Lawson, John, and Silver, Harold. 1973. *A social history of education in England*. London: Methuen.
Lawson, M. D. 1984. "John Ruskin, education and manual labour." *Education Research and Perspectives* (11) 2.
Leach, Mary S. 1991. "Mothers of in(ter)vention: Women's writing in philosophy of education." *Educational Theory* (41) 3.
Levine, Daniel. 1971. *Jane Addams and the liberal tradition*. Madison, Wisconsin: State Historical Society of Wisconsin.
Lipset, Seymour Martin. [1950] 1968. *Agrarian socialism*. New York: Doubleday.
Lloyd, Henry Demarest. [1894] 1936. *Wealth against commonwealth*. Washington, DC: National Home Library Foundation.
Lloyd, T. O. [1979] 1989. *Empire to welfare state: English history 1906-1985* 3rd. ed. Oxford: Oxford University Press
Locke, John. [1690] 1977. *Letter concerning toleration*. Ann Arbor, MI: University Microfilms International.
———[1695] 1978. *Thoughts concerning education*. London: Printed for A. and J. Churchill. Ann Arbor, MI: University Microfilms International.
London, Jack. 1903. *The people of the abyss*. New York: Macmillan.
———1906, September. "Apostate." *Woman's Home Companion*.
———[1908] 1957. *Martin Eden*. New York: Macmillan.
———1909, January-February. "The dream of Debs." *International Socialist Review*.
———[1934] 1948. *The iron heel*. New York: Grayson.
Low-Beer, Ann. 1969. *Herbert Spencer*. London: Collier-Macmillan.
Lyell, Charles. [1830] 1889. *Principles of geology*. New York: D. Appleton.
MacIntyre, Alasdair. 1984. "The relationship of philosophy to its past." In *Philosophy in history*. Eds. Richard Rorty, J. B. Schneewind, and Quentin Skinner. Cambridge: Cambridge University Press.
Mackie, Margaret. 1966. *Education in the inquiring society: An introduction to the philosophy of education*. Hawthorn, Victoria: Australian Council for Education Research.
———1968. *Educative teaching*. Sydney: Angus & Roberts.
———1970. *What is right?* Sydney: Angus & Roberts.
———1977. *Philosophy and school administation*. St. Lucia: University of Queensland Press.
Mackie, Robert. Ed. 1981. *Literacy & revolution*. New York: Continuum Press.
Macmillan, C. J. B. 1991. "PES and the APA—An impressionistic history." *Educational Theory* (41) 3.
Mann, Arthur. Ed. 1963. *The Progressive era: Liberal renaissance or liberal failure?* New York: Holt, Rinehart, and Winston.
Marcuse, Herbert. 1955. *Eros and civilization*. Boston: Beacon Press.
———1964. *One dimensional man*. Boston: Beacon Press.
Marshall, James. 1982. "Philosophy of education in New Zealand." *Educational Analysis* (4) 1.
———1987. *Positivism or Pragmatism: Philosophy of education in New Zealand* (vol. 2). New Zealand Educational Research Association.
Marwick, Arthur. [1982] 1988. *British society since 1945*. London: Pelican.
Matthews, Michael R. 1980. *The Marxist theory of schooling*. Brighton, Sussex: Harvester Press.
May, Henry F. 1959. *The end of American innocence*. New York: Alfred A. Knopf.
Mayhew, Henry. [1851] 1967. *London labour and the London poor*, (vol. 4). London: Frank Cass & Co.
Mayhew, Katherine, Camp and Edwards, Anna Camp. 1936. *The Dewey school*. New York: D. Appleton-Century.
McCalman, Janet. 1989. "Old school ties and silver spoons: A statistical footnote from darkest Victoria." *Australian Cultural History* (8).

McCaul, Robert L. 1959. "Dewey's Chicago." *School Review* (67).
McGuinnis, Brian. 1988. *Wittgenstein: A life*. London: Duckworth.
McGregor, P. 1985. Is our school curriculum out of control? *IPA Review* (39).
McLaren, Ian A., 1974. *Education in a small democracy: New Zealand*. London: Routledge & Kegan Paul.
McMurray, Foster. 1981. "Animadversions on the Eightieth Yearbook of the NSSE." *Educational Theory* (31) 1.
McNair, A. (chair). 1944. *Teachers and youth leaders*. London: Her Majesty's Stationery Office.
McQueen, Humphrey. 1970. *A new Britannia*. Ringwood, VIC: Australia: Penguin Books.
———1990. "Tomorrow, tomorrow & tomorrow." *Futures* (22).
Mead, Margaret. [1928] 1968. *Coming of age in Samoa*. New York: William Morrow and Company.
Melby, Ernest. Ed. 1943. *Mobilizing educational resources*. Sixth yearbook of the John Dewey Society. New York: Harper Brothers.
Mill, John Stuart. [1843] 1884. *System of logic*. London: Longmans, Green & Co.
———[1848] 1891. *Principles of political economy* (v. 1-2). New York: D. Appleton.
———[1859] 1947. *On liberty*. New York: Appleton-Century-Crofts.
———[1867] 1985. "Inaugural address at St. Andrews University." In *John Stuart Mill: A selection of his works*. Ed. John M. Robson. New York: Macmillan.
Miller, Henry. [1934] 1961. *Tropic of Cancer*. New York: Grove Press.
Millett, Kate. 1969. "Sexual politics." *New American Review* (7).
———1970. *Sexual politics*. Garden City, NY: Doubleday.
Mills, C. Wright. 1964. *Sociology and pragmatism*. New York: Paine-Whitman.
Morison, Samuel Eliot. 1965. *The Oxford history of the American people*. New York: Oxford University Press.
Morrison, Arthur. 1895. *Tales of mean street*. New York: R. F. Fenno.
Murphy, Arthur E. 1945. "Special courses and programs of study." In *Philosophy in American education*. Ed. Brand Blanshard New York: Harper & Brothers Publishers.
Murphy, Marjorie. 1981. "Taxation and social conflict: Teacher unionism and public school finance in Chicago 1898-1934." *Journal of the Illinois State Historical Society* (74).
———1990. *Blackboard unions*. Ithaca, NY: Cornell University Press.
Nakosteen, Mehdi. 1965. *The history and philosophy of education*. New York: The Ronald Press.
Niblett, Roy W., Humphreys, Darlow W., and Fairhurst, John R. 1975. *The university connection*. UK: NFER Publishing.
Nietzsche, Friedrich. [1872] 1968. "The birth of tragedy." In *Basic writings of Nietzsche*. Ed. and Tr. Walter Kaufmann. New York: Random House.
Noble, David W. 1958. *The paradox of Progressive thought*. Minneapolis: University of Minnesota Press.
Norris, Frank. 1901. *The octopus*. Sun Dial Press.
———[1903] 1956. *The pit*. New York: Grove Press.
Norwood, Cyril. (chair) 1943. *Curriculum and examination in secondary schools*. London: His Majesty's Stationery Office.
Nunn, Percy. [1920] 1947. *Education: Its data and first principles* (3rd ed). London: Edward Arnold.
O'Connor, D. J. 1957. *An introduction to the philosophy of education*. London: Routledge & Kegan Paul.
Ortega y Gasset, José. 1932. *The revolt of the masses*. New York: W. W. Norton.
Owen, Robert. 1818. *A new view of society*. London: R. and A. Taylor.
Parry, David Hughes, Andrew, Geoffrey C. and Harman, Roy H. 1960. *Report of the committee on New Zealand universities—December 1959*. Wellington, New Zealand: R. E. Owen, Government Printer.
Partington, G. 1982, August. "Our ailing schools." *Quadrant*.

Passmore, John. 1965. "Analytic philosophies of education." *Studies in Philosophy of Education*. Carlton, VIC: Melbourne University Press.
——1967a. "Anderson, John." *The encyclopedia of philosophy* (vol. 1). Ed. Paul W. Edwards. New York: Macmillan.
——1967b. "Historiography of philosophy." *The encyclopedia of philosophy* (vol. 6). Ed. Paul W. Edwards. New York: Macmillan.
——1980. *The philosophy of teaching*. London: Duckworth.
Pearson, Karl. [1892] 1900. *The grammar of science*. London: A.C. Black.
Peters, R. S. 1958. *The concept of motivation*. London: Routledge & Kegan Paul.
——[1959] 1966. *Authority, responsibility, and education*. New York: Atherton Press.
——1966. *Ethics and education*. London: George Allen & Unwin.
——1967. "What is an education process?" In *The concept of education*. Ed. R. S. Peters. London: Routledge & Kegan Paul.
——1973. *The philosophy of education*. London: Routledge & Kegan Paul.
——1983. "Philosophy of education." In *Educational theory and its foundations*. Ed. Paul Hirst. London: Routledge & Kegan Paul.
Philip, Neil, and Neuburg, Victor. 1986. *Charles Dickens, A December vision: His social journalism*. London: William Collins.
Phillips, A. A. 1988. "Cultural nationalism in the 1940s and 1950s: A personal account." In *Intellectual movements and Australian society*. Eds. Brian Head and James Walter. Melbourne: Oxford University Press.
Phillips, D. C. 1970. *Theories, values and education*. Melbourne: Melbourne University Press.
Philosophy of Education Society of Australasia (PESA). 1972a. Minutes of the ordinary general meeting. Philosophy of education Society of Australasia. Christchurch, New Zealand.
——1973. Minutes of the ordinary general meeting. Philosophy of Education Society of Australasia. Hobart, Australia.
——1974. Minutes of the ordinary general meeting. Philosophy of Education Society of Australasia. Canberra, Australia.
——1981. Minutes of the ordinary general meeting. Philosophy of Education Society of Australasia. La Trobe, Australia.
——1972. Proceedings (1) 1.
Philosophy of Education Society Great Britain (PESGB). 1964a. Minute of: Meeting of the Steering Committee, Wednesday 11th November, 1964, at 5.30 p.m. in Room 365: Attachment. Secretary, Paul Hirst. Archive: Philosophy of Education Society of Great Britain.
——1964b. Minute of: First annual general meeting, 13th December 1964, at 10.00 a.m. at 'Uplands,' High Wycombe. Secretary, Paul Hirst. Archive: Philosophy of Education Society of Great Britain.
Plowden, J. P. (chair). 1967. *Children and their primary schools*. London: Her Majesty's Stationery Office.
Potter, Robert E. 1967. *The stream of American education*. New York: American Book Company.
Pratte, Richard. [1979] 1981. "Analytic philosophy of education: A historical perspective." In *Philosophy of education since mid-century*. Ed. Jonas F. Soltis. New York: Teachers College Press.
Price, Derek J. De Solla. 1961. *Science since Babylon*. New Haven, CT: Yale University Press.
——[1963] 1986. *Little science, big science*. New York: Columbia University Press.
——1965. "Is technology historically independent of science?" *Technology and Culture* (6).
Price, Kingsley. 1967. "Philosophy of education: History of." *The encyclopedia of philosophy* (vol. 6). Ed. Paul W. Edwards. New York: Macmillan.
Pring, Richard. 1972. "Education as control of knowledge: Knowledge out of control." *Education for Teaching* (89).

Pugh, Patrica. 1984. *Educate, agitate, organize: 100 years of Fabian socialism*. New York: Methuen.

Raup, R. Bruce. 1936a. *Education and organized interests in America*. New York: G. P. Putnam's Sons.

————1936b, January. "Shall we use the class dynamic." *The Social Frontier* (3).

————1940, November 4. Private letter, (unpublished), Philosophy of Education Society, Archives.

————1966. [taped interview]. Philosophy of Education Society, Archives.

Reid, Louis Arnaud. 1923. *Knowledge and truth*. London: Macmillan.

————1931. *A study in aesthetics*. London: George Allen & Unwin.

————1937. *Creative morality*. London: George Allen & Unwin.

————1939. *A preface to faith*. London: George Allen & Unwin.

————1945. *A rediscovery of belief*. Great Britain: London: Lindsey Press.

————1960. *Ways of knowledge and experience*. London: George Allen & Unwin.

————1962. *Philosophy and education*. London: Heinemann.

————1966. *Education*. (Unpublished manuscript).

————1970. *Meaning in the arts*. London: George Allen & Unwin.

————1986. *Ways of understanding education*. London: Heinemann.

————N.d. *Yesterdays today: Journey into philosophy*. Unpublished autobiography.

Rice, J. M. 1893. *The public-school system of the United States*. New York: The Century Company.

Riesman, David. 1953. *Thorstein Veblen: A critical interpretation*. New York: Charles Scribner's Sons.

Riis, Jacob A. (1903) 1970. *How the other half lives*. Ed. Sam Bass Warner, Jr. Cambridge, MA: The Belknap Press of Harvard University.

Roach, John. 1957. "Liberalism and the Victorian intelligentsia." *The Cambridge Historical Journal* (13).

Robbins, C. B. (chair). 1963. *Higher education*. London: Her Majesty's Stationery Office.

Robbins, Keith. 1989. *Nineteenth-century Britain*. Oxford: Oxford University Press.

Roderick, Gordon, and Stephens, Michael. 1981. *Where did we go wrong?: Industry, education and economy of Victorian Britain*. London: Falmer Press.

Rolt, L. T. C. 1980. *Victorian engineering*. Harmondsworth, Middlesex, England: Penguin Books.

Ronan, Colin A. 1983. *The Cambridge illustrated history of the world's science*. Cambridge: Cambridge University Press.

Rorty, Richard. 1967. *The linguistic turn*. Chicago: University of Chicago Press.

————[1976] 1982a. "Keeping philosophy pure." In *Consequences of pragmatism*. Ed. Richard Rorty. Brighton, Sussex: Harvester Press.

————[1976] 1982b. "Professionalized philosophy and transcendental culture." In *Consequences of pragmatism*. Ed. Richard Rorty. Brighton, Sussex: Harvester Press.

————[1977] 1982. "Dewey's metaphysics." In *Consequences of pragmatism*. Ed. Richard Rorty. Brighton, Sussex: Harvester Press.

————1980. *Philosophy and the mirror of nature*. Oxford: Basil Blackwell Publisher.

————[1980] 1982. "Pragmatism, relativism and irrationalism." In *Consequences of pragmatism*. Ed. Richard Rorty. Brighton, Sussex: Harvester Press.

————[1981] 1982. "Philosophy in America today." In *Consequences of pragmatism*. Ed. Richard Rorty. Brighton, Sussex: Harvester Press.

————Ed. 1982. *Consequences of pragmatism*. Brighton, Sussex: Harvester.

————1984. "The historiography of philosophy: Four genres." In *Philosophy in history*. Eds. Richard Rorty, J. B. Schneewind, and Quentin Skinner. Cambridge: Cambridge University Press.

————1989. *Contingency, irony, and solidarity*. Cambridge: Cambridge University Press.

Rorty, Richard, Schneewind, J. B., & Skinner, Quentin. 1984. "Introduction." In *Philosophy in history*. Eds. Richard Rorty, J. B. Schneewind, and Quentin Skinner. Cambridge: Cambridge University Press.

Ross, Dorothy. 1991. *The origins of American social science*. New York: Cambridge University Press.

Rothblatt, Sheldon. 1968. *The revolution of the dons*. London: Cambridge University Press.

———1976. *Tradition and change in English liberal education*. London: Faber and Faber.

———1988. "Supply and demand: The 'two histories' of English education." *History of Education Quarterly* (28) 4.

Rousseau, Jean-Jacques. [1762] 1907. *Emile*. Trans. William H. Payne. New York: D. Appleton.

———[1762] 1987. *Social contract*. Trans. and ed. Donald A. Cress. Indianapolis/Cambridge: Hackett.

Royce, Josiah. 1904. *Herbert Spencer: An estimate and review*. New York: Fox, Duffield & Company.

Rubenstein, David. 1979. *Education & equality*. Harmondsworth, Middlesex, England: Penguin Books.

Rugg, Harold. 1931. *Culture and education*. New York: Harcourt, Brace and Company.

———Ed. 1939. *Democracy and the curriculum*. Third yearbook of the John Dewey Society. New York: D. Appleton-Century.

———1952. *The teacher of teachers*. New York: Harper & Brothers.

Rugg, Harold with Shumaker, Ann. 1928. *The child-center school*. Chicago: World Book Company.

Ruskin, John. [1852] 1904. "Modern education," *Stones of Venice* (vol. 11: 258-263). In *The works of Ruskin*. Eds. E. T. Cook and A. Wedderburn. London: George Allen.

———[1865] 1905. *Sesame and lillies*, In *The works of Ruskin* (vol. 18: 401-428). Eds. E. T. Cook and A. Wedderburn. London: George Allen.

———[1866] 1905a. *The crown of wild olive*. In *The works of Ruskin* (vol. 18). Eds. E. T. Cook and A. Wedderburn. London: George Allen.

———[1866] 1905b. *The ethics of the dust*. In *The works of Ruskin* (vol. 18). Eds. E. T. Cook and A. Wedderburn. London: George Allen.

———[1867] 1905a. "Of public education irrespective of class-distinction." *Time and tide*. In *The works of Ruskin* (vol. 17: 394-401). Eds. E. T. Cook and A. Wedderburn. London: George Allen.

———[1867] 1905b. "The relations of education to position of life." *Time and tide*. In *The works of Ruskin* (vol. 17: 394-401). Eds. E. T. Cook and A. Wedderburn. London: George Allen.

———[1867] 1905c. "The harmful effect of servile employment." *Time and tide*. In *The works of Ruskin* (vol. 17: 405-409). Eds. E. T. Cook and A. Wedderburn. London: George Allen.

———1907. *Fors Clavigera*. In *The works of Ruskin* (vol. 27-29). Eds. E. T. Cook and A. Wedderburn. London: George Allen.

Russell, Bertrand. 1926. *On education: Especially in early childhood* (also: *Education and the good life*). London: George Allen & Unwin.

———1932. *Education and the modern world* (also: *Education and the social order*). New York: W. W. Norton.

———[1949] 1968. *Authority and the individual*. New York: AMS Press.

———1987. *On ethics, sex, and marriage*. Ed. Al Seckel. New York: Prometheus Books.

Russell, Bertrand, and Whitehead, Alfred [1910-1913] 1927. *Principia mathematica* (3 vols. 2nd ed). Cambridge: Cambridge University Press.

Ryan, William. 1969. *Blaming the victim*. New York: Random House.

Ryle, Gilbert. [1949] 1964. *The concept of mind*. New York: Barnes and Noble.

Safford, John Lugton. 1987. *Pragmatism and the Progressive movement in the United States.* New York: University of America Press.

Salwak, Dale. 1992. *Kingsley Amis.* Latham, MD: Barnes & Noble.

Sammons, Morris. 1981. "A new role for the philosophy of education." *Texas Tech Journal of Education* (8) 2.

Scheffler, Israel. 1958. *Philosophy of education.* Boston: Allyn and Bacon.

———1960. *The language of education.* Springfield, IL: Charles C. Thomas.

———1974. *Four pragmatists.* London: Routledge & Kegan Paul.

Schlesinger, Arthur M. Jr. [1957] 1988. *The crisis of the old order (1919-1933): The age of Roosevelt.* Boston: Houghton Mifflin.

———1963, 8 February. "The administration and the left." *New Statesman.*

Schrader, George Alfred. Ed. 1967. *Existential philosophers.* New York: McGraw-Hill.

Seaman, L. C. B. [1973] 1985. *Victorian England.* London: Methuen.

Selleck, R. J. W. 1968. *The new education: 1870-1914.* London: Sir Isaac Pitman & Sons.

Senn, Peter R. 1958. "The earliest use of the term 'social science.'" *Journal of the History of Ideas* (19).

Shapin, Steven, and Schaffer, Simon. 1985. *Leviathan and the air-pump: Hobbes, Boyle, and the experimental life.* Princeton, NJ: Princeton University Press.

Shapiro, Charles. 1962. *Theodore Dreiser: Our bitter patriot.* Carbondale: Southern Illinois University Press.

Sharp, Rachel. 1980. *Knowledge, ideology and the politics of schooling.* London: Routledge & Kegan Paul.

Shelton, Robert. 1986. *No direction home: The life and music of Bob Dylan.* London: Penguin.

Sidgwick, Henry. [1874] 1962. *The methods of ethics.* Chicago: University of Chicago Press.

———[1886] 1892. *Outlines of the history of ethics for English readers.* London: Macmillan.

Siegel, Harvey. 1981a. "The future and purpose of philosophy of education." *Educational Theory* (31) 1.

———1981b. "How 'practical' should philosophy of education be?" *Educational Studies* (12).

———1983. "On the obligations of the professional philosopher of education." *Journal of Educational Thought* (18) 2.

Silver, Harold. 1969. *Robert Owen on education.* Cambridge: Cambridge University Press.

———1983. *Education as history.* London: Methuen.

———1990. *Education change and the policy process.* New York: Falmer Press.

Simon, Brian. 1965. *Education and the labour movement 1870-1920.* London: Lawrence & Wishart.

———1974. *The politics of educational reform 1920-1940.* London: Lawrence & Wishart.

———1983. "The study of education as a university subject in Britain." *Studies in Higher Education* (8) 1.

———1991. *Education and the social order 1940–1990.* New York: St. Martin's.

Sinclair, Upton. 1906. *The jungle.* New York: Doubleday, Page and Company.

———1922. *The goose-step: A study of American education.* Pasadena, CA: Author.

———[1924] 1970. *The goslings: A study of the American schools.* New York: AMS Press.

Sizer, Theodore R. 1970. "Low-income families and the schools for their children." *Public Administration Review.* 340-347.

Sloan, Douglas. 1971. *The Scottish Enlightenment and the American college ideal.* New York: Teachers College Press.

————1980. "The teaching of ethics in the American undergraduate curriculum, 1876-1976." In *Ethics teaching in higher education*. Eds. Daniel Callahan, and Sissela Bok. New York: Plenum Press.

Small, Albion. 1897. "Some demands of sociology upon pedagogy." *The American Journal of Sociology* (2) 6.

Smart, John C., and McLaughlin, Gerald W. 1982. "Educational specialty areas." *Educational Researcher* (1) 7.

Smith, Mike. 1977. *The underground and education*. London: Methuen.

Snook, I. 1966a. "Education and the philosopher: A reply to J. P. Powell." *Australian Journal of Education* (10) 2.

————1966b. "Philosophy, education and a myth." *Australian Journal of Higher Education* (2).

————1969. "Philosophy of education: Today and tomorrow." *New Zealand Journal of Educational Studies* (4) 1.

————1972a. *Concepts of indoctrination*. London: Routledge & Kegan Paul.

————1972b. *Indoctrination and education*. London: Routledge & Kegan Paul.

————1986. [Taped telephone interview with the author].

Snow, C. P. [1959] 1961. *The two cultures and the scientific revolution*. New York: Cambridge University Press.

Soffer, Reba N. 1978. *Ethics and society in England*. Berkeley: University of California Press.

Soltis, Jonas. 1971. "Analysis and anomalies in philosophy of education." *Proceedings of the twenty-seventh annual meeting of the Philosophy of Education Society*. Normal, IL: The Philosophy of Education Society.

————[1979] 1981. *Philosophy of education since mid-century*. New York: Teachers College Press.

————1981. *Philosophy and education. The eightieth yearbook of the National Society for the Study of Education*. Ed. Kenneth J. Rehage. Chicago: University of Chicago Press.

Spaull, Andrew. 1982. *Australian education in the Second World War*. St. Lucia: University of Queensland.

Spencer, Herbert. [1851] 1969. *Social statics*. New York: Augustus M. Kelley.

————[1861] 1897. *Education: Intellectual, moral, and physical*. New York: D. Appleton.

————[1862] 1880. *First principles*. New York: A.L. Burt.

————[1873] 1904. *The study of sociology*. New York: D. Appleton.

————1876-1896. *The principles of sociology*, v: 1-8. London.

————[1892] 1940. *The man versus the state*. Caldwell, ID: Caxton.

Spens, W. (chair) [1938] 1959. *Secondary education*. London: Her Majesty's Stationery Office.

Spring, Joel. 1969. "Education and progressivism." *History of Education Quarterly* (10) 1.

Stearns, Peter N. Ed. 1988. *Expanding the past: A reader in social history*. New York: New York University Press.

Steffens, Lincoln. 1904. *The shame of cities*. New York: McClure, Phillips & Co.

Steinbeck. John. 1939. *The grapes of wrath*. New York: The Viking Press.

Steinberg, Ira S. 1982. "From our American correspondent." *Educational Analysis* (4) 1.

Stewart. W. A. C. 1989. *Higher education in postwar Britain*. London: Macmillan.

Strike, Kenneth A. 1989. *Liberal justice and the Marxist critique of education*. New York: Routledge, Chapman and Hall.

Suchodolski, Bogdan. 1979. "Philosophy and education." *International Review of Education* (25) 2 & 3.

Summers, Anne. [1975] 1976. *Damned whores and God's police: The colonization of women in Australia*. Blackburn, VIC, Australia: Penguin Books.

Tanner, Daniel. 1991. *Crusade for democracy*. Albany, NY: State University of New York Press.

Tarbell, Ida M. 1902, 1903, 1904. "The history of Standard Oil Company." *McClure's* (20, 21, 22, 23).

———1904. *The history of Standard Oil*. New York: McClure, Phillips & Co.

Tawney, R. H. [1918] 1964a. "Keep the workers' children in their place." In *The radical tradition*. Ed. Rita Hinden. London: George Allen & Unwin.

———[1918] 1964b. "The problem of the public schools." In *The radical tradition*. Ed. Rita Hinden. London: George Allen & Unwin.

———([1922] 1988) *Secondary education for all*. London: Hambledon Press.

Taylor, Harold. 1952. "The philosophical foundations of general education." In *General education*. The fifty-fifth yearbook of the National Society for the Study of Education. Chicago: University of Chicago Press.

Tholfsen, Trygve R. 1961. "Transition to democracy in Victorian England." *International Review of Social History* (6).

Thomas, Lawrence G. Ed. 1972. *Philosophical redirection of educational research*. The seventy-first yearbook of the National Society for the Study of Education. Ed. Herman G. Richey. Chicago: University of Chicago Press.

Thoreau, Henry David. 1863. "Walking." In *Excursions*. Boston: Ticknor and Fields.

———[1863] 1866. "Life without principle." In *A Yankee in Canada with anti-slavery and reform papers*. Boston: Ticknor and Fields.

———[1849] 1866. "Civil disobedience." In *A Yankee in Canada with anti-slavery and reform papers*. Boston: Ticknor and Fields.

Tice, Terrence N., and Slavens, Thomas P. 1983. *Research guide to philosophy*. Chicago: American Library Association.

Toulmin, Stephen E. 1967. "The evolutionary development of natural science." *American Scientist* (55) 4.

———1969. "Innovation and the problem of utilization." In *Factors in the transfer of technology*. Eds. William H. Gruber and Donald G. Marquis. Cambridge: MIT Press.

———1972. *Human understanding*, (vol. 1). Princeton, NJ: Princeton University Press.

———1990. *Cosmopolis: The hidden agenda of modernity*. New York: The Free Press.

Toulmin, Stephen and Goodfield, June. [1965] 1983. *The discovery of time*. New York: Octagon Books.

Tozer, Steven. 1991. "PES and school reform." *Educational Theory* (41) 3.

Tozer, Steve and McAninch, Stuart. 1986. "Social foundations of education in historical perspective." *Educational Foundations* (1) 1.

———1987. "Four texts in the social foundations of education in historical perspective." *Educational Studies* (18) 1.

Trow, Martin. 1987. *Higher education and the comparative study of unique traditions*. Paper presented at International conference of the Swedish National Board of Universities and Colleges on "Higher education: Creativity, legitimation and systems transformation." Dalaro, Sweden.

———1988. "Comparative perspectives on higher education policy in the UK and the US." *Oxford Review of Education* (14) 1.

Tynan, Kenneth. 1969. *Oh! Calcutta*. New York: Grove Press.

Ulich, Robert Ed. [1947] 1982. *Three thousand years of educational wisdom*. Cambridge, MA: Harvard University Press.

Vandenberg, Donald. [1979] 1981. "Existential and phenomenological influences in educational philosophy." In *Philosophy of education since mid-century*. Ed. Jonas F. Soltis. New York: Teachers College Press.

———1987. "Interpretive, normative theory of education." *Educational Philosophy and Theory* (19)1.

Veblen, Thorstein. [1899] 1922. *The theory of the leisure class*. New York: B. W. Huebsch.

———1918. *The higher learning in America*. New York: B. W. Huebsch.

Veysey, Laurence R. 1965. *The emergence of the American University*. Chicago: University of Chicago Press.
Villemain, Francis. 1988. [Taped interview with the author].
Walker, James. 1985. [Taped interview with the author].
Ward, Lester F. 1883. *Dynamic sociology*. New York: D. Appleton.
——1903. *Pure sociology*. New York: Macmillan.
Ward, Russell. 1958. *The Australian legend*. Melbourne: Oxford University Press.
Wesley, Edgar B. 1957. *NEA: The first hundred years*. New York: Harper & Brothers.
White, John. 1987. "The medical condition of philosophy of education." *Journal of Philosophy of Education* (21) 2.
——1989. [Taped interview with the author].
Whitehead, Alfred North. [1929] 1957. *The aims of education*. New York: The Free Press.
Wilenski, H. 1964-1965. "The professionalization of everyone."*American Journal of Sociology* (70): 137-8.
Williams, Bruce. 1985. "Wealth, invention, and education." *Daedalus* (14) 1.
Williams, Raymond. 1958. *Culture and society*. London: Chatto & Windus.
——1967. "John Ruskin." *The encyclopedia of philosophy* (vol. 7). Ed. Paul W. Edwards. New York: Macmillan.
Williams, Trevor I. 1982. *A short history of twentieth-century technology: 1900-c. 1950*. Oxford: Clarendon Press.
Wilson, John. 1979. *Preface to the philosophy of education*. London: Routledge & Kegan Paul.
Winch, Peter. 1958. *The idea of social science and its relation to philosophy*. London: Routledge & Kegan Paul.
Windschuttle, Keith. 1979. *Unemployment: A social and political analysis of the economic crisis in Australia*. London: Harmondsworth.
Wise, Winifred E. 1935. *Jane Addams of Hull House*. New York: Harcourt, Brace and Company.
Wittgenstein, Ludwig. [1921] 1974. *Tractatus logico-philosophicus*. London: Routledge & Kegan Paul.
Woelfel, Norman. 1933. *Molders of the American mind*. New York: Columbia University Press.
Young, M. F. D. 1972. *Knowledge and control*. London: Collier-Macmillan.
Ziman, J. M. 1968. *Public knowledge*. Cambridge: Cambridge University Press.
Zinn, Howard. 1980. *A people's history of the United States*. New York: Harper & Row.
Zukav, Gary. [1979] 1986. *The dancing Wu Li masters*. New York: Bantam Books.

# Index

**About the Author**

JAMES S. KAMINSKY is head of the Department of Educational Foundations, Leadership, and Technology at Auburn University.